David McCants

WILLIAM McCANTS directs the Project on U.S. Relations with the Islamic World at the Brookings Institution. He is adjunct faculty at Johns Hopkins University and a former U.S. State Department senior adviser for countering violent extremism. McCants has a Ph.D. in Near Eastern Studies from Princeton University and lives in the Washington, D.C. area.

THE ISIS
APOCALYPSE

THE ISIS

APOCALYPSE

THE HISTORY, STRATEGY, AND DOOMSDAY VISION OF THE ISLAMIC STATE

WILLIAM McCANTS

Picador

St. Martin's Press
New York

picadorusa.com • picadorbookroom.tumblr.com
twitter.com/picadorusa • facebook.com/picadorusa

Picador® is a U.S. registered trademark and is used by St. Martin's Press under license from Pan Books Limited.

For book club information, please visit facebook.com/picadorbookclub or e-mail marketing@picadorusa.com.

Design by Letra Libre, Inc.

The Library of Congress has cataloged the St. Martin's Press edition as follows:

McCants, William Faizi, 1975–
   The ISIS apocalypse : the history, strategy, and doomsday vision of the Islamic State / William McCants.
      p. cm.
   ISBN 978-1-250-08090-5 (hardcover)
   ISBN 978-1-4668-9270-5 (e-book)
   1. IS (Organization)—History. 2. Terrorism—Religious aspects—Islam.
3. Terrorism—Middle East. 4. Jihad. 5. Strategy. 6. Islamic Empire. 7. End of the world—Political aspects—Middle East. 8. Political messianism—Middle East.
9. Middle East—Politics and government—21st century. I. Title.
   HV6433.I722M35 2015
   363.3250956—dc23   2015015281

Picador Paperback ISBN 978-1-250-11264-4

Our books may be purchased in bulk for promotional, educational, or business use. Please contact your local bookseller or the Macmillan Corporate and Premium Sales Department at 1-800-221-7945, extension 5442, or by e-mail at MacmillanSpecialMarkets@macmillan.com.

First published by St. Martin's Press

First Picador Edition: August 2016

10 9 8 7 6 5 4 3 2

For Mom, who's always asking me simple,
difficult questions about the Middle East.
As the Arabic saying goes,
al-sahl al-mumtani',
the easy is elusive.

CONTENTS

Preface to the 2016 Edition   xi

Acknowledgments   xv

Transliteration   xix

Introduction   1

1   Raising the Black Flag   5

2   Mahdi and Mismanagement   31

3   Bannermen   47

4   Resurrection and Tribulation   73

5   Sectarian Apocalypse   99

6   Caliphate Reborn   121

Conclusion   145

Appendices: Sunni Islamic Prophecies of the End Times   161

Appendix 1: The Final Days   163

Appendix 2: The Victorious Group   173

Appendix 3: The Mahdi Is Preceded by an Islamic State   177

Appendix 4: Twelve Caliphs   179

Notes   183

Index   235

PREFACE TO THE 2016 EDITION

As I finished writing this book early last year, I had a stylistic decision to make. What tense would I use to describe the Islamic State's capabilities and intentions? The State's enemies had not yet dented the group's government in Syria and Iraq, so perhaps better to use the present tense to convey the gravity of the moment or the future tense to titillate readers with visions of a darker future. But the historian in me worried. What if the group's behavior and priorities suddenly changed? My caution won out, and I used the past tense throughout most of the book, satisfied with explaining why the group had succeeded so spectacularly in establishing a state in 2014.

I made the right call, if only because of what followed a month after the book was published: the Islamic State's affiliate in Egypt's Sinai Peninsula brought down a Russian airliner by smuggling a bomb on board. The attack killed all 224 passengers. The Islamic State revealed that its Sinai affiliate had initially planned to attack a Western airliner but made a last-minute change after the Russians began bombing rebel positions in Syria.[1]

Two weeks later, Islamic State operatives who had trained in Syria coordinated an attack in France. Nine men split into three teams and stalked the crowds enjoying the Parisian nightlife. "You could hear someone methodically reloading his gun so he could start firing at us again," remembers one survivor of the massacre.[2] The attackers killed 130 and wounded 368 more using assault rifles and suicide vests. The

Islamic State claimed the attack was in reprisal for Western "strikes against Muslims in the lands of the Caliphate with their jets."[3]

The attack in Paris made many non-Muslims in the West more fearful of their fellow Muslim citizens and more hostile to Muslims fleeing violence from the East. The fear in the United States intensified to near 9/11 levels after two isolated Islamic State supporters in San Bernardino, California—a husband and wife—killed more than a dozen of the husband's coworkers.

In Europe and the United States, politicians on the right exploited the paranoia for political gain—some went so far as to call for a ban on Muslim refugees. The Islamic State, which had been dismayed by earlier European and American openness to the refugees, gleefully watched as the "gray zone" Western Muslims inhabited between assimilation and alienation sharpened to a black-and-white choice. More alienated youth meant more potential recruits for the Islamic State.

The seeds of the Paris and Sinai attacks were planted a year before in the summer of 2014, when America first dropped bombs on Islamic State soil in Syria and Iraq. Perhaps worrying that it was too vulnerable, the State looked for ways to alleviate the pressure. In September, its spokesman publicly urged supporters around the world to attack Western countries in revenge; privately, he began organizing European operatives in Syria to return home to coordinate attacks.[4] A month later, the Islamic State announced its expansion into new territories throughout the Middle East and North Africa.

The loss of a quarter of its territory in Syria and Iraq over the following year and the death of thousands of its fighters deepened the Islamic State's sense of urgency. Always hoping to expand its caliphate and attack the infidel West, the group had the resources and the need to accelerate its timetable.

If necessity is the mother of terrorist innovation, money is the father. The Islamic State's $2 billion war chest, though diminished, was more than enough to fund deadly new start-ups on the battlefield that will mature and migrate if given enough time. The group reportedly has a team of scientists developing chemical weapons[5] and it has flown surveillance drones that could be rigged with explosives.[6] Less exotic and less expensive attacks would be no less deadly. The Paris attack may have cost as little as $10,000.[7]

The Islamic State's attack in Paris touched off a debate about the group's intent. What did it hope to achieve by murdering dozens of civilians? Did it want to deter Western nations from carrying out more strikes against the Islamic State or to provoke them into a large-scale ground invasion? Unhelpfully, the Islamic State offered both explanations for the attack in its online magazine.[8] Bin Laden had done the same after 9/11. He, like the Islamic State, wanted the United States to go all out or all in, no mushy middle. Politicians and the public don't like the mushy middle either. They want to know for certain why the Islamic State attacked the West, and they want an equally clear response—all out or all in.

Dissatisfied with the ambiguity, some turned to the Islamic State's apocalyptic prognostications to divine the group's intent. A candidate for the American presidency repeatedly asserted from the debate stage that the Islamic State wanted to trigger an "apocalyptic showdown" with the West in Syria. A *New York Times* reporter confidently cited the Islamic State's love for the prophecy as evidence that it wants "the United States and its allies to be dragged into a ground war."[9] But prophecy is not a reliable guide to the group's intent—it has also cited other prophecies of a truce with the "Roman" West as another possible outcome of the current conflict. The future is written but it depends on what prophecy one reads.

Though reluctant to use the future tense when writing the book, I ventured my own predictions about the fortunes of the Islamic State. I anticipated its government in Syria and Iraq would collapse and its "provinces" abroad would multiply and spread. Both are proving true, and I derive some small satisfaction that I was right to go against the prevailing skepticism of the war against the Islamic State in Syria and Iraq. But my accurate guess about the spread of the Islamic State in the Middle East and North Africa is not a testament to my predictive prowess. It was obvious to anyone who has watched how capably the Islamic State capitalizes on the chaos roiling the region.

If I am right that the Islamic State pushed to expand its territory and terror network abroad in response to Western nations attacking its lands in Syria and Iraq, then we should anticipate more expansion to compensate for fresh setbacks on the battlefield. As of this writing, its strongest province in Libya already has an estimated 6,500 fighters, controls 173 miles of coastline, and governs a city and several towns. And an Islamic State defector disclosed that the group is urging would-be jihadist immigrants to stay home—they are more useful building cells abroad than dying in battle.[10] The more the United States and its allies succeed in destroying the Islamic State's government, the more terrorism it will face. That is not an argument to do nothing but rather an acknowledgment that success will come at a bloody price.

I look forward to the day that I can write about the Islamic State in the past tense alone. But that day is far distant.

ACKNOWLEDGMENTS

Readers will decide if this book is any good, but I'm certain it would have been much poorer were it not for the help of my family, friends, and colleagues. Assad Ahmed, Cole Bunzel, Ali Chaudrey, and Shadi Hamid all get gold stars and my eternal gratitude for reading and commenting on the early draft, which really helped me clarify my thoughts. Their enthusiasm and encouragement propelled me toward the finish line. Michael O'Hanlon is also in the gold-star club for reading the entire manuscript and reminding me that I couldn't leave the "so what?" question unanswered. I never showed the manuscript to my Dad, but he kept urging me to answer the equally important question, "Why do they do that?"

Anne Peckham and Elizabeth Pearce not only read and commented on the entire manuscript in detail; they also shouldered many of my office duties to give me time to write it. I couldn't have done it without them.

Daniel Benjamin, Ryan Evans, Stephanie Kaplan, Daniel Kimmage, Robert McKenzie, and Clint Watts—nonalarmists all—read individual chapters and let me know when I was getting too carried away or not carried away enough. I sent my research assistant Kristine Anderson on lots of wild goose chases in the thickets of Twitter and YouTube and she managed to come back with some fantastic cyberfowl. Superstar intern Nouf Al Sadiq helped me decipher some awfully blurry screen shots of some awfully messy Arabic handwriting. And Jennifer Williams went above and beyond the call of duty when she put everything on hold to help me tame my unruly footnotes before deadline.

Dan Byman, Mike Doran, Jeremy Shapiro, and Tamara Wittes all heard various parts of the book in their nascent form and encouraged me to keep at it. Tamara loved the idea of telling the story of the Islamic State through its flag. Dan didn't love it enough but found lots of other things he did love. Jeremy, who usually doesn't love anything, thought I had a few smart things to say, which was just as gratifying. And Mike, who has long been a mentor and a friend, urged me to write something that people would want to actually read. I hope you're all pleased with how things turned out.

I'm grateful to Suzanne Maloney and Khaled Elgindy, who gave me the right compliments at the right moment, when things were tough going. Martin Indyk and Bruce Jones asked hard questions and nudged me to defend my ideas in front of the great scholars at Brookings, which kept me on my toes. And Strobe Talbott's enthusiasm for the project not only encouraged me but also made me hopeful that Brookings will want to keep me around a bit longer.

There are plenty of people who kindly answered my questions or generously shared their findings. I especially want to thank Volkmar Kabisch, who passed along the documents he and his team had gathered in Iraq, and Peter Neumann, who put us in touch and shared his own research. J. M. Berger graciously responded to my queries, Thomas Hegghammer pushed me to be more precise, Sam Helfont helped me better understand Ba'athist religious politics in Iraq, and Jomana Qaddour kept me up to date on the Syrian civil war.

A special thanks to my agent extraordinaire, Bridget Matzie, who not only read and commented on the manuscript but also connected me with the wonderful Karen Wolny and her outstanding team at St. Martin's. Readers can thank Karen for constantly reminding me that people like stories and explanations that don't leave them more confused than when they started.

There's a reason why authors usually thank their immediate family last: every subsequent thank you would dim in comparison.

Casey and my three sweet little kids spent a very cold winter in DC tiptoeing around the house so I could write this book. I can never thank you enough for your understanding—well, at least Casey understood. My kids just laughed loudly when I shushed them. Now it's time to take that much-delayed summer vacation!

TRANSLITERATION

generally followed the guidelines of the *International Journal of Middle East Studies*, although I've capitalized proper nouns. Outside of book and article titles, I haven't used initial *ayn* because I find it too distracting. *Hamza* and *ayn* are represented by an apostrophe.

THE ISIS

APOCALYPSE

INTRODUCTION

June 2014 was going to be quiet. Government employees in Washington, DC, disperse for the summer to beat the heat, which means those of us who make a living commenting on the government do too. It'd be a good time to play with my kids and get back to my hobby, writing a scriptural history of the Qur'an. Articles about al-Qaeda and the civil war in Syria, my usual beat, could wait. No one cared.

They cared a few days later when the so-called Islamic State group marched across Iraq and conquered its second-largest city, Mosul. Mass executions, enslaved women, and crucifixions soon followed, parading across cable news and Twitter. The danse macabre hasn't stopped since. Black flags rose, and government buildings were painted the same somber shade. The Islamic State's leaders proclaimed the establishment of God's kingdom on earth, called the caliphate. Prophecy was fulfilled, they said, and Judgment Day approached.

The new caliphate was expansive and flush with weapons and cash, reportedly in the billions. At its head was the self-styled caliph Ibrahim al-Baghdadi, an Iraqi religious scholar who took up arms after the United States invaded Iraq in 2003. Councils and governors advised the caliph, whose provinces stretched from Mosul to the outskirts of Aleppo in Syria, the distance from Washington, DC, to Cleveland, Ohio. Baghdadi's followers inside the caliphate numbered in the tens of thousands. Thousands more applauded him in Europe and the Middle East. The group threatened to topple American allies in the Middle East, destabilize world energy markets, foment revolution abroad, and launch attacks against Europe and the United States.

Questions flew. How had the Islamic State conquered so much land? Why was it so brutal? Why would such a murderous group claim to do God's bidding and fulfill prophecy? Did it really have anything to do with Islam, the world's second-largest religion? And what threat did it pose to the international community?

Readers who want more than sound-bite answers to these questions face a daunting challenge. Much of the Islamic State's propaganda is in Arabic and cloaked in medieval theological language that confuses Arabic-speaking Muslims, much less English-speaking non-Muslims. The Islamic State's bureaucracy is layered in secrecy, and few details have emerged about its inner workings. But like any bureaucracy, the Islamic State leaves a paper trail of emails and couriered messages. Some of them have been leaked by dissenters who post private Islamic State memoranda on password-protected discussion forums; other memos were released by the U.S. government, which captured them during raids. Followers and critics of the Islamic State have taken and posted pictures of its fatwas that were never meant to circulate online. Making sense of it all would require a guide proficient in Islamic theology and history, modern jihadism, clandestine bureaucracies, and Arabic.

That's what I am, and I am going to take you on a tour of the Islamic State. We will explore its origins, meet its leaders, boo its fans, and cheer its detractors. You will read its propaganda, study its strategies, eavesdrop on its internal debates, and follow its tweets. Along the way, I will explain its obscure allusions to Islamic history and theology so you can understand the ways the Islamic State uses and abuses Islam. You will be able to appreciate how the Islamic State thinks of itself, how its self-understanding has affected its political fortunes, and what will happen if those fortunes change again.

Like most of what the Islamic State does, its extreme brutality defies the conventional jihadist playbook. We're used to thinking of al-Qaeda's former leader Osama bin Laden as the baddest of the bad, but the Islamic State is worse. Bin Laden tamped down messianic fervor and sought popular Muslim support; the caliphate was a distant dream. In contrast, the Islamic State's members fight and govern by their own version of Machiavelli's dictum, "It is far safer to be feared than loved." They stir messianic fervor rather than suppress it. They want God's kingdom now rather than later. This is not Bin Laden's jihad. In what follows, I will tell you why the Islamic State's jihad is different and why that difference matters.

ONE
RAISING THE
BLACK FLAG

On a mild August morning in 2014, a passerby noticed a black flag hanging outside a rundown duplex in suburban New Jersey. He could not make out the flag's black-and-white Arabic, but he recognized the design from the news. All summer, American televisions and computer screens had been filled with reports of horrific acts committed by a renegade al-Qaeda group in Syria and Iraq, accompanied by foreboding images of masked jihadists waving the flag. From Morocco to Mindanao, jihadists were fighting under the banner to realize their dark vision of God's rule on earth. Alarmed, the passerby sent a picture of the house and its flag to his friend Marc Leibowitz, a former Israeli paratrooper working as an investment manager in New Jersey, who promptly tweeted the picture and the address with the caption "Scary!" The prospect of a jihadist proudly displaying his colors in America guaranteed the tweet went viral. Leibowitz also informed Homeland Security.[1]

When the police arrived, the flag's owner, Mark Dunaway, had no idea anyone had tweeted a picture of it. Dunaway had converted to Islam a decade ago, he explained, and flew the flag to mark Muslim holidays. "Every Muslim uses that black flag," he said. "You'll find it in any mosque in the world. I am an American citizen and I love my country, but I am also a Muslim and I use that flag to say I'm a Muslim." Still, Dunaway could see why people would be concerned, and he took down the flag. "I understand now that people turn on CNN and see the flag associated with jihad, but that's not the intention of that flag at all. It says 'There is only one god, Allah, and the prophet Muhammad is his messenger.' It's not meant to be a symbol of hate. Islam is all about unity and peace. I am not a part of any group like that, and I'm not anti-American. I love my country, but I am a Muslim."[2]

Doubtless, Dunaway sincerely believed he did not support a militant group by flying the flag, as attested by the police's disinterest in the case and his neighbors' testimonials. Dunaway, like many Muslims and even Middle East experts, did not know the flag was designed by an al-Qaeda offshoot, the Islamic State, after it proclaimed its statehood in 2006. It certainly wasn't in every "mosque in the world" as Dunaway thought. He and others were confused because the Islamic State had used terror and Twitter to advertise its brand and Islamic tradition to obscure its meaning.

Before the Islamic State declared itself the caliphate reborn that summer, it had been ambiguous about the flag's meaning and the cause it represented. Was it the flag of *an* Islamic state or the flag of *the* Islamic state, the caliphate that had once ruled land from Spain to Iran and whose prophesied return would herald the end of the world? The Islamic State encouraged the second interpretation but let the global community of jihadists read into the flag and the "state" what they would.

And read into them they did, with many taking up the flag and promoting the Islamic State as the fulfillment of prophecy long before it declared itself as such. The Islamic State's cause proved so compelling among jihadists that in 2014 the organization supplanted its former master, al-Qaeda, to lead the global jihadist movement. The spread of the flag, then, traces the spread of an idea and chronicles a major changing of the guard in the global jihadist movement

over the past nine years. It also represents a revolution in how jihadists think about acquiring power and holding onto it.

Although it took nearly a decade to play itself out, the Islamic
State was destined to fall out with al-Qaeda from the start. Al-Qaeda
leader Osama bin Laden and his deputy Ayman al-Zawahiri wanted
to build popular Muslim support before declaring the caliphate.
The Islamic State wanted to impose a caliphate regardless of what
the masses thought. The dispute that divided parent from child was
there from the Islamic State's conception.

PROBLEM CHILD

In 1999, a hotheaded Jordanian street-tough-turned-jihadist, Abu
Mus'ab al-Zarqawi, arrived in Qandahar, Afghanistan, seeking an
audience with al-Qaeda's leaders. The young Zarqawi wanted to foment revolution in the Fertile Crescent, the land stretching from
the eastern Mediterranean through Iraq. Zarqawi had been to Afghanistan before, just after the defeat of the Soviets in 1989.[3] Too
late to fight in the war, he soon returned to Jordan, where he failed
as a terrorist and spent time behind bars for his effort. Now out of
prison, Zarqawi had come back to Afghanistan to gather money and
recruits for his cause.[4]

Al-Qaeda's man in Qandahar, Sayf al-Adl, did not contact Zarqawi immediately. A former special forces colonel in the Egyptian
military,[5] Sayf had learned to watch and wait. He had Zarqawi
followed.[6]

Sayf's spy reported that Zarqawi frequently argued with other
jihadists because of his extreme views on who should count as a good
Muslim. Zarqawi especially disliked the Shi'a, one of the two major
sects in Islam. Zarqawi, a Sunni, disagreed with the Shi'i doctrine
that Muhammad's son-in-law and some of his male descendants were
infallible and the only legitimate political and religious leaders of the
early Muslim community. He also believed the modern Shi'i state of
Iran colluded with the West to oppress Sunnis. When Sayf finally

met Zarqawi, he found him a man of few words who sincerely wanted to bring Sunni Islam back to "the reality of human life." But Zarqawi did not have a lot of specific ideas for how to do it.

Sayf relayed his impressions of Zarqawi to his bosses in al-Qaeda. Al-Qaeda's leader, Bin Laden, was the son of a wealthy Saudi building contractor, and his deputy, Ayman al-Zawahiri, was a surgeon who had run an Egyptian terror group before merging part of it with al-Qaeda. Both men would oversee the 9/11 attacks, which were premised on their belief that the American infidel should be killed wantonly. But when it came to Muslims, Bin Laden and Zawahiri were more cautious. They believed Muslim support was crucial for driving the Americans out of the Middle East and establishing Islamic states. It wouldn't do to make enemies on all sides, especially over theological differences. Some have even speculated that Bin Laden's own mother grew up in a small Shi'i sect.[7] Unity of mission rather than unity of mind was what was needed.

Despite their misgivings about Zarqawi's extreme views, Sayf recommended his bosses support the Jordanian hothead because they had so few Palestinian or Jordanian allies. They consented but would not invite Zarqawi to join al-Qaeda; he would have refused anyway. Rather, they coordinated and cooperated with him "in serving our common goals."[8]

Sayf and his companions came up with a plan for Zarqawi to establish a training camp in Afghanistan to attract jihadists from Jordan, Palestine, Syria, Lebanon, and Turkey. Herat was chosen because of its proximity to the Iranian border, where it was easy to move men and materiel across. Over time, Syrians, Jordanians, Palestinians, Lebanese, and Iraqis arrived. Zarqawi also reached out to the Kurdish Ansar al-Islam organization in northern Iraq.[9]

By the beginning of 2001, Zarqawi was no longer a jihadist neophyte in the eyes of Sayf. He had "begun to think and plan strategically for the future." Reading widely about world events and Islamic history, Zarqawi was struck by the figure of Nur al-Din Zengi, the ruthless medieval ruler of a dominion stretching from Aleppo in Syria to Mosul in Iraq who had driven the crusaders from Syria.[10]

Zarqawi undoubtedly admired Nur al-Din's ambition and remorseless efficiency. In one account, Nur al-Din had besieged a crusader citadel in Syria. The crusaders finally capitulated and approached Nur al-Din to discuss terms. "He would not consent to their request," as a medieval Muslim historian euphemistically put it. When crusader reinforcements arrived to lift the siege, they saw the citadel wall "and the dwelling of its inhabitants were entirely in ruins."[11]

"[Zarqawi] was always asking for any book available about Nur al-Din and his protégé Saladin," Sayf recalled, referring to the ruler of Egypt who battled Richard the Lionheart during the Crusades. "I believe that what he read about Nur al-Din and his launch from Mosul in Iraq played a big role in influencing Abu Mus'ab [al-Zarqawi] in his decision to go to Iraq after the fall of the Islamic Emirate in Afghanistan" in 2001.[12]

The "Islamic Emirate of Afghanistan" had been established in 1996 by the Taliban, conservative Sunnis who swept to power in the chaotic aftermath of the Soviet withdrawal from the country in 1989. In medieval Islamic thought, an "emirate" (*imara*), or government of a region, is subordinate to the "state" (*dawla*), the empire ruled by the caliph. But in the absence of a caliph, jihadists today sometimes use "state" and "emirate" interchangeably when talking about the government of a country they'd like to create.[13] The Taliban's emirate brought order to Afghanistan by strictly enforcing Islamic law. It also gave shelter to likeminded jihadist groups such as al-Qaeda and Zarqawi's outfit.

After the fall of the Taliban, Zarqawi and Sayf fled Afghanistan for Iran. There they discussed where Zarqawi should go next. After "long study and deliberation," Sayf later wrote, Zarqawi's group decided to relocate to Iraq, where their "appearance" and "dialect" would help them blend in. Zarqawi and Sayf anticipated that the Americans would "invade Iraq sooner or later" to overthrow the regime. "It was necessary for us to play a major role in the confrontation and resistance," Sayf recalled. "This is our historical opportunity . . . to establish the state of Islam, which would play the greatest role in lifting injustice and bringing truth to this world, by God's permission. I was in agreement with brother Abu Mus'ab [al-Zarqawi] in this analysis."[14]

For Sayf and presumably for Zarqawi, the "state of Islam" was the caliphate itself.[15] Sayf used to believe that "the Islamic state of the caliphate" would develop from the Taliban's Islamic emirate in Afghanistan. But the American invasion in 2001 had ended that dream.[16] Iraq was a second chance.

In 2002 and early 2003, Zarqawi set about building his clandestine network in Iraq. When the Americans invaded in March 2003, Zarqawi's cells in Baghdad were ready to greet them. Zarqawi himself arrived in June.[17] By the end of August, his new group, Monotheism and Jihad, had bombed the Jordanian embassy and the United Nations headquarters in Baghdad, as well as the mosque of Imam Ali, one of the holiest shrines of Shi'i Islam. The subsequent departure of the UN mission and rising fury of Iraq's majority Shi'a signaled the beginning of a bloody sectarian civil war.

Zarqawi's group had not pulled off the attack alone. It had help from former security officers in Saddam Hussein's government, casualties of the Bush administration's purge of Saddam party loyalists. They, like other disenfranchised Arab Sunnis, feared the rise of the country's Shi'i population who had lived under the yoke of Saddam and minority Sunni rule for decades. There was a reckoning coming, and Sunni jihadists and nationalists were willing to put aside their ideological differences for the time being to unite against a common foe: the Americans and the majority Shi'a who stood to benefit from the occupation.[18]

Zarqawi's hatred of the Shi'a was all-consuming. To his mind, the Shi'a were not just fifth columnists, selling out the Sunnis to the Americans. They were servants of the Antichrist, who will appear at the end of time to fight against the Muslims. The Americans served the same master.[19]

Zarqawi's hatred of the Shi'a made him lose sight of his long-term political goals. When he applied for membership in al-Qaeda in February 2004, he did not mention an Islamic state or a plan for achieving it. Rather, he explained his strategy for winning over the Sunnis, defeating the transitional government, and driving the infidels from Iraq: Provoke the Shi'a. "If we are able to strike them with one painful blow after another until they enter the battle, we will be able to reshuffle the cards. Then, no value or influence will remain to the Governing Council or even to the Americans, who will enter a second battle with the Shi'a. This is what we want, and, whether they like it or not, many Sunni areas will stand with the mujahidin."[20] (Mujahidin, or "those who fight in a jihad," is how jihadists refer to themselves.)

Zarqawi knew he would be criticized as "hasty and rash," "leading the Muslim community into a battle for which it is not ready, a battle that will be revolting and in which blood will be spilled." So be it. "This is exactly what we want, since right and wrong no longer have any place in our current situation. The Shi'a have destroyed all those balances."[21]

If al-Qaeda's leaders would assent to his strategy, Zarqawi offered to swear allegiance to them, joining his group to theirs: "If you agree with us on it, if you adopt it as a program and path, and if you are convinced of the idea of fighting the sects of apostasy, we will be your readied soldiers, working under your banner, complying with your orders, and indeed swearing fealty to you publicly and in the news media, vexing the infidels and gladdening those who preach the oneness of God."[22]

Al-Qaeda's leaders were wary. Bin Laden and Zawahiri wanted to compel the U.S. military to leave the Middle East and to stop supporting local autocrats. Their strategy was to attack the Americans and stir Muslim resentment against them. Building popular Muslim support for their cause was vital; the caliphate could not be established without it. In contrast, Zarqawi wanted to first overthrow local autocrats and eliminate the "traitorous" Shi'a, whom he believed were collaborating with the Americans to subjugate the Sunnis. His strategy was to ignite a sectarian civil war. Popular support mattered far less to Zarqawi than it did to Bin Laden and Zawahiri. He could will a caliphate into being regardless of what its subjects might say.

Despite their reservations, Bin Laden and Zawahiri accepted Zarqawi's oath of allegiance, joining his Monotheism and Jihad group to their own in October 2004. Al-Qaeda had just mounted a disastrous terror campaign in Saudi Arabia and was desperate for a role in the growing Sunni insurgency in Iraq.[23] Zarqawi may have wanted to tap into al-Qaeda's network of private Gulf funders, operational expertise, and recruitment apparatus.[24] Thus, al-Qaeda in Iraq was born.

Zarqawi was elated. "Our noble brothers in al-Qaeda understand the strategy of the Monotheism and Jihad group in the land of the two rivers, the land of the caliphs," he declared in his pledge to al-Qaeda's leaders, "and their hearts are overjoyed by its method there." "Perhaps," wrote Zarqawi, the group would establish the "caliphate according to the prophetic method."[25] As we will see later, Zarqawi was alluding to an Islamic prophesy of the caliphate's return shortly before the End of Days.

Although Bin Laden and Zawahiri shared Zarqawi's desire to re-establish the caliphate, they advised him to proceed slowly and build popular support. In July 2005, Zawahiri wrote Zarqawi, urging him to establish an Islamic "emirate" only after the jihadists had expelled the United States from Iraq. The jihadists were to then "develop" and "consolidate" the emirate as far as they could inside the Sunni areas of Iraq until it reached "the level of the caliphate." The mission of the jihadists thereafter was to protect the caliphate's domain and expand its borders until the Day of Judgment.[26]

Despite encouraging Zarqawi to establish an emirate after the American withdrawal, Zawahiri warned him not to attempt it before securing the support of the Sunni masses. Al-Qaeda's "two short-term goals" of "removing the Americans and establishing an Islamic emirate or caliphate in Iraq" both required "popular support from the Muslim masses in Iraq and the surrounding countries." "In the absence of this popular support," Zawahiri predicted, "the Islamic mujahid movement would be crushed in the shadows."[27]

Zawahiri counseled Zarqawi to overlook the heresies of Sunni religious scholars, whose support al-Qaeda needed, and to cooperate with Sunni community leaders. Zarqawi should also stop broadcasting hostage beheadings. The beheadings may thrill "zealous young men," Zawahiri chided, but the Muslim masses "will never find them palatable." In general, the jihadists "shouldn't stir questions in the hearts and minds of the people about the benefit of our actions . . . we are in a media battle in a race for the hearts and minds of our [Muslim] community."[28]

Zawahiri even went so far as to question Zarqawi's attacks on Shi'i civilians, the cornerstone of Zarqawi's strategy to provoke a sectarian civil war. "My opinion is that this matter won't be acceptable to the Muslim populace however much you have tried to explain it, and aversion to this will continue." In addition to jeopardizing public support, Zawahiri doubted the morality of these sectarian attacks. "Why kill ordinary Shi'a considering that they are forgiven because of their ignorance? And what loss will befall us if we did not attack the Shi'a?"

Another al-Qaeda leader in Bin Laden's inner circle, Atiyya Abd al-Rahman, was blunter in a December 2005 letter to Zarqawi. Echoing the nineteenth-century Prussian military theorist Carl von Clausewitz, Atiyya reminded Zarqawi that "policy must be dominant over militarism. This is one of the pillars of war that is agreed upon by all nations, whether they are Muslims or unbelievers." Atiyya cautioned that unless the jihadists' "short-term goals and successes" serve their "ultimate goal and highest aims," they would simply exhaust themselves to no effect.[29]

Atiyya reminded Zarqawi of the fate of the Algerian jihadists in the 1990s. After Algerian Islamists had won the first round of voting for parliament in 1991, the military had cancelled the elections. Some Islamists turned to violence and, as the civil war dragged on, a jihadist faction began to murder civilians. Their short-term tactical successes won through brutality blinded them to how much they had alienated the Muslim masses. As Atiyya reminded Zarqawi, "They destroyed themselves with their own hands, with their lack of reason, delusions, their ignoring of people, their alienation of them through oppression, deviance, and severity, coupled with a lack of kindness, sympathy, and friendliness." It was not their enemy that defeated them; "they defeated themselves."[30]

Atiyya knew what he was talking about. In 1993, al-Qaeda had sent the young Libyan to Algeria to liaise with the jihadist groups there. Rather than welcoming Atiyya, the worst of the groups imprisoned him. Atiyya managed to escape months later, but he was haunted by the experience. "I think [he] is still having nightmares about it," recounted someone who knew Atiyya's story.[31]

Like Zawahiri, Atiyya reminded Zarqawi of the long-term objective he was fighting for: the establishment of the caliphate. "My brother," Atiyya wrote, "what use is it for us to delight in some operations and successful strikes when the immediate repercussion is a defeat for us of our call, and a loss of the justice of our cause and its logic in the minds of the masses who make up the people of the Muslim nation?" "You need all of these people," Atiyya observed, if you want "to destroy a power and a state and erect on its rubble the state of Islam."[32]

"What am I commanding you to do?" Atiyya asked rhetorically. "Remedy the deficiency."[33]

Atiyya detailed what he and other al-Qaeda leaders expected of Zarqawi. He should make no major strategic decisions without first consulting Bin Laden and Zawahiri. And he was to win over and work with influential Sunnis in Iraq, even the heterodox. Stop killing them, "no matter what."[34]

Atiyya also counseled Zarqawi to stop insisting Sunni rebels join his organization and leave other jihadist groups: "Whether they come into the organization with us or not . . . they are our brothers."[35]

Zarqawi initially agreed with Zawahiri and Atiyya that expelling the Americans was the priority. "First, we will expel the enemy," he explained in an interview. "Then we will establish the State of Islam." After that, the jihadists would "embark on conquest of Muslim lands to reclaim them," and then set their sights on the infidels.[36]

But by April 2006, Zarqawi had changed his mind. When he announced a consultative council composed of several jihadist groups including al-Qaeda, he described it as the "nucleus for establishing an Islamic state."[37] That state, he proclaimed, would be established in three months.[38]

After the United States killed Zarqawi on June 7, 2006, al-Qaeda in Iraq carried out its leader's dying wish. Rather than wait to establish the Islamic state until after the Americans withdrew and the Sunni masses backed the project, as Bin Laden and Zawahiri wanted, the Islamic State was proclaimed on October 15, 2006. As we will see in the following chapter, the timing of the Islamic State's announcement was based on an apocalyptic schedule. The al-Qaeda front group that made the announcement insisted that Muslims in Iraq pledge allegiance to a certain Abu Umar al-Baghdadi and acknowledge him as "commander of the faithful."[39] No one had ever heard of him, not even other jihadists.

STATE OF CONFUSION

The Islamic State called its mysterious leader the "commander of the faithful" to encourage jihadists to think of him as the caliph without explicitly saying so.[40] Historically, Muslims reserved that title for the early Islamic caliphs, the spiritual and temporal heads of a vast empire. Abu Umar al-Baghdadi's alleged descent from the Prophet's tribe, which many Muslims consider a prerequisite for the caliph, hinted at his entitlement to the position. Abu Umar even claimed descent from one of the Prophet's grandsons, Husayn, in an attempt to appeal to those who would confine leadership of the Muslim world to descendants from Muhammad's family, just as medieval caliphs had done.

The name of the Islamic State was equally ambiguous. The group had called itself a state rather than an emirate, the latter a more common word used by jihadists to describe small territory ruled by an emir. The word "state" in Arabic, *dawla*, can either mean a modern nation-state or evoke the memory of medieval caliphates like the Dawla Abbasiyya, which spanned Mesopotamia, the Persian Gulf, and North Africa. The Islamic State played on this ambiguity to encourage its followers to view it as the proto-caliphate, sometimes calling itself "the Islamic State *in* Iraq" rather than its official name of "the Islamic State *of* Iraq."[41]

Although most of the Islamic State's members at this time were part of al-Qaeda in Iraq, the Islamic State made no mention of al-Qaeda or of members' preexisting oaths of allegiance to Bin Laden or to Mullah Omar, the head of the Taliban.[42] Only four months earlier, Abu Ayyub al-Masri (aka Abu Hamza al-Muhajir), the head of al-Qaeda in Iraq after Zarqawi and later the founder of the Islamic State, had proclaimed his undying loyalty to Mullah Omar as "commander of the faithful" and to Bin Laden as the head of al-Qaeda. "We . . . are an arrow in your quiver. Shoot us where you wish for we are naught but an obedient soldier."[43]

Al-Qaeda's supporters around the globe were confused. Was the new Islamic State part of al-Qaeda or something different? The jihadist pundit Akram Hijazi complained that al-Qaeda had not released an official statement and there was no sign of official co-ordination between al-Qaeda and the Islamic State. Bin Laden and Zawahiri had pledged oaths of allegiance to Mullah Omar, as had the head of al-Qaeda in Iraq. Were those oaths dissolved now? Who was in charge? Why, Hijazi wondered, was the hitherto unknown Abu Umar al-Baghdadi not just named a governor under the authority of the commander of the faithful, Mullah Omar?[44]

Another jihadist Internet commentator summarized the confusion rampant in the private discussion boards where jihadists hung out before the advent of Twitter. "How can we pledge allegiance to Abu Umar al-Baghdadi when we may have pledged allegiance to Mullah Omar? What do we do with the pledge of allegiance to Shaykh Osama if we want to pledge allegiance to Shaykh Abu Umar?"[45]

The truth was that Bin Laden and Zawahiri had been caught by surprise. "The decision to announce the State was taken without consulting the leadership of al-Qaeda," American al-Qaeda spokesman Adam Gadahn confided in a private letter. As he saw it, the un-authorized announcement "caused splits in the ranks of the mujahids and their supporters inside and outside Iraq."[46] Zawahiri would later recall that "the general command of [al-Qaeda] and its emir Shaykh

Osama bin Laden (God bless him) were not asked for permission, consulted, or even warned just prior to the announcement of the establishment of the Islamic State of Iraq."[47]

Behind the scenes, the Islamic State sought to heal its rift with Bin Laden and Zawahiri. The former head of al-Qaeda in Iraq and the actual leader of the new Islamic State, Abu Ayyub al-Masri, assured his bosses that the "commander of the faithful," Abu Umar al-Baghdadi, had pledged an oath of allegiance to Bin Laden in front of the jihadist brothers in Iraq. They did not announce it publicly "due to some political considerations that they saw in Iraq at that time."[48]

Masri was attempting to preserve the Islamic State's ties to al-Qaeda while encouraging the public to think of it as a separate entity. He wanted the world to view his group as a state and not a terrorist franchise. Ambiguity, again, was critical to the Islamic State's early propaganda.

Masri used the same strategy in his public statements. A month after the Islamic State's founding, Masri hailed it as an important step in the "program of the Islamic caliphate." In the same statement, Masri pledged his allegiance to the shadowy "commander of the faithful," Abu Umar al-Baghdadi, announced the dissolution of al-Qaeda, and reassigned all its fighters to the Islamic State of Iraq. "All of them have pledged allegiance unto death in the path of God," Masri assured the commander of the faithful. "You will only find us listening to what you say and obeying what you command."[49]

In the five succeeding months, Abu Umar al-Baghdadi and the Islamic State hammered home the same point: Al-Qaeda in Iraq was no more. "Al-Qaeda is but one of the groups in the Islamic State," Abu Umar declared in December 2006."[50] "It is more correct to say," instructed the Islamic State's ministry of media, "that the brothers previously in the organization of al-Qaeda in Iraq became part of the 'army of the State,' which includes dozens of battalions and thousands of fighters from the remaining jihadist groups that pledged loyalty to the commander of the faithful after the announcement of the State."[51] On April 19, 2007, an Islamic State spokesman announced that Masri was now the minister of war in the State's first cabinet.[52]

Al-Qaeda's leaders were not only angered that the Islamic State had challenged Bin Laden's authority by not seeking his approval. They were also convinced the Islamic State had declared itself too soon. In the spring of 2007, a senior al-Qaeda leader, Abu al-Walid al-Ansari, asked a string of pointed questions of the group. Why had the state been declared now rather than later? Had its appointment of the commander of the faithful followed Islamic rules? Why had the Islamic State announced that anyone who opposed it was a sinner? Ansari reminded the Islamic State that it needed the broad support of the people it wished to govern and the consent of their leaders if it was going to survive. By declaring itself prematurely, the Islamic State had taken on the burdens of governing and invited foreign intervention, both of which could prove lethal to the nascent enterprise.[53]

Other jihadists were even more pointed in their criticisms. The Kuwaiti scholar Hamid al-Ali argued that an authentic Islamic State should be able to impose its authority over those it governs. The Islamic State did not meet that standard. The Islamic State also failed to meet classical Islamic requirements for establishing an Islamic government, at least according to al-Ali. "It is not recognized in Islam to pledge allegiance to an unknown, concealed leader who has no authority . . . [or] established state" capable of imposing Islamic law, al-Ali wrote. Mullah Omar could declare a state in Afghanistan in the 1990s because he actually ruled it at the time; Abu Umar al-Baghdadi ruled nothing. Declaring a state in Iraq under false pretenses, al-Ali charged, had divided the jihadist movement in Iraq, which should be united under the banner of jihad rather than the banner of a single group.[54]

Al-Qaeda's leaders in Pakistan looked on in shame and dread as its problem child stumbled in its first few months. Atiyya Abd al-Rahman, Bin Laden's chief of staff who had sent the 2005 letter upbraiding Zarqawi, shared his worry with a confidant "about the brothers making political gaffes." "You must have heard Abu Umar's recent sermon," he wrote, referring to the Islamic State's nominal leader, Abu Umar al-Baghdadi. "In my view, it was filled with obvious errors. There were things in it that a commander should never say." The speech gave the impression that they were "extremists and gave life to the notion that they are self-absorbed and too hasty!" Atiyya worried that if "they continue in this way, they will become corrupt and . . . lose the people," allowing the enemy to turn the populace against them. "None of the enemies scare me, I swear, no matter who they are, or how intimidating they may be. . . . But I do worry about our and our brothers' mistakes, bad behavior, and lack of wisdom at times."[55] Reminiscent of the letter he had written Zarqawi, Atiyya confided that he himself had chastised the Islamic State's leaders: "I was a little hard on them."[56]

Despite al-Qaeda's private misgivings, its leaders presented a united front in public and endorsed the establishment of the State.[57] They probably wanted to keep a hand in the Iraq game and avoid further dissension in the ranks. "I want to clarify that there is nothing in Iraq by the name of al-Qaeda," said Zawahiri in a December 2007 question-and-answer session. "Rather, the organization of [al-Qaeda in Iraq] merged, by the grace of God, with other jihadist groups in the Islamic State of Iraq, may God protect it. It is a legitimate emirate established on a legitimate and sound method. It was established through consultation and won the oath of allegiance from most of the mujahids and tribes in Iraq."[58]

Al-Qaeda's affiliate in Iraq may have become part of the Islamic State and the Islamic State may have privately joined al-Qaeda, but the public would not know the nature of the relationship between the two groups for years to come. The Islamic State itself never addressed the question publicly, again relying on ambiguity to imply greater power and autonomy than it possessed. The Islamic State's ambiguous audacity would capture the jihadist imagination and become crucial in its later rise to power. Nothing embodied the propaganda strategy better than the Islamic State's flag.

MAKING THE BLACK FLAG

When the Islamic State first announced itself on October 15, 2006, it had no flag of its own.[59] It was not until January 2007 that al-Qaeda's media distribution arm, al-Fajr, released a picture of the Islamic State's new flag. Anonymous authors affiliated with the Islamic State explained its design.[60]

Unsurprisingly, the Islamic State had turned to the Prophet's example for inspiration, quoting passages from Islamic scripture and historical accounts. "The flag of the Prophet, peace and blessings be upon him, is a black square made of striped wool," according to one account. Another depicts Muhammad "standing on the pulpit preaching" surrounded by fluttering black flags. "On the flag of the Prophet was written 'No god but God, and Muhammad is the Messenger of God.'" The flag even had a name: "the eagle."[61]

Although the authors acknowledged other reports of green, white, and yellow flags, they concluded the Islamic State's flag will be black because most of the reports about Muhammad mention a black flag. "The commander of the faithful [Abu Umar al-Baghdadi] issued his decree, informed by knowledgeable people, that the flag of the Islamic State is black." The authors were equally confident when explaining the banner's text, which is the Muslim profession of faith. "What is written on the flag is what is written on the flag of the Messenger of God, peace and blessings be upon him: 'No god but God, Muhammad is the Messenger of God.'"[62]

The Islamic State's design of the Muslim profession of faith is unique, different from every other attempt to replicate the Prophet's flag: "No god but God" is scrawled in white across the top and "Muhammad is the Messenger of God" is stacked in black inside a white circle. As the authors noted, they took the circle's design from a seal of the Prophet used on letters supposedly written on his behalf and housed in Topkapi Palace in Turkey. The seal's design, the authors argued, comports with historical reports of what the Prophet's seal looked like. Never mind that modern scholars doubt the letters' authenticity.[63] We are meant to believe the Islamic State had inherited the Prophet's seal, just as the early caliphs had.[64]

Why make a flag? In addition to following the Prophet's example, the Islamic State wanted a symbol to rally people to its cause. The State quoted a nineteenth-century Ottoman historian and official,

Ahmad Cevdet Pasha, to make the point: "The secret in creating a flag is that it gathers people under a single banner to unify them, meaning that this flag is a sign of the coming together of their words and a proof of the unity of their hearts. They are like a single body and what knits them together is stronger than the bond of blood relatives."[65]

Like all fundamentalist attempts to revive the early days of their faith, the Islamic State's leaders had to choose among contrasting scriptures and histories from their religion's past to paint a portrait of what they aspired to in the present and future. Their choices display the cultural biases and modern sensibilities they try so hard to displace. They selected a stark black for the flag rather than green, yellow, or white; the color suits their Manichean worldview, which permits no gray areas between the binaries of right and wrong, believer and unbeliever. The white scrawl across the top, "No god but God," is deliberately ragged, meant to suggest an era before the precision of Photoshop even though the flag was designed on a computer.

Even the Islamic State's quotation of Ahmad Cevdet Pasha unwittingly betrays modern sensibilities. Influenced by European notions of nationalism yet desiring to hold together the multi-ethnic Ottoman Empire under sovereign Turkish rule, Cevdet Pasha imagined Islam and its symbols to be the glue. The sentiment underlies his utilitarian outlook on religion. "The only thing uniting Arab, Kurd, Albanian and Bosnian is the unity of Islam. Yet the real strength of the Sublime State lies with the Turks."[66] Try as they might to re-create the imagined utopian era of the Prophet, the people who designed the Islamic State's flag were still captives of their age. The quest for authenticity is a very modern pursuit.

As with its flag, the Islamic State unwittingly organized and described itself in modern ways. A jihadist pundit complained that the Islamic State used modern words to describe its bureaucracy: "[Words] in the expressions 'Spokesman on behalf of the Islamic State of Iraq' and 'the Minister of Education' are found in Arab and Islamic history but their form appears closer to the reality of today than any Islamic reality." The same pundit also griped that confining the state to Iraq was too close to modern notions of the state.[67] The original caliphal state had been a large empire with ever-expanding borders, not a state contiguous with any particular nation like the modern nation-state.

Despite its ambiguity, the Islamic State was dropping hints that it aspired to be more than a modern nation-state. Its flag carried the seal of the Prophet, a sign of authority inherited by the caliphs. As we will see, the flag's color also evoked a powerful early caliphate. But there was something more. The Islamic State ended its explanation of its flag's design with a prayer: "We ask God, praised be He, to make this flag the sole flag for all Muslims. We are certain that it will be the flag of the people of Iraq when they go to aid . . . the Mahdi at the holy house of God." The house of God is the Ka'ba in Mecca, the holiest shrine in Islam, and the Mahdi is the Muslim savior who will appear there in the years leading up to the apocalypse. The Islamic State was signaling that its flag was not only the symbol of its government in Iraq and the herald of a future caliphate; it was the harbinger of the final battle at the End of Days.[68]

THE RIGHTLY GUIDED ONE

Legends of the black flag and the Muslim savior, the Mahdi, first circulated during the reign of the Umayyad dynasty, which ruled the Islamic empire from the ancient city of Damascus in the seventh and eighth centuries AD. The dynasty's founders, the Umayya clan, had seized the caliphate from Muhammad's son-in-law and grandsons, which infuriated many Muslims. The father of the dynasty's founder Mu'awiya had persecuted Muhammad and his early followers before he later converted. The founder's mother had even eaten the liver of Muhammad's uncle.

People unhappy with Umayyad rule and the way they had seized power circulated prophecies of a man of the Prophet's family who would return justice to the world. They called the man the Mahdi, Arabic for "the Rightly Guided One." Many of the prophecies envision the Mahdi appearing in the End of Days to lead the final battles against the infidels. It is the Islamic version of the Christian Battle of Armageddon. The Final Hour and Day of Judgment will soon follow.

To give the prophecies added heft, they were often attributed to Muhammad. "[The Mahdi's] name will be my name, and his father's name my father's name" went one. "He is a man from my family" went another.[69]

Like most Islamic prophecies of the End of Days, those about the Mahdi are not found in the preeminent scripture of Islam, the Qur'an, which Muslims believe preserves God's revelation to Muhammad.[70] Rather, the prophecies are found in voluminous compendia of the words and deeds of the Prophet and his companions, known as *ahadith*. Because the *ahadith* were written down decades or even centuries after the Prophet's death, they often reflect later political, social, and theological developments rather than what actually happened. Muslims argue over the veracity of individual *ahadith* and the contradictions between them the way some Christians debate the reliability of the Gospels and their discrepancies.

End-Time prophecies were an especially inviting target for fabricators. In the internecine wars that tore apart the early Muslim community, each side sought to justify its politics by predicting its inevitable victory and the other side's preordained defeat. What better way to do this than to put the prophecy in the mouth of the Prophet? Prophecies proliferated, reaching into the thousands. When the politics evaporated, the prophetic residue remained. Throughout the centuries, new politics would give the residue new meaning, a phenomenon familiar to readers of the Christian Book of Revelation for nearly two millennia.

Over the years, the prophecies of the Mahdi have inspired many claimants. How could they resist? Whether the claimant was sincere or not, claiming the spiritual and political power of the Mahdi made a potent recruiting pitch. Think Jesus and George Washington rolled into one.

"The common people, the stupid mass, who make claims with respect to the Mahdi," wrote the medieval Muslim historian Ibn

Khaldun, "assume that the Mahdi may appear in a variety of circumstances and places." Because the masses are gullible, he observed, leaders wrap themselves in the savior's mantel to mobilize them.[71]

Militant messiahs are not unique to Islam. Whether in the Middle Ages or the modern world, groups that want to overturn the social and political order often use apocalyptic language. The Jewish "messiah" Bar Kokhba led an insurgency against the Romans, which the emperor Hadrian brutally repressed, reportedly killing hundreds of thousands, desecrating holy sites, and banning Jews from Jerusalem.[72] The 100,000 European foreign fighters who flooded into Palestine under the banner of the First Crusade believed they were hastening the End of Days.[73] In modern times, some members of the Israeli settler group Gush Emunim sought to hasten the coming of the messiah by blowing up the Dome of the Rock, one of the holiest sites in Islam.[74] The megalomaniacal Christian "savior" Joseph Kony still hides in the Central African Republic, leading the child soldiers in his Lord's Resistance Army.[75]

The two main sects in Islam, Sunni and Shi'a, each had numerous messianic aspirants in the Middle Ages, some of whom established caliphates. These aspirants often claimed the title of Mahdi. "I am Mahdi of the end of time" proclaimed the Sunni founder of the Almohad caliphate in Spain and North Africa.[76] The Shi'i founder of the Fatimid caliphate in Egypt claimed the same for himself and later for his son.[77] Muslims who opposed them were apostates deserving death, a consequence of defying God's anointed.[78]

The first Mahdi didn't actually claim the title himself. In AD 685, a little over fifty years after Muhammad's death, a man named al-Mukhtar led a rebellion against the Umayyads in Iraq in the name of the Mahdi, whom he identified as a grandson of Muhammad. Al-Mukhtar claimed to be the Mahdi's vizier. In addition to leading a rebellion, he is also remembered for prophesying in verse and parading an Ark of the Covenant around Kufa, Iraq. Many of those who rallied to his cause were non-Arab or Jewish converts to Islam who chafed at being treated like second-class citizens in the Arab-dominated government.[79] "They used to say that only three things interrupt prayer," records an early Spanish-Arab historian: A donkey, a dog, and a non-Arab convert to Islam.[80]

The discontent only reinforced the Umayyads' sense of entitlement and fueled their resentment of the new converts who supported the Prophet's family. Were it not for us, complained an early Umayyad caliph, the entire Muslim world would be subservient to the non-Arabs rallying around the Prophet's family. They have become uppity, he allegedly wrote his governor in Iraq, and need to be put in their place.[81]

Supporters of the Prophet's family loosely aligned themselves in what historians call the Hashimite movement, which believed the Mahdi would be a descendent of Muhammad's great-grandfather Hashim. Many of the movement's supporters were from Iran, where Zoroastrian legends prophesied the coming of a club-wielding savior who would appear at the End of Time followed by sable-clad disciples. Influenced by the prophecies, the Hashimite supporters donned black clothes, flew black flags, and carried around wooden clubs called "infidel-bashers."[82]

Iranians and descendants of the Arab conquerors of Iran felt alienated from the remote Umayyad clan ruling from Damascus. "These lands belonged to our ancient fathers!" protested an Arab rebel commander who had grown up in Iran. The early Arab caliphs had once ruled Iran justly, he recalled, and "helped the oppressed." But the Umayyads had made pious people fear the family of the Prophet, so Iranians and Arabs alike had to rise up against them to restore the rule of Muhammad's progeny.[83]

As the revolutionaries built support for their cause, they circulated prophecies of soldiers fighting under black flags who would come from the East to overthrow the Umayyads. Some were put in the mouth of Muhammad's son-in-law Ali, who allegedly foretold the coming of an army from Khorasan, the "land of the rising sun" that includes parts of modern eastern Iran and most of Afghanistan. "The companions of the black flags that will approach from Khorasan are non-Arabs. They will seize power from the Umayyads and kill them under every rock and star."[84] Other black flag prophecies were attributed to the Prophet himself. "The black banners will come from the East, led by men like mighty camels, with long hair and long beards; their surnames are taken from the names of their hometowns and their first names are from kunyas" or teknonyms in the form of Abu So-and-So.[85] "If you see the black banners coming from Khorasan," instructs another, "go to them immediately even if you must crawl over ice because indeed among them is the caliph, al-Mahdi."[86]

In early Islam, the color black was associated not just with mourning but also with revenge for a wrongful death. The pre-Islamic poet Imru al-Qays donned black when he went out to negotiate with the tribe that had murdered his father. When the Arab pagans defeated Muhammad's army at Uhud, his supporters dyed their clothes black to signal their desire to avenge the loss.[87] According to the historian Ibn Khaldun, the opponents of the Umayyads adopted black as their color to avenge the Umayyads' persecution of the Prophet's family. "Their flags were black as a sign of mourning for the martyrs of their family, the Hashimites, and as a sign of reproach directed against the Umayyads who had killed them."[88]

Black flags were also flown by the Prophet in his war with the infidels.[89] "Do not flee with [the flag] from the infidels and do not fight with it against the Muslims," Muhammad reportedly told one of his generals.[90]

When Muslims raised the black flag against the Umayyad caliphs, the caliphs understood the doubly implied threat: vengeance for the family of the Prophet against the "infidel" Muslim rulers who had usurped them.[91]

The seeds of anti-Umayyad propaganda had been sown by a secret network of revolutionaries. The network was led by a shadowy imam, or spiritual leader, descended from the Prophet's uncle Abbas who hoped to use the Hashimite movement to come to power. His agent, Abu Muslim, conducted the propaganda effort and eventually commanded the armed revolt. Their revolutionary agitation on behalf of the Abbasid family came to a head in the Islamic year 129 (AD 746–747), when the imam sent a black "flag of victory" to Abu Muslim in Iran. The flag arrived with a message: "The time has come." Abu Muslim unfurled the black flag, dubbed "the Shadow," on a lance fourteen cubits high and publicly proclaimed the Abbasid's revolutionary call on June 9, 747, the twenty-fifth day of Ramadan, the Muslim month of fasting. After unfurling a second flag, "the Clouds," Abu Muslim and his companions donned black robes. "As the clouds cover the earth, so would the Abbasid preaching," the people were told. "And as the earth is never without a shadow, so it would never be without an Abbasid caliph to the end of time."[92]

Fighting under the black flag, Abu Muslim's armies swept westward into Syria and Iraq. They overthrew the Umayyad caliph and pledged allegiance to a new one, al-Saffah, a brother of the Abbasid imam, who had been executed. The caliph proclaimed himself the Mahdi of the Muslim community, supposedly filling the world with justice and inaugurating the "blessed revolution," *dawla mubaraka*, from which the new empire took its name, Dawla Abbasiyya.[93] It's thanks to the Abbasids that *dawla* came to mean "state."[94]

There are striking parallels between the Abbasid revolution and the Islamic State revolution. They share a name (*dawla*), symbols and colors, apocalyptic propaganda, clandestine networks, and an insurgency in Syria and Iraq. They also claim the right to rule as the Prophet's descendants. The Abbasids had provided a blueprint for how to overthrow a Muslim ruler, establish a new caliphate, and justify both. Apocalypse, caliphate, and revolution were inseparable, just as they are for the Islamic State.

Apocalyptic messages resonate among many Muslims today because of the political turmoil in the Middle East. In 2012, half of all Muslims in North Africa, the Middle East, and South Asia expected the imminent appearance of the Mahdi.[95] And why wouldn't they, given the revolutions sweeping the Arab world? The signs that herald his coming have only multiplied since. A great sectarian war tears Syria asunder. Iraq is in chaos. The "infidel" West has invaded. The "tribulations" (*fitan*) are too awful and apparent to brook mundane explanations.

Despite the propaganda value of apocalyptic messages, al-Qaeda's leaders were reluctant to use them. Sure, al-Qaeda held press conferences in "Khorasan," part of which is in Afghanistan, backed by a different version of the black flag. The name of al-Qaeda's magazine, *Vanguards of Khorasan*, evokes the same prophecies, and its media outlet is called al-Sahab, or "the Clouds," perhaps alluding to the Abbasid flag.

But all these examples merely hint at the apocalypse. Al-Qaeda's leaders rarely referred to Islamic End-Times prophecies in their propaganda and never suggested the Mahdi was just around the corner. As one scholar of modern Islamic apocalypticism observes, "al-Qaida, so far as one can judge from its internal correspondence, was for many years impervious to the apocalyptic temptation."[96]

Bin Laden's and Zawahiri's disdain for apocalypticism reflects their generation and class. Until the Iraq war, apocalypticism was unpopular among modern Sunnis, who looked down on the Shi'a for being obsessed with the Mahdi's return. Sunni books on the apocalypse were commercial failures.[97]

Bin Laden and Zawahiri grew up in elite Sunni families, who sniffed at messianic speculation as unbecoming, a foolish pastime of the masses. Their attitude is captured in an article distributed by an al-Qaeda propaganda outfit that discourages Muslims from speculating on who the Mahdi is or when he will appear: "Many people think that the State of Islam will not be established until the Mahdi appears. They neglect to take action, instead raising their hands in prayer that God will hasten his appearance."[98]

Bin Laden had another, more personal reason for disliking messianism. In 1979, the year he graduated from college in Saudi Arabia, a group of Sunni radicals captured the Grand Mosque in Mecca. The mosque encloses Islam's holiest shrine, the Ka'ba. The radicals were there to consecrate one of their number as the Mahdi. Elite Saudi soldiers ended the weeks-long siege with the help of tear gas and French special forces; the Mahdi lay among the dead.[99] The humiliating defeat became a cautionary tale among jihadists: It is too risky to claim the fulfillment of prophecy and then fail.

Although al-Qaeda's leaders downplayed the apocalypse, some of their followers celebrated it. Group members quoted the black flag prophecies when interrogated by members of the Federal Bureau of Investigation (FBI). "If you see the black banners coming from Khorasan, join the army," recited Abu Jandal, a former Bin Laden bodyguard, to FBI agent Ali Soufan. Soufan remembers another Bin Laden associate, Ali al-Bahlul, citing the prophecy during his interrogation in Guantanamo Bay as evidence that al-Qaeda was fighting the final battles of Armageddon.[100]

Senior al-Qaeda officers also cited Islamic prophecies. "The Islamic armies must gather, rely on God, and support His religion and their brothers in Jerusalem" wrote Fadil Harun, Bin Laden's man in Somalia. The "awaited Mahdi" would then appear and lead "an ideological struggle, which will continue until the [Final] Hour as long as an inch of Muslim land in the Holy Land is under the control of the enemies."[101]

Perhaps the most prolific apocalypticist in the al-Qaeda orbit was Abu Mus'ab al-Suri, a Syrian jihadist who devoted over a hundred pages to the End Times in his massive 2004 tome on terrorist strategy. Although the book enjoyed immense popularity among jihadists for its strategic insights, many looked askance at his taste in prophecies.[102] Suri cited the medieval *Book of Tribulations* written by Nu'aym bin Hammad, which contains prophecies many Muslims consider spurious. But Suri read broadly in the canonical prophecies too and concluded that jihadists should reorient their fight toward the Fertile Crescent, which is where many prophecies locate the final battles of the Apocalypse, as we will see in chapter 5.[103]

Given the rise of messianism in the Middle East and the historical precedent of the Abbasids, it makes sense that the Islamic State would appeal to prophecy to justify its cause. But did the leaders of the Islamic State actually believe what they were saying, or were they cynically cloaking their ambition in messianic garb? And if they were sincere, how could they reconcile the urgent imperatives of the Apocalypse with the patient care required to run a state?

TWO
MAHDI AND MISMANAGEMENT

One way to measure the performance of a terror CEO is by the bounty his enemies put on his head. By that measure, the man who ran the Islamic State in its first year, Abu Ayyub al-Masri, was an abject failure. In 2007, the United States offered $5 million for information leading to Masri's location. In May 2008, the amount had fallen to $100,000.[1] A variety of reasons could be given for the precipitous fall in Masri's stock: He was a terrible manager, isolated from the battlefield, and facing the most powerful military on earth—that of the United States. But many of Masri's bad decisions that first year of the Islamic State's existence can be traced to something more fundamental: his apocalypticism and dogmatic belief that the Islamic State was an actual state.

Masri was an old hand at terrorism. In 1982, he had joined the Islamic Jihad organization later run by fellow Egyptian Ayman al-Zawahiri. When Zawahiri merged his organization with al-Qaeda, Masri went with him, learning to make bombs at an al-Qaeda training camp in the late 1990s. While in Afghanistan, Masri met Abu Mus'ab al-Zarqawi, who later founded al-Qaeda in Iraq. When the United States invaded Iraq in 2003, Masri was already in Baghdad ready to help Zarqawi set up shop. Zarqawi put him in charge of recruiting suicide bombers and overseeing operations in Iraq's Shi'i south. Masri allegedly built the bombs detonated at the United Nations headquarters and the Jordanian embassy in 2003 and oversaw terror campaigns against the Shi'a.[2] As we saw in the last chapter, the attacks paved the way for Iraq's descent into sectarian civil war.

Masri took over al-Qaeda in Iraq after Zarqawi died in June 2006, only to dissolve the group a few months later when the Islamic State was declared. According to the Islamic State's chief judge, Masri rushed to establish the State because he believed the Mahdi, the Muslim savior, would come within the year. To his thinking, the caliphate needed to be in place to help the Mahdi fight the final battles of the apocalypse. Anticipating the imminent conquest of major Islamic cities as foretold in the prophecies, Masri ordered his men to build pulpits for the Mahdi to ascend in the Prophet's mosque in Medina, the Umayyad Mosque in Damascus, and the Aqsa Mosque in Jerusalem. He also ordered his commanders in the field to conquer the whole of Iraq to prepare for the Mahdi's coming and was convinced they would succeed in three months. The Islamic State's forces fanned out across the country, only to be recalled a week later because they were spread too thin. When those close to Masri criticized him for making strategic decisions on an apocalyptic timetable, Masri retorted, "The Mahdi will come any day."[3]

In his public propaganda, Masri's apocalypticism was more restrained but still on display. When Masri was appointed the Islamic State's minister of war, he proclaimed, "The war is in its early stages . . . and this is the beginning of the battles" that herald the Day of Judgment. "We are the army that shall hand over the flag to the servant of God, the Mahdi," he asserted. "If the first of us is killed, the last of us will deliver it."[4]

Masri technically answered to the Islamic State's "commander of the faithful." The original statement announcing the Islamic State did not give the commander's real name, only his nom de guerre Abu Umar al-Baghdadi, which suggested he hailed from Baghdad, the capital of Islam's greatest caliphate, the Abbasid dynasty. At the time, Masri confided to his chief judge that he was still looking for a suitable candidate for the job. "A man will be found whom we will test for a month. If he is suitable, then we will keep him as the commander of the faithful. If not, we will look for someone else."[5]

The man Masri chose, Hamid al-Zawi, was "a normal person and not a leader" in the organization, according to a former member of the Islamic State.[6] Zawi had been a police officer in the Sunni farming town of Haditha until he was fired in the early 1990s for his ultraconservative religious views. Zawi repaired electronics to make ends meet before the Americans invaded in 2003, when he joined al-Qaeda in Iraq and then the Islamic State.[7] "Everyone was astonished [Masri] gave an oath of allegiance to him," the former member recalled. "What were his qualifications?"[8] The selection of Zawi for the post of commander of the faithful was more like a casting call than anything resembling an Islamic procedure for choosing an emir or leader.

In its propaganda, the Islamic State had equivocated on whether it was just a state or something more. In private, Masri equivocated too. Sometimes he said that the announcement of the Islamic State was merely an announcement. Most of the jihadist "brothers" in Iraq took that to mean the Islamic State was just an extension of the emirate declared by Mullah Omar, to whom they had pledged allegiance, just as Bin Laden had done. But at other times Masri claimed that the Islamic State in Iraq was an actual entity unto itself. Masri even confided to his chief judge that he believed Abu Umar al-Baghdadi to be the caliph, although Masri did not intend to proclaim him as such until after the Americans left Iraq.[9]

Because the leaders of the Islamic State thought of it as an actual state, they were high-handed and brutal in dealing with Sunnis who did not want to pledge allegiance to it. In the beginning of 2007, the Islamic State informed the other Sunni rebel groups that they had "no choice." As the State's spokesman put it, "they have to either join us in forming the Islamic State project in the Sunni areas or hand over their weapons to us before we are forced to act against them forcefully." To make its point, the Islamic State began killing or kidnapping insurgent leaders.[10] The Islamic Army, one of the largest Islamist insurgent groups in Iraq, was a particular target. When the Islamic Army refused to bow to the Islamic State's authority, the State killed thirty of its members. In April 2007, the harassed group wrote an open letter to Bin Laden criticizing his Iraqi franchise. "They threaten some members of the group with death if they do not swear allegiance to al-Qaeda or its other names." The Islamic Army also accused the Islamic State of attacking civilians, "especially easy targets such as the imams of mosques, the prayer callers, and unarmed Sunnis." "They try to kill anyone who criticizes [the Islamic State] or goes against them."[11]

It is a major taboo in Islam to kill a fellow Muslim. But the Islamic State argued that those who defied its rule were apostates or rebels so it could kill them without blame.

Still, Abu Umar al-Baghdadi tried to reconcile with the Islamic Army, doubtless worried it would join forces with the United States and the Iraqi government to fight the Islamic State. "Know that I am prepared to shed my blood to spare yours," he told them. "By God, you will hear from us only what is good, and you will see from us only what is good."[12] But the rift quickly turned into a chasm as Islamic State fighters continued attacking their competitors.

Even when the State's leaders wanted to be conciliatory, they often didn't know when their commanders were behaving badly. Part of the problem was that the Islamic State had allowed too many people to join without vetting them properly. A clandestine terrorist group is usually picky about who joins, worried that it will be penetrated by spies or destroyed from the inside by idiots. Because it saw itself as something more than a terrorist group, the Islamic State had opened wide the doors for membership. Former Saddam loyalists from the military and intelligence services rushed in, as did insurgents who took orders from other countries. Some believed in the cause, but many were corrupt or had divided loyalties.[13]

At times, Masri didn't know what his subordinates were doing because he was "totally isolated" and "almost absent from the details of what goes on in the battlefield," recalled his chief judge.

Those close to Masri painted a rosy picture that distorted "his view of things and of reality." The reports from the field were similarly filled with happy talk. They didn't "mention the negatives and the problems as they really are."[14]

Compounding the problem, Masri didn't fire or discipline subordinates who abused their power. When his chief judge told Masri that a senior official had confiscated goods from a Sunni merchant in Anbar Province who had been on good terms with the Islamic State, Masri told the judge to mind his own business or face demotion. According to the judge, going over Masri's head to the commander of the faithful, Abu Umar al-Baghdadi, would have been pointless because Abu Umar didn't "know what [was] going on around him."[15]

Already in 2006, Masri was receiving complaints from other Sunni insurgent groups. "Dear Brother [Masri], the mistakes in the field of battle have come to the point [where we are] fed up" wrote a leader of the militia Ansar al-Sunna. A one-time ally of the Islamic State that had considered joining its ranks, the militia was furious at the arrogant and murderous behavior of the State toward it and other Sunni insurgent groups fighting the Americans in Iraq. "Individuals from your group have kidnapped, tortured, and killed people from our group with their [full] knowledge that they were from the Ansar [al-Sunna] group." Fearful of losing the Islamic State's last important ally, Masri apologized profusely in his January 2007 response: "I pledge to become a faithful servant and a loyal guard to you. I would carry your shoes on my head and kiss them a thousand times."[16]

Whether the Islamic State's heavy-handedness came from the top or from rogue elements in the organization (probably a mix of both), the effect was the same. The group's bullying had eroded its base of support among Iraq's Sunnis, which was crucial for keeping alive its state-building enterprise. Ansar al-Sunna, the Islamic Army, and other militias that had complained to the Islamic State began to talk to the Americans in late 2006 and early 2007 about finding a way to rid themselves of the group.[17]

Sunni support was already tepid after years of al-Qaeda murdering Sunni civilians. In the early days of the Sunni insurgency,

Zarqawi had pioneered the strategy of provoking the Shi'a into a fight and had warned against attacking Sunnis.[18] His plan worked initially, as Sunnis sought any port in the sectarian storm. But when al-Qaeda began to try to impose its rule in Sunni areas, the locals soured on the organization. In 2004, the inhabitants of Fallujah and the local insurgents who represented them were among the first to resist al-Qaeda, which controlled much of the city. Among their list of complaints were al-Qaeda's religious requirements that were at odds with local Islamic customs, such as full-body veiling.[19] Beatings and broken bones brought reluctant citizens into line but bred resentment. The same happened a year later in 2005 in the city of Qaim on the border of Syria. Islamic State fighters burned down a beauty parlor and torched stores selling music; men who drank alcohol were lashed.[20] By September 2006, Iraqi prime minister Nuri al-Maliki had received pledges of support from over a dozen Sunni tribal leaders, prompting al-Qaeda to issue a statement threatening their lives.[21]

In October 2006, just days before the establishment of the Islamic State, a masked jihadist going by the name Abu Usama al-Iraqi released a video addressed to Bin Laden. Whether a clever government propagandist or a true jihadist insider, Abu Usama channeled the jihadists' mounting frustration with al-Qaeda in Iraq. "From the moment the commander of that group swore an oath of allegiance to you," Abu Usama said to Bin Laden, "we have been faced with a nightmare."[22]

Abu Usama detailed atrocities so awful they "may cause children's hair to turn white." Al-Qaeda in Iraq had liquidated "religious scholars," followed by "acts of persecution against Sunni Muslims, harming their livelihood." The group "had planted explosives in front of homes, schools and hospitals, or under electric transformers, without taking any account of the consequences for society." Al-Qaeda in Iraq even used mothers and sick children as human shields. The group had utterly forgotten Zawahiri's "counsel that they should serve the population and protect it." Without support of the Sunnis, the jihadists had become "easy prey for the crusader occupation and its helpers, the vicious Shi'a."[23]

Abu Usama also accused al-Qaeda in Iraq of greed and sacrilege. Its fighters had confiscated the salaries of government employees, looted religious endowments, "driven out worshippers . . . killed dozens of imams and preachers," and used the mosques to store weapons.[24]

Abu Usama informed Bin Laden that many of the jihadist factions were biting their tongues, waiting for the al-Qaeda leader to censure his Iraqi affiliate. "The other factions are watching the Sunnis sinking deep into hunger and oppression. If any of them speak out in opposition he is silenced . . . He is kidnapped [and placed] in the trunk of a car, and is subjected to severe torture or killed. What kind of behavior is this? Is this religious behavior?"[25]

Abu Usama recounted several stories of al-Qaeda killing or beating other rebels, including a sixty-five-year-old man in the 1920 Revolution Brigade, a Sunni insurgent group. Tired of the abuse, the rebel group began killing al-Qaeda members after mosque prayers in one city after another, which pushed al-Qaeda to further terrorize "people in order to deter them." Rumors circulated that the Americans and the Shi'a were working with al-Qaeda. Surely no Sunni fighters would do this to other Sunnis. Abu Usama counseled Bin Laden to dissociate himself from the group.[26]

The establishment of the Islamic State did nothing to silence the critics. Its nominal head, Abu Umar al-Baghdadi, released an audio statement on March 13, 2007, to refute the "lies" circulating about the group's intolerance and brutality. He also laid down nineteen tenets the Islamic State's subjects were to abide by.[27] All Shi'a and those who assisted the American occupiers were infidels. Christians and Jews living in the Islamic State had to submit to its authority and pay a protection tax or be killed. Any form of secularism, in which Abu Umar included mainstream political Islam and Arab socialism, would not be tolerated. Shari'a law was to be the law of the land and "anything encouraging deviance" was forbidden, such as satellite television and the uncovered faces of women.[28] In the eyes of Iraq's beleaguered Sunnis, Abu Umar's charm offensive was more offensive than charming.

Abu Umar's directives were of a piece with the Islamic State's political theory. In a January 2007 document,[29] the State argued that Islam requires a government to perform the following functions: impose the fixed punishments specified in Islamic scripture, the so-called *hudud;* resolve conflicts and quarrels; provide security; and prosecute criminals and sinners.[30] The government should also tend to the economic welfare of its subjects. In its own words, the government should "oversee the provision of foodstuffs and relief materials and organize the selling of oil and gas and the other necessities of life to ease the suffering of the people."[31] Because the Islamic State attempted to fulfill the duties of a state, it believed it should be treated as one.

The Islamic State never really controlled any cities so it couldn't do much to improve local economies. But it could dress up its terrorism in religious garb to subdue the locals and lay claim to statehood. The pillar of this strategy was imposing the *hudud:* beheading or crucifying bandits who kill people while robbing them; death by stoning for adultery; cutting off a hand or foot for theft; and flogging for fornication, drinking alcohol, and falsely accusing someone of fornication or adultery. (Some also say Islamic scripture prescribes death or lesser penalties for apostasy and rebellion.) There had to be two eyewitnesses for all of the crimes except adultery, which required four. Because the evidentiary standards were so high, especially for adultery, it was hard to get a conviction in premodern times.[32] But because the penalties have to be enforced by a state, ultraconservative Muslims see their implementation as a touchstone for an authentic Islamic government. Imposing the *hudud*, therefore, could burnish one's ultraconservative credentials and bolster one's claims to be a state. The penalties are also frightening, and some of them, such as the punishment for apostasy, can be used against enemies, which makes them handy for subjugating people.

Unfortunately for the Islamic State, it was too zealous in applying the *hudud* and therefore scared too many people. As one Sunni explained, "I saw an Al Qaeda man behead an 8-year-old girl with my own eyes. . . . We want American support because we fought the most vicious organization in the world here . . . I would rather work with the Americans than the Iraqi Army. The Americans are not sectarian people."[33] Sunni tribal leaders were furious at the abuse of their fellow tribesmen and annoyed that the Islamic State had horned in on their illicit smuggling activities.[34] Local "Awakening" councils of Sunni tribal militias, so-called because they awoke to the threat of al-Qaeda and then the Islamic State, formed to expel Islamic State fighters from their towns. Their cause was helped immeasurably by the Islamic State falling out with the other Sunni insurgent groups, which were now far less inclined to close ranks with it.

DISGRUNTLED

In November 2007, al-Qaeda's leaders in Afghanistan and Pakistan received word that a certain Abu Sulayman al-Utaybi had arrived and was on his way to see them. Abu Sulayman, a Saudi in his late twenties, had served as the chief judge of the Islamic State in its first year. Although he had publicly defended the group from its detractors,[35] Abu Sulayman was privately worried about its missteps and declining popularity. When he raised his concerns with Abu Ayyub al-Masri, the shadow leader of the Islamic State, Masri brushed him off. Incensed, Abu Sulayman tried to send a letter to al-Qaeda bad-mouthing his boss. When Masri got wind of the letter Abu Sulayman intended to send, he fired him.[36] The former chief judge packed his bags and set out for Afghanistan and Pakistan to hand deliver his complaints to al-Qaeda's leaders.

Although al-Qaeda's leaders knew Abu Sulayman had been fired, they were surprised when he showed up on their doorstep. Before meeting with him, they wrote Masri. "Why did [Abu Sulayman] leave you and come here?" they asked. "Is it perhaps something bad or some problems? What is your recommendation on the brother? . . . What was the reason that you dismissed him from his work?"[37]

When al-Qaeda's leaders got no answer from Masri, which a messenger blamed on "encrypted files that did not open,"[38] they went ahead and met with Abu Sulayman.

Abu Sulayman's allegations against Masri—some of which were already presented in this chapter—were damning.[39] Al-Qaeda in Iraq had declared the Islamic State under false pretenses, he charged. People think many militias and tribes pledged allegiance to the Islamic State; in fact, he claimed, only the heads of a few militias, some of which did not even exist, pledged their allegiance. "Among them were those who had never carried weapons in their entire lives." As for the tribes, they never pledged their support for establishing the Islamic State.[40]

As you'll recall, al-Qaeda had repeatedly warned its Iraqi franchise not to declare a state until it had the support of the Sunni masses and their leaders. Abu Sulayman was alleging they had neither, despite the Islamic State's claims to the contrary. The Islamic State had not just defied its bosses; it had risked undermining the project of restoring the caliphate by turning the enterprise into a joke.

Beyond accusing Masri of declaring the Islamic State under false pretenses, Abu Sulayman claimed his former boss had made poor strategic decisions because he believed the apocalypse was imminent. As Abu Sulayman explained to al-Qaeda's leaders, Masri was unduly influenced by prophecies "about the tribulations [preceding the Day of Judgment], especially regarding the Mahdi."[41]

For Abu Sulayman, Masri's greatest sin was his tolerance of corruption in the Islamic State. Several of the State's deputies were depraved and irreligious, Abu Sulayman alleged. They "corrupt the organization and the State from the inside, intellectually, methodologically and ethically," and they hurt the Islamic State's "public relations." Masri would not stand up to them, Abu Sulayman complained, because he was "weak." Masri himself set a poor example, reissuing old propaganda footage "as though it were new operations."[42]

Not once did Abu Sulayman blame the figurehead of the Islamic State, Abu Umar al-Baghdadi, for failing to lead; he understood that Masri was truly in charge. By Abu Sulayman's estimation, the Islamic State was "approaching an abyss" and would not last much longer if al-Qaeda did not get Masri under control. The Islamic State's leaders were corrupt, apocalypse addled, or just incompetent. They had lied to al-Qaeda about the public's support for their cause, and they actually believed their terror group was the caliphate reborn.[43]

After reading Abu Sulayman's letter and a summary of his complaints, Ayman al-Zawahiri cautioned the other al-Qaeda leaders to "not rush to accept everything [Abu Sulayman] says until we verify it and ask [Masri] and his brothers and see their opinion and response. . . . Maybe [Abu Sulayman] is being unfair or is carrying a grudge or something else."[44]

In a letter to Masri, al-Qaeda's leaders demanded he address Abu Sulayman's allegations point by point. Apocalyptic thinking is "very dangerous," they warned, because it "corrupts policy and leadership" and makes for hasty decisions.[45] Corrupt leaders in the Islamic State should be expelled; otherwise their bad behavior would destroy the organization and "deface al-Qaeda and its method."[46] Ever mindful of Muslim public opinion, al-Qaeda worried its rogue affiliate would irreparably tarnish its brand.

Al-Qaeda's leaders ordered Masri to put them in direct contact with the Islamic State's nominal head, Abu Umar, and with the other "trusted brothers" in the organization. Al-Qaeda's leaders worried they did not have enough points of contact in the Islamic State. They were also concerned that if Masri and Abu Umar died, the line of succession would be unclear.[47] The subtext was that Masri had gathered too much power to himself.

Al-Qaeda's leaders received contact information for Abu Umar al-Baghdadi but no answers to their questions. Frustrated, Zawahiri bypassed Masri and wrote directly to Abu Umar on March 6, 2008, to get answers to Abu Sulayman's accusations. "We want to have a full response from you about them."[48] The answer finally came not from Abu Umar but from Masri, who responded to al-Qaeda's letter and Abu Sulayman's charges by playing for time—or "slow rolling," in American bureaucratese. "A letter reached us containing the accusations of Abu Sulayman and many requests for explanation. Before answering those requests, I want you to tell me: has [al-Qaeda's leadership] read this letter before it was sent? If not, I want you to disclose the text to them because it contains many matters and it is important that we know they agree with all of it."[49]

Exasperated, al-Qaeda's leaders responded on March 10. "As I have explained to you," one of them wrote, "[they] have all seen Abu Sulayman's words and they have asked us to write you in order to inquire about these words, claims, and accusations." When Masri once again failed to respond to their satisfaction, al-Qaeda's leaders summoned him to the woodshed in "Khorasan" (Afghanistan or Pakistan) to answer the charges directly.[50] Abu Sulayman, who had started the row, was killed by U.S. forces in Afghanistan before his former boss could confront him.[51]

WHAT WENT WRONG?

We don't know if Masri ever met with al-Qaeda's leaders, but it didn't matter. He was never able to turn the Islamic State around. From a high of 2,500 civilians killed per month by the Islamic State in early 2007, the rate had declined to about 500 a month by the end of 2008.[52] The Sunni tribes, backed by the U.S. surge and Iraqi troops, had constrained the State's movements, and American special operations forces had demolished its leadership. By 2009, jihadists were derisively calling the Islamic State a "paper state." Even Masri's Yemeni wife was giving him a hard time. "Where is the Islamic State of Iraq that you're talking about?" she reproached him in their mud hut south of Tikrit. "We're living in the desert!"[53]

Pessimism also filled the jihadist discussion boards online. "The Painful Truth: Al-Qaeda Is Losing the War in Iraq," wrote one commenter.[54] Another lamented, "The people of Iraq completely betrayed the mujahids and allied with everyone who had turned away from religion, except those whom my Lord had mercy on. . . . The situation of the mujahids has become extremely difficult."[55] Jihadists couldn't understand why a group that had God's support was failing: "The Islamic State of Iraq is still in the right," forum members wondered. "So why are things becoming so difficult for it [and] its enemies joining against it from all sides?"[56]

The jihadist discussion boards were usually friendly territory for the Islamic State and its predecessor al-Qaeda in Iraq, where they had pioneered the distribution of propaganda. They opted for snuff films rather than al-Qaeda's usual pedantry and uploaded multiple links to videos in numerous sizes and formats. Extreme violence attracted eyeballs to the propaganda, and redundant links and decentralized distribution kept it online.[57] The Islamic State would use many of the same techniques a few years later to recruit on Twitter. But at the moment, the private discussion boards had turned against the State and become a water cooler around which discontented jihadists gathered to grouse about the group's failures.

The Islamic State's own members were complaining too. In an analysis captured by U.S. forces, a member of the Islamic State cataloged an array of reasons for the State's failure: The organization did not understand Iraqis well; foreign fighters attracted by Islamic State propaganda did not get along with local members of the group; the Islamic State's commanders did not coordinate well with one another and their large number weakened the chain of command; and, finally, good old-fashioned bureaucratic stovepiping prevented commanders from knowing what one another were doing.[58]

From abroad, al-Qaeda's inner circle watched in horror as the Islamic State dragged the al-Qaeda brand through the dust. Al-Qaeda owned the Islamic State's every excess and failure because outsiders still called the State by its old name: al-Qaeda in Iraq. And al-Qaeda had yet to denounce the group.

In Pakistan, al-Qaeda's American propagandist, Adam Gadahn, seethed. A former death metal fan from California, Gadahn had converted to Islam in his late teens, gravitating toward an ultraconservative version of the religion. Two years after his conversion, Gadahn moved to Pakistan, where he married and soon joined al-Qaeda. No softy, Gadahn had celebrated al-Qaeda's atrocities for years in videos distributed online. But the Islamic State was too extreme even for him. Privately commenting on the reign of Abu Umar al-Baghdadi, Gadahn thought it was absurd that the Islamic State had believed "the authenticity of their fictitious State" when it could not even

"defend itself" or others. The Islamic State had demanded a protection tax from Christians, a right reserved only for a real Islamic state,
and it treated Muslims who disagreed with it like infidels, "targeting
[their] mosques with explosives." Al-Qaeda had not ordered these
actions, but its reputation would "be damaged more and more as a
result of the acts and statements of this group." Gadahn advised al-
Qaeda's leader to "cut its organizational ties" to the Islamic State for
such behavior.[59]

Gadahn's sentiments were echoed a world away in Somalia,
where the secret al-Qaeda affiliate al-Shabab controlled much of the
country. In its midst was Fadil Harun, one of the earliest members
of al-Qaeda. Harun had grown up in the Comoros, a former French
colony off the coast of Mozambique. Like Gadahn a decade later,
Harun embraced an ultraconservative version of Islam in his teens
and traveled to Pakistan, where he joined al-Qaeda and learned to
make bombs. Harun became one of al-Qaeda's most skilled operatives, helping to plan the bombing of the U.S. embassy in Nairobi
and later running al-Qaeda's cell in east Africa.[60]

Harun had known Masri from his time in Afghanistan during
the Taliban era. "He was very close to us, as we lived with him in
Afghanistan during the second period when the [Taliban's] Islamic
Emirate was established." Harun admired Masri's piety but worried
when he heard his old friend had taken over leadership of al-Qaeda in
Iraq and then the Islamic State. Masri was part of al-Qaeda's Egyptian contingent, which was known to be too strict and too indiscrim-
inate in its killing of Muslim civilians. "We know very well that the
group is strict in some controversial issues where there is room for
disagreement," Harun recounted in his memoir. "They only stick to
their opinion," Harun lamented when his worries were later justified
by the Islamic State's excesses.[61] The State should have learned from
the "mistakes of others" and not "ignore the people of a country."[62]

Bin Laden too privately bemoaned the Islamic State's brutality,
especially its rough treatment of the Sunni tribes. In a 2010 letter, he
reflected on early American missteps with the tribes that had given
the jihadists an opportunity to win them over: "The enemy entered

Iraq without any knowledge of the area or the Iraqi people, who have a strong tribal background; therefore, the Iraqis supported the mujahidin." But when the Islamic State attacked tribal youth in Anbar for signing up with the Awakening militias, their tribes retaliated. The youth were "going to join the security forces for financial reasons," complained Bin Laden, and presented no "imminent threat" to the jihadists. The incident taught the jihadists a hard lesson in not initiating a blood feud with tribal members.[63]

Despite his private misgivings, Bin Laden doggedly refused to renounce the Islamic State. Watching the train wreck from afar, al-Qaeda's leader could only offer the chagrined executive's passive excuse: "Mistakes were made."[64]

Masri's and Abu Umar al-Baghdadi's disastrous reign was ended by American and Iraqi soldiers who killed the men in a joint raid on Masri's mud hut in April 2010. In the following three months, thirty-four more Islamic State leaders would be killed or captured,[65] crippling the organization but also making room for new leadership. The Islamic State announced the appointment of its new commander of the faithful, Abu Bakr al-Baghdadi,[66] in May although it would be two years before he issued a public statement.[67] Like his predecessor, most jihadists had never heard of him.

In the three years since its birth in the autumn of 2006, the Islamic State had managed to humiliate its absentee lords in al-Qaeda and lose every bit of territory it claimed to rule. An authoritarian, arrogant style coupled with mismanagement, apocalyptic zeal, and unfocused brutality against an ever-widening circle of enemies was poorly matched against the strength and resolve of the State's opponents. Although the organization would come back to life again as the last American troops departed in 2011, for the moment its prospects were bleak.

But just as the flag of the Islamic State was trampled underfoot in Iraq, jihadist fanboys and al-Qaeda's own affiliates began to lift it up, keeping the dream of the caliphate alive during a bleak period for all of al-Qaeda's affiliates preceding the chaos of the Arab Spring, which would renew the fortunes of the global jihadist movement.

THREE
BANNERMEN

Friends and family remembered nineteen-year-old Nayif al-Qahtani as "quiet" and "shy," the kind of guy who obeys his mom and doesn't get into trouble. "I never saw any change in his behavior or any inclination toward extremism," remembered Qahtani's brother. The Saudi teen was the last guy you'd expect to stand in front of the emir of al-Qaeda's branch in Yemen, about to pitch a bold idea.[1]

You need an online magazine, Qahtani said, and I'm the man to do it.

The emir of al-Qaeda in Yemen, Nasir al-Wuhayshi, liked the idea. Every terrorist organization worthy of the name needs a magazine to needle its enemies and attract recruits. But Wuhayshi probably had misgivings about the young Saudi's ability to pull it off. Qahtani had no university education, having left Saudi Arabia at age seventeen to join the jihad in Yemen.[2] He also had no skill at designing magazines. Still, Wuhayshi admired Qahtani's pluck, perhaps seeing a little of himself in the teen. When Wuhayshi was around the young man's age, he had left his native Yemen for Afghanistan, serving as Bin Laden's secretary for six years. Modest "with flashes of sarcastic humor," Wuhayshi had endeared himself to the al-Qaeda rank and file.[3]

Wuhayshi blessed Qahtani's proposal in late 2007. Over the next few months, Qahtani worked feverishly to find and format the content. To give the magazine some added heft, the teen even conducted an "Interview with One of the Most Wanted People in [Saudi Arabia]"—which was actually an interview with himself.[4] The magazine debuted in January 2008. Its title, *The Echo of Battles*, alluded to the final battles of the apocalypse.

Anonymous jihadists online applauded the magazine in their private discussion forums. Most of them lived in the Arab world, so they could appreciate the Arabic text. If anyone disliked the magazine, they either were silenced by the jihadists who administered the forums or kept quiet. Such uniformity was typical, achieved through censorship or self-censorship. Freewheeling jihadist debates online would come later with the advent of Twitter.

There was plenty to criticize in the magazine, especially its visual presentation. The layout was ugly, with pictures floating across a vacuum of white interspersed with blue and black text. Qahtani's inexperience as a graphic designer was showing.

Over the next few months, Qahtani either vastly improved as a graphic designer or he had some help. When the second issue of *Echo* was released in March 2008, the title dripped with fire and blood, and colorful borders corralled the text. On the masthead and silhouetted on every page was the new logo of al-Qaeda in Yemen: two scimitars crossed over outlines of Yemen and Saudi Arabia. Fluttering between the scimitars was the black flag of the Islamic State.[5] When the leaders of al-Qaeda in Yemen released a video the following year announcing the group's merger with the moribund al-Qaeda in the Arabian Peninsula (AQAP), the Islamic State's flag hung in the background. At the very moment the Islamic State was stumbling in Iraq, another al-Qaeda affiliate had taken up its standard.

Why had al-Qaeda in Yemen adopted the flag of another al-Qaeda affiliate? Why not create its own flag, or use the black flag Bin Laden displayed in his press conferences? After all, al-Qaeda in Yemen answered to Bin Laden, just as the Islamic State did. Perhaps the leaders of al-Qaeda in Yemen just liked the design of the Islamic

State's flag and the notoriety attached to it. But more likely they admired what the flag represented: the imminent return of the caliphate. As we will see, soon after al-Qaeda in Yemen adopted the Islamic State's flag, it attempted to establish its own Islamic government—as would several other al-Qaeda affiliates that began displaying the flag around the same time in other countries. By flying the Islamic State's symbol, the al-Qaeda affiliates were embracing what it represented. They were not joining the Islamic State in Iraq but rather endorsing its project. It was not a project Bin Laden liked.

TWELVE THOUSAND

Two and a half years after Qahtani debuted his first issue of *The Echo of Battles*, AQAP launched its second online magazine, *Inspire*. Another young man, twenty-four-year-old Samir Khan, was at the helm.

Like Qahtani, Khan was born in Saudi Arabia. But as a child he had moved to New York and later to North Carolina with his Pakistani parents. Despite being raised in the West, Khan ended up in the same place as Qahtani. Entranced by the 9/11 attacks and infuriated by the American invasion of Iraq, Khan started a website devoted to jihadist propaganda, which he edited from his parents' home in North Carolina. Ignoring the pleas of his parents and local Muslim leaders to renounce jihadism, Khan left for Yemen in 2009 to join his hero, Anwar al-Awlaki.[6]

Born in America, Awlaki had returned to his parents' homeland of Yemen during his teens and again in 2004. A skilled preacher, he had one foot in radical Islamist eddies and another in the Muslim mainstream.[7] By the time Khan arrived, Awlaki had fully radicalized, joining AQAP and recruiting disciples online to carry out attacks in Europe and the United States. The propagandist and the blogger began to collaborate on a new way to reach Muslim youth in the West. AQAP's first English magazine, *Inspire*, was born.

Awlaki's article in the inaugural issue was directed to the "American people and Muslims in the West." For the Muslims in the West, his message was stark: "You either leave or you fight." Those who stay in "infidel" lands should follow the example of Awlaki's acolytes Nidal Hasan and Umar Farouk Abdulmutallab. Hasan was a Palestinian-American soldier in the U.S. military who killed thirteen people at Fort Hood, Texas. Abdulmutallab was a British-educated son of a wealthy Nigerian banker who attempted to blow up an airplane over Detroit.

As for Muslims who leave infidel lands, Awlaki invited them to come to Yemen. The Prophet had prophesied the appearance of an army of "twelve thousand" men who would "come out of Aden-Abyan" in the south to "give victory to Allah and His Messenger," Muhammad. Awlaki believed the fulfillment of the prophecy was fast approaching.[8]

The prophecy was a favorite of Awlaki's comrades in AQAP. The group's Arabic magazine, *Echo of Battles*, frequently quoted it,[9] especially after AQAP clashed with government forces in Abyan Province in the summer of 2010.[10] In July, an AQAP leader announced, "An army of 12,000 fighters is being prepared in Aden and Abyan. By this army, we will establish an Islamic Caliphate."[11]

Jihadist anticipation of a caliphate in Yemen was rising. AQAP's *Echo* magazine published an exchange on the subject between a pseudonymous Yemeni jihadist and the world's most influential jihadist scholar, Abu Muhammad al-Maqdisi.[12] The jihadist asked if the fighting in southern Yemen was a fulfillment of the "twelve thousand" prophecy and whether it meant the caliphate would be established in Yemen.[13]

Maqdisi was well equipped to answer. The Palestinian had spent most of his adult life studying Islamic scriptures and jihadist treatises. His knowledge had attracted jihadist protégés, including Abu Mus'ab al-Zarqawi, although the two had fallen out over Zarqawi's excesses in the Iraq war. If anyone knew what the "twelve thousand" prophecy portended for the future of the caliphate in Yemen, it would be Maqdisi.

On the question of the caliphate, Maqdisi responded cautiously:

Some of those who talk about this hadith say that it contains
a subtle allusion that the caliphate will happen in Aden Abyan
and Yemen will be the capital of the caliphate because the
armies will usually start out from the seat of the caliphate. . . .
That is not necessarily so; rather perhaps it means Yemen will
help the caliphate or help its people and its Muslim army, or
recruit the like of this army for repelling the enemy attacking
some of the lands of Muslims or for driving away an occupier
or apostate.[14]

Not wanting to discourage his questioner, Maqdisi was more en-
thusiastic in his response to the question about whether AQAP was
fulfilling the "twelve thousand" prophecy. Affirming the glorious
destiny of the jihadists in Yemen, Maqdisi quoted a second prophecy
in which Muhammad instructs faithful Muslims to go to Syria in
the End Times. If they can't go to Syria, Muhammad advised, they
should go to Yemen. AQAP was fulfilling the prophecy, Maqdisi
argued, because the "crusaders" feared the growing strength of
the fighters gathering in Yemen, "who fight beneath the banner of
monotheism."[15]

Maqdisi closed his essay by recommending that the jihadists in
Yemen follow the advice of Abu Mus'ab al-Suri. A Syrian, Suri was
the red-haired Carlos the Jackal of the global jihad, turning up in
one conflict after another. He's the author of the large book on jihadist strategy and End-Time prophecy we met in chapter 1. Having
witnessed many failed revolutions, Suri had developed a keen sense
for what not to do.

In an October 1999 essay on how to wage a jihad in Yemen, Suri
quoted the same prophecies mentioned by Maqdisi and explained
why Yemen was the ideal place for launching a revolution in the
Arabian Peninsula.[16] Suri was convinced that the jihadists should be
fighting to mobilize popular support against the crusaders and their
local allies. It is the "key of jihad." Rather than attacking the government in Yemen, Suri advised the jihadists to view the country as a

base in which to gather their forces and launch attacks on the rest of the Arabian Peninsula.[17] If any Arab countries retaliated against the jihadists in Yemen, the Yemeni people would view those countries as lackeys of the crusaders. Suri ended his analysis by quoting the "twelve thousand" prophecy.[18]

Bin Laden broadly agreed with Suri's strategic perspective and discouraged al-Qaeda's affiliate in Yemen, AQAP, from overthrowing the local government or establishing a state. The head of AQAP, Nasir al-Wuhayshi, had written Bin Laden sometime in 2010, "If you want Sana'a, today is the day."[19] (Sana'a is the capital of Yemen.) Bin Laden replied, "We want to establish the Sharia of God in Sana'a only if we are able to preserve [the state we create]." Bin Laden reminded Wuhayshi that no Islamic government founded by jihadists will endure as long as America "continues to possess the ability to topple any state we establish."[20] "We have to remember that the enemy toppled the Taliban and Saddam's regime."[21]

This was a big change from Bin Laden's public position in 2007, when he had defended the Islamic State in Iraq against charges that it had been established prematurely. At that time, he had acknowledged that the United States could "make war on any state and bring down its government." But that was no excuse for not trying.[22] The subsequent dismantlement of the Islamic State had made him more cautious.[23]

Instead of establishing a state in Yemen, Bin Laden preferred to use it as a base for operations against the United States: "I believe that Yemen should remain peaceful and kept as a reserve army for the [Muslim] community. It is well known that one of the requirements for plunging into wars is to have a reserve army and to continue exhausting the enemy in the open fronts until the enemy becomes weak, which would enable us to establish the state of Islam. Therefore, the more we can escalate operations against America, the closer we get to uniting our efforts to establish the state of Islam, God willing."[24] Bin Laden acknowledged that, from a jihadist perspective, Yemen's president is an apostate. But he is an ineffectual one, which gives jihadists room to maneuver. "It is not in our interest to rush in bringing down the regime. In spite of this regime's mismanagement, it is less dangerous to us than the one America wants to exchange it with. . . . The Salafists and the jihadist Salafists were able to take advantage of his regime and target America from Yemen, as some of the mujahidin went to Somalia or traveled to us, which allowed us to assign our brothers to conduct international operations."[25]

If the Yemeni government attacks the jihadists, then they should defend themselves, Bin Laden counseled. But they should not go on the offensive against the government, which would only turn the population against their enterprise.[26]

Note the importance of popular support in Bin Laden's strategic thinking and his focus on driving the Americans from the Middle East. Toppling local Muslim regimes and establishing states would have to wait. Those goals would only alienate the locals because achieving them would require attacking fellow Muslims. And even if the jihadists were successful, the United States still stood in the way.

Bin Laden was angered by news that AQAP members had attacked Yemeni government forces in the summer of 2010, which contradicted his guidance. He couldn't believe AQAP's leaders had disobeyed him, so he blamed the group's youth for carrying out the operations. Perhaps they weren't sufficiently apprised of al-Qaeda's America-first policy, Bin Laden wrote. Such operations were excusable if they were "for the mujahidin's self-defense only."[27]

Just as AQAP should avoid attacks on the local government, Bin Laden advised them to "avoid killing anyone from the tribes."[28] To his mind, the tribes were pivotal to the success of the jihadist state-building enterprise, which would be doomed without their backing. "We must gain the support of the tribes who enjoy strength and influence before building our Muslim state," wrote Bin Laden.[29] Muhammad's predecessors had ignored this maxim at their peril, Bin Laden observed. The Prophet had succeeded because he had been able to co-opt the tribes in Medina in whole or in part.[30]

Bin Laden was right. When Muhammad's own tribe in Mecca turned against him, the Prophet allied with tribal factions to the north in the town of Medina. Using a mix of religious persuasion, the promise of spoils, marriages, intimidation, and violence, Muhammad succeeded in bringing many of the tribes of the Arabian Peninsula over to his side by the end of his life.

Bin Laden's counsel to avoid alienating the tribes was part of his larger strategy to win popular Muslim support. Many of Yemen's citizens are members of tribes, which enjoy more autonomy than in most Arab countries.[31] Bin Laden was also wary of triggering a blood feud, a form of retaliatory justice that tribes sometimes initiate when one of their members is killed.[32]

In a draft letter to AQAP's leader, Bin Laden mused at length on the insurmountable challenges facing any Islamic state established in the Arab world. The state would have to meet the "demands and needs of its people." Because Arab states have made people dependent on them for everything, any Islamic state that does not deliver public goods efficiently would quickly lose support. The inevitable sanctions and aerial bombardment would further hasten the state's demise.[33]

A revolutionary movement today needs more than just military might to topple a government or control a country. While putting aside the external enemy, a movement needs to have the resources in place to meet the needs and demands of the society, as it makes its way to controlling a city or a country. A movement cannot expect, however, a society to live without for a long time, even if that society happens to be a great supporter of that movement. People often change when they see persistence in a shortage of food and medicine, and the last thing they want to see is having their children die for lack of food or medicine.[34]

Failure would be costly, warned Bin Laden. "The impact of losing a state can be devastating, especially if that state is at its infancy. . . . The public often has all sorts of interpretations for the word failure. Nonetheless, the public does not like losers. The public is only interested in the results and it often ignores the details and conditions which led to one's success or failure. If the public stigmatizes a group, the group will likely fail to rally that public for support, be it to build or defend a state."[35]

Behind the scenes, at least one member of al-Qaeda's senior leadership was unhappy with the guidance Bin Laden gave to AQAP. Atiyya Abd al-Rahman, Bin Laden's chief of staff who had chastised Zarqawi and the Islamic State in Iraq for their excesses, worried his boss was too obsessed with attacking the Americans. Bin Laden was ignoring opportunities to establish Islamic governments, which was out of step with what the jihadist rank and file wanted. In their eyes, the whole point of jihad was to establish Islamic governments. "The young men want to go to the 'front' and they want 'operations,'" Atiyya reminded Bin Laden. "Is it proper to say: stop the escalation, we do not want war in Yemen!? I do not support this choice. None of the brothers here, who gave you their opinions, supports it. We definitely see it as a mistake." Giving the Yemeni government a pass and allowing other Islamists to take over, which is what Bin Laden's strategy amounted to, should not be an option.[36]

Despite his misgivings, Atiyya deferred to Bin Laden's wishes. AQAP did not. In early 2011, popular protests broke out in the capital of Yemen as part of the Arab Spring uprisings. Taking advantage of the political crisis, AQAP seized parts of Abyan Province in the South, including one of its major towns, Ja'ar. "As soon as we took control of the areas," confided AQAP's leader, Nasir al-Wuhayshi, "we were advised by the General Command [of al-Qaeda] here not to declare the establishment of an Islamic emirate or state for a number of reasons."[37] The reasons al-Qaeda's General Command gave Wuhayshi echoed Bin Laden's earlier guidance: "We wouldn't be able to treat people on the basis of a state since we would not be able to provide for all their needs, mainly because our state is a state of the downtrodden. Moreover, we fear failure in the event that the world conspires against us. If this were to happen, people may start to despair and believe that jihad is fruitless."

AQAP's leaders "deemed that [al-Qaeda's] advice was wise and decided not to declare a state." But they did declare several "emirates"[38] in the areas they controlled, breaking with the spirit of the advice in the letters from Bin Laden and al-Qaeda's senior leaders. A senior jihadist ideologue ominously warned AQAP: "You have seized territories even though you know from prior experience that you will not be able to protect them or your presence in them."[39] Despite Bin Laden's warning and the Islamic State's failure, AQAP couldn't resist the opportunity to take power.

Although AQAP unilaterally seized territory, it was not inured to the need to burnish its public image. Mindful of the mistakes of the Islamic State in Iraq, AQAP vowed to win "hearts and minds" and garner the support of the tribes in the South, whom AQAP's leaders saw as a greater threat to their enterprise than the United States.[40]

As part of its new public relations strategy, AQAP created a front group in 2011 called Supporters of the Shari'a (Ansar al-Shari'a). We don't know exactly why the group chose that name, but we can guess. Western media was in the habit of shortening al-Qaeda's full name, Qa'idat al-Jihad (Base of Jihad), which annoyed Bin Laden because the word "al-Qaeda," or "base," has nothing to do with Islam. Bin Laden privately acknowledged the al-Qaeda brand was toxic, needlessly bringing down heat on groups that adopted it.[41] He had actually considered changing his group's name to something else, such as "Monotheism and Jihad" or "Restoration of the Caliphate." Doing that, he believed, would force the media and the U.S. government to acknowledge the Islamic nature of the group and reinforce the idea that the West was at war with Islam. The same considerations were likely behind AQAP's choice of Ansar al-Shari'a as the name for its new front group.

The term "Ansar," or "supporters," harkens back to the Ansar of Medina, the people who helped Muhammad and his followers in their time of need when they emigrated from Mecca to escape persecution for their beliefs. The Shari'a is God's guidance for humanity, which includes prohibitions and ethical teachings. The whole point of setting up an Islamic state is to enforce the Shari'a.

Islam was born in a tribal society that lacked formal laws or a state to enforce them. Each tribe abided by its own customs and cult.

The founder of Islam, Muhammad, was able to create a state because he appealed to a greater religious identity to unite the fractious tribes. Doing that required him to promulgate laws that could transcend tribal identity and regulate a state. As a consequence, Islam's scriptures cover everything from inheritance to warfare. (Judaism emerged in a similar environment, which accounts for some of the parallels between the two religions.) Although some of Muhammad's legislation is harsh by modern standards, jihadists view it as a ready-made kit for enforcing rule in tribal societies. And Muhammad's life provides a model for how to do it successfully.

AQAP's decision to set up a front group reflected its shift away from terrorism and toward state building. In an April 2011 interview,[42] one of AQAP's senior religious leaders, Adil al-Abab, explained the group's change in focus. At times, Abab sounded like any politician tasked with tending to the mundane aspects of governing: "The largest problem that we face here is the lack of public services such as sewage and water, and we are trying to find solutions."[43] AQAP could govern even more territory, he asserted, were it not for the lack of "administrative staff and financial resources that would make us able to provide services to the people."[44] Abab made a special plea to wealthy Muslims to donate to their cause: "We have here in Ja'ar full plans for projects we want to achieve for the people such as water, sewage and cleaning, and we want to make contracts with investors so as to arrange these affairs. These projects are ready, and the regime has failed in carrying out these services. Now we have toppled the regime here and we are waiting for your investments."[45] Still, Abab reminded his listeners that bread and butter alone would not feed the Muslim soul; they must also submit to the *hudud*, the fixed punishments mandated by Islamic scripture. But this was also part of AQAP's hearts-and-minds strategy, according to Abab:

> Three days ago, here in Ja'ar, the Ansar al-Sharia caught a thief stealing while drunk, and I met him the next day. I asked him whether he was drunk, and he said "yes." I said did you know that drinking alcohol is prohibited, and he also said "yes." I

said did you know that your punishment would be whipping, he said: "Yes but cleanse me please." May God reward him. We whipped him forty lashes and that was the first implementation of *hudud* here. So we catch some people and chase others, we apply *hudud* as much as we can whenever we have the ability.[46]

In Abab's telling, the drunk was not alone in his desire to be punished in accordance with the Qur'an. "People are very happy with this, and they ask us: 'Where have you been all this time?' They never thought of us as such moral people with these ethics. They always thought that the al-Qaeda organization was evil because of the distortions they have been hearing about us. Whenever we meet people today, they rejoice at our existence and we talk to them about the Sharia and that if it is applied, God will send rain with welfare to the earth."[47]

AQAP developed an online media campaign to disseminate interviews with the happy inhabitants of the emirates they established. "How is it working for you now?" an AQAP interviewer asked a Ja'ar resident after the group turned the power back on. "Wonderfully!" the man replied.[48] A resident in the town of Seehan enthused, "Even the children, look at the children, they are happy! We used to wish for this, our grandfathers used to wish for this."[49]

Of course, there were fewer smiles off camera. Men could no longer wear soccer shorts. Music and dancing were banned.[50] Alleged spies were shot and then crucified, women accused of witchcraft were beheaded, and the hands of thieves were amputated. "They accused me of stealing," said one. "They detained me in a room for five days. They kept beating me hard . . . and tortured me with electric shocks. They would pour some water on my chest and then place a wire on it and I would feel as if I had been thrown hard. After five days, they gave me an injection, and I slept. When I woke up, my hand was not there."[51]

Predictably, AQAP's brutal rule turned the population against it within a year. As one Ja'ar resident put it, "In the beginning when they came here, they were simple people and weak. We were one of those people who were harmed by the government, because the government stole from us, and we were without work. We aligned with them in the beginning. We found out, thank God, before we did anything with them, we found out that they are liars . . . they love blood, and they are terrorists."[52]

AQAP also managed to alienate the local tribes despite wooing them with food and water.[53] In Ja'ar, the tribes were roused in 2011 by the cousin of a man AQAP executed for allegedly spying.[54] By the summer of 2012, southern tribal militias dubbed Popular Committees worked with the Yemeni government and the United States to overrun AQAP positions, ending the group's experiment in state building.[55]

After AQAP lost its territories, Adil al-Abab, the spokesperson for its Ansar al-Shari'a front group, ruminated on its failed effort to govern. Abab acknowledged that "some will wonder what were the gains achieved by the Ansar al-Sharia?" He spun AQAP's failure as a good first attempt, dispelling the criticism that jihadists could not govern. They implemented Islamic law, supplied swift justice and competent security, and provided public goods. Abab agreed that AQAP had not governed perfectly, but how could it when the Yemeni government had bombarded the cities under AQAP's control? Abab did not explicitly blame the tribes' betrayal for AQAP's losses, but he came close: "Know, O shaykhs of the tribes, that there is a project run by national security that aims in the first place to corrupt your sons and employ them as lackeys and agents."[56]

In private, AQAP's leaders were less sanguine. Yes, the jihadists had acquired some valuable experience in governing, and their subjects saw they cared about more than fighting. "But after that, the West and the East gathered against us, and fought us with one hand," lamented AQAP's leader Wuhayshi.[57] "After four months of fighting, we were forced to withdraw." "The whole world was against us."

"The most effective weapon of the enemy," Wuhayshi admitted, were the Popular Committees formed of disgruntled tribesmen and some Islamist opponents of AQAP.[58] "Those are the groups which were gathered by the enemy to become a de facto army of the area."

In Iraq, Sunni tribal militias backed by the United States and the central government had ended the Islamic State's attempt to rule in 2007. In Yemen, the same strategy had worked against another al-Qaeda affiliate.

In the end, the reasons for the collapse of the AQAP state were similar to the reasons for the Islamic State's failure in Iraq: fickle tribal allies, resentful subjects, and powerful foreign enemies—all reasons Bin Laden had cited for delaying the establishment of an Islamic state in Yemen.

The prophesy of "twelve thousand" wouldn't be fulfilled any time soon. No matter—the young founders of AQAP's online magazines who cherished the prophesy did not live long enough to be disappointed. Nayif al-Qahtani, Samir Khan, and Anwar al-Awlaki all died in American air strikes before the nascent AQAP state collapsed in 2012.

"TRY TO WIN THEM OVER THROUGH THE CONVENIENCES OF LIFE"

Just before AQAP lost its territory in 2012, its leader offered advice on governing to al-Qaeda's branch in North Africa, called al-Qaeda in the Islamic Maghreb (AQIM). Flush with weapons from the storehouses of Libya's fallen president and working with other jihadist groups, AQIM had just invaded and occupied northern Mali. "The places under your control are a model for an Islamic state," Wuhayshi wrote in a private letter to AQIM's leader, Abu Mus'ab Abd al-Wadud.[59] "The world is waiting to see what you'll do next and how you'll manage the affairs of your state." But "your enemies want to see you fail," Wuhayshi cautioned. "They are throwing obstacles in your path to prove to people that the mujahideen are people that are only good for fighting and war, and have nothing to do with running countries and the affairs of society."

Wuhayshi recommended a hearts-and-minds strategy: Win people over by providing public goods and by leniently applying Islamic law. The people are "hard-pressed by their needs and by the hard toil of making a living." So the jihadists should "try to win them over through the conveniences of life and by taking care of their daily needs like food, electricity and water." "What we've observed during our short experience," Wuhayshi related, is that "providing these necessities will have a great effect on people, and will make them sympathize with us and feel that their fate is tied to ours." AQAP had learned it was better to be loved and feared than feared alone.[60]

Wuhayshi advised AQIM to apply Islamic law very gradually because the people in the region were not used to its strictures. "You can't beat people for drinking alcohol when they don't even know the basics of how to pray." Wuhayshi recounted his group's own experience in Yemen: "Only after monotheism took hold of people's hearts did we begin enforcing these punishments. Shari'a rule doesn't mean enforcing punishments, as some people believe, or have been made to believe. We have to correct this misconception for the sake of the people. Try to avoid enforcing Islamic punishments as much as possible, unless you are forced to do so."[61]

Wuhayshi was less upbeat in a letter written a few months later, after the United States and its allies helped local tribesman drive AQAP from its territories. "We advise you not to be dragged into a prolonged war. Hold on to your previous bases in the mountains, forests, and deserts and prepare other refuges for the worst-case scenario. This is what we came to realize after our withdrawal."[62]

Whether or not AQIM's leader Abd al-Wadud ever received the advice,[63] he shared Wuhayshi's outlook. For over twenty years, Abd al-Wadud had fought in jihadist insurgencies against Algeria and other North African governments. Although an admirer of the ruthless Zarqawi and commander of his own brutal terrorist organization,[64] Abd al-Wadud had come to see the wisdom of the light touch. In 2012, he issued a "set of directions and recommendations" to "the brother emirs in the Sahara by which they should operate."[65]

Abd al-Wadud cautioned against monopolizing "the political and military stage." "We should not be at the forefront" of the movement to liberate northern Mali from the government's control.[66] Instead, the jihadists should build a broad coalition and abstain from excommunicating others.[67] "The aim of building these bridges is to make it so that our mujahideen are no longer isolated in society, and to integrate with the different factions, including the big tribes and the main rebel movement and tribal chiefs." Abd al-Wadud reminded the emirs that "the people of jihad serve as the directing and leading vanguard that works to implement this project amid our Islamic nation and among the various sectors of its people."[68] The jihadists simply do not have the "military, financial, and structural capability" to govern the state alone and stand up to the inevitable foreign pressure.[69]

AQIM and its cohorts had mixed success in rallying the support of the diverse tribes of the Sahel, the belt of semi-arid land cutting across Mali that separates North Africa from sub-Saharan Africa. In the years leading up to the fall of Timbuktu in 2012, jihadists were at times able to capitalize on racial and economic tensions to attract tribal recruits. However, internal tribal divisions and preexisting prejudices frustrated their efforts.[70] Racial and ethnic tensions among tribes proved a major problem, as the jihadists treated darker-skinned recruits worse than their light-skinned counterparts.[71] Black fighters were reportedly assigned insultingly menial tasks and were even abandoned in Timbuktu after jihadist forces left town.

The need for local support weighed heavily on Abd al-Wadud's mind. He chastised the jihadists for "the extreme speed with which you applied Shari'a, not taking into consideration the gradual evolution that should be applied in an environment that is ignorant of religion, and a people which hasn't applied Shari'a in centuries."[72] Failure to apply the Shari'a gradually would inevitably "engender hatred toward the mujahideen." Citing examples of what not to do, Abd al-Wadud rebuked the jihadists for severely applying religious punishments and for destroying the shrines of saints venerated by locals.[73]

In the months preceding Abd al-Wadud's letter, jihadists in Timbuktu had harshly punished male and female "adulterers," lashing a young couple for having a child out of wedlock and stoning another young couple to death for alleged premarital sex.[74] They flogged locals who dared to indulge in less egregious but still "un-Islamic" activities such as smoking or walking around without a veil.[75] The jihadists even banned music, integral to the beloved rituals associated with the animist-infused version of Islam commonly practiced in Mali.[76]

Locals were especially incensed when the jihadists razed the shrines of local Muslim saints. "All Muslims know the tomb is a holy place," a local religious scholar complained. "It's not something you attack and destroy. It's anti-Islamic. People in the community are angry."[77]

Visiting the shrines of saints is a major no-no in the ultraconservative Islam practiced by Salafi jihadists, so the shrines become targets when jihadists take over. Destroying them demonstrates the jihadists' religious bona fides to other ultraconservatives and lets the locals know who's boss. That Abd al-Wadud would criticize his fellow jihadists for destroying shrines shows how sensitive he was to popular sentiment. In the same vein, he criticized commanders for going beyond the requirements of Islamic law by preventing "women from going out" and "children from playing." "Your officials need to control themselves."[78]

Despite their fear, locals were not always shy about expressing their discontent: In Gao, a group protested after a young man accused of theft was sentenced to amputation, and a young woman defiantly removed her veil in public, which she had previously worn by choice.[79] Concerned citizens in Goundam tried to stop the public flogging of Sufis, followers of a mystical practice in Islam, only to be driven away by gunfire.[80] When a woman was beaten for not veiling, she dropped her baby, who nearly died. In response, crowds gathered at the local mosques to prevent the jihadists from saying their prayers. When firing in the air didn't disperse them, the jihadists took shelter in the house of a local official.[81]

Abd al-Wadud reminded his emirs to "take into account in our overall picture" the ever-present threat of hostile foreign powers. Invasion was "probable, perhaps certain;" if not, hostile foreign powers would still put in place a complete "economic, political, and military blockade." The invasion or blockade would "either force us to retreat to our rear bases," "provoke the people against us," or "enflame conflict between us and the other armed political movements in the region." Even if the armed groups initially closed ranks, the foreign powers would use "a carrot-and-stick policy with them to incite them against us."[82] To avoid that outcome, the jihadists should allow their local allies to publicly take the lead to give the appearance of a broad-based nationalist movement rather than a global jihadist enterprise that would provoke foreign intervention. "Better for you to be silent and pretend to be a 'domestic' movement that has its own causes and concerns. There is no call for you to show that we have an expansionary, jihadi, al-Qaeda or any other sort of project."[83]

Abd al-Wadud's "directions and recommendations" came too late. AQIM and its affiliates were never able to truly win over the locals, despite a shared a resentment of Mali's central government. When the French sent in fighter jets and special forces in early 2013, the jihadist proto-state in northern Mali collapsed. The jihadists either fled for neighboring Algeria and Libya or turned to guerrilla warfare.[84] Another al-Qaeda experiment in state building had ended in disaster.

FAILED STATE

In a now-familiar pattern, al-Qaeda's franchise in Somalia, the Shabab, also tried and failed to govern the territory it conquered. In 2008, the Shabab controlled a large expanse of land in central and southern Somalia,[85] prompting one of its most powerful leaders, Mukhtar Robow (aka Abu Mansur), to predict the imminent establishment of an "emirate."[86] Jihadists online also speculated that the emirate's establishment would come any day.[87] In the fall of 2009, the Shabab's leader, Ahmed Abdi Godane, publicly called Bin Laden the group's emir, and Shabab fighters began carrying the Islamic State's flag.[88] The Shabab's leaders secretly asked Bin Laden whether he would recognize them publicly as an al-Qaeda affiliate. They also asked if they could declare themselves an emirate.[89]

Bin Laden mulled the two questions for months, despite gentle reminders from his chief of staff that he needed to respond.[90] Bin Laden knew that, to garner popular support, the Shabab had provided basic services to citizens in rural areas outside the reach of Somalia's weak government. The southern countryside where the group operated its training camps and aggressively recruited was a particular area of focus. Justice and humanitarian relief were the orders of the day, which were in line with Bin Laden's thinking. The strategy initially seemed to work, winning over the public and local tribal leaders, which enabled the Shabab to function as the de facto government in southern rural areas.[91]

But like the other al-Qaeda affiliates, the Shabab squandered its support by meting out harsh punishments for violating its austere brand of Islamic law. Muslims who repeatedly failed to pray the required five times per day were imprisoned with no food until they prayed correctly.[92] The Shabab beat women for not fully covering themselves and stoned them to death for alleged extramarital sex,[93] including a thirteen-year-old girl who had been raped by Shabab men.[94] The Shabab also publicly amputated the feet and hands of people accused of theft.[95] There were protests against the Shabab's brutality, but they usually happened outside of areas the Shabab controlled.[96] People living in Shababaland were scared.

In addition to imposing harsh punishments, the Shabab put in place social restrictions that infuriated the locals in less conservative parts of the country.[97] It forbade music, prohibited smoking and playing sports, required women to don the hijab, closed cinemas showing international films,[98] and banned the Internet just as Internet use was spreading in Somalia.[99]

Mirroring the poor example of the Islamic State, AQAP, and AQIM, the Shabab also alienated local Somali tribes. When it began in 2006, the Shabab militia allied with the powerful Hawiye clan, one of the largest in Somalia. After the Ethiopian invasion in 2006, the Shabab exploited nationalist hatred of the occupiers to gather members of different, sometimes hostile, tribes under its umbrella to combat the invaders. The unity was temporary; interclan disputes in the group erupted soon after the 2009 Ethiopian withdrawal. Things continued to go downhill: The Shabab pitted clans against one another, capitalizing on the grievances of one clan to garner support and recruits, which would anger the clan's enemies. The Shabab also stabbed allies in the back; for example, in late 2009, it pushed out its erstwhile friend, the clan-based Islamist militia Hizb al-Islam, from a strategic port city and then made nice with local tribes to maintain its hold on power.[100]

The Shabab's behavior bothered Bin Laden because it went against everything he believed was necessary for establishing long-lived states. So when he finally responded to the Shabab in August 2010, he cautioned them against declaring a state even though he tepidly acknowledged that "a functioning state exists on the ground."[101] But the Shabab didn't have enough judges to administer the large territory it controlled, observed Bin Laden. Even the judges it had didn't "show lenience" toward the locals, especially toward those who didn't practice the Shabab's austere version of Islam. Such practices would only "push [the locals] closer to the enemies."[102]

Bin Laden also felt the Shabab was making a mess of Somalia's economy. The Shabab dominated the charcoal trade, cutting down scarce trees to manufacture fuel to send to the Gulf states. It also heavily taxed local businesses.[103] The charcoal monopoly and the onerous taxes not only bred resentment but also stifled the economy. Bin Laden recommended easing the taxes, relying on religious tithes instead. He also encouraged the Shabab to abandon its monopoly, citing the negative effects of state ownership in the Arab world. Rather than chopping down Somalia's scarce trees for short-term economic gain, Bin Laden suggested planting other kinds of trees that would encourage economic growth and stop deforestation. "You don't fail to notice that due to climate change, there's drought in some areas and floods in others," Bin Laden observed. If you didn't know he ran the world's most notorious terrorist organization, you'd think Bin Laden was an officer working for the United States Agency for International Development.[104]

Despite Bin Laden's misgivings about the Shabab, he was willing to allow it to secretly join al-Qaeda. But he wouldn't announce the merger publicly. To do otherwise, he explained, would needlessly cause "the enemies to escalate their anger and mobilize against you."[105]

Privately, Bin Laden continued to worry the Shabab wasn't doing enough to improve the livelihoods of the people in its lands. In a letter Bin Laden wrote to his chief of staff a week before he died, he observed that "improving the livelihood of people is one of the important goals of the Shari'a and the most prominent duty of the emir, so there must be an effort to establish an economic power."[106] Bin Laden also fretted the Shabab was still too quick to apply the harsh *hudud* punishments. As he rightly observed, the Prophet had established a high standard for proof that made it hard to implement his punishments. In contrast, the Shabab wasn't giving people the "benefit of the doubt when it comes to dealing with crimes and applying Shari'a."[107]

Like other al-Qaeda affiliates that attempted to govern, the Shabab undermined its efforts by antagonizing powerful foreign governments. In July 2011, Shabab operatives detonated three bombs in Kampala, the capital of Uganda, killing at least seventy-six people as they watched the World Cup finale.[108] Uganda had contributed peacekeepers to Somalia, whom the Shabab wanted to leave. But the attack only stiffened the resolve of African nations to rid themselves of the Shabab.[109] In late 2011, Kenyan forces entered southern Somalia, and the United States began drone strikes soon after. Over the course of 2012, Kenyan, African Union, and Somali government troops seized control of most major Shabab-held cities. By January 2015, the African Union claimed its troops had reclaimed "85 percent" of territory previously held by the Shabab, isolating the group in remote areas in the north and south.[110] The Shabab, like its brethren in Mali and Yemen, managed to survive as a guerrilla group, carrying out periodic terrorist strikes on select targets in Somalia, Kenya, and neighboring states.[111] But its proto-state had vanished.

When the Shabab and the other al-Qaeda affiliates launched rebellions and tried to govern, they flouted some of al-Qaeda Central's directives for winning hearts and minds. But some flouted less than others. Consider Bin Laden's and Zawahiri's advice for insurgencies: Cooperate with other Sunni rebel groups; don't kill tribesmen even if they collaborate with the enemy; don't broadcast the execution of prisoners; and avoid attacks on Muslim civilians even if they're "heretics." AQAP came closest to the al-Qaeda ideal. It collaborated with local rebel groups and sought the support of the tribes, but it also killed tribesmen who worked with its enemies.[112] It beheaded opponents and spies[113] but usually didn't broadcast the acts.[114] It bombed two Shi'i religious processions, but such attacks were rare.[115] After it lost its territory, AQAP's leaders would denounce the filming of beheadings[116] and attacks on Shi'i worshippers.[117] In both cases, they drew a distinction between themselves and the Islamic State, which we can put at the other end of the hearts-and-minds spectrum. Think of AQAP as attempting to win hearts and minds and the early Islamic State as trying to cut them out.

The same holds true for governance. Bin Laden had discouraged his affiliates from establishing Islamic governments before they had popular support. But when his affiliates insisted, he counseled them to prioritize the economic well-being of their subjects and apply the *hudud* punishments leniently. AQAP had tried to provide public services and to manage their local economies, but it was not lenient when applying the *hudud* punishments, a failure its leader later came to regret. As for the early Islamic State, it never really had a chance to govern. But it did burn down local businesses and harshly apply the *hudud*. Again, AQAP was closer to the al-Qaeda ideal, and the Islamic State was far from it.

Either way, all the al-Qaeda affiliates failed to create durable governments. The jihadists could interpret the failure as proof that al-Qaeda's leaders were right all along. Had the affiliates hewed more closely to the hearts-and-minds strategy advocated by Bin Laden and Zawahiri, they would have succeeded. AQAP's and AQIM's leaders certainly felt that way when they evaluated their successes and failures. But the jihadists could also interpret the failures as proof that the al-Qaeda affiliates hadn't been brutal enough. As we'll see, that's pretty much what the Islamic State would decide, although it would do better than it had in its first attempt at providing government services and co-opting the tribes.

Although al-Qaeda's leaders, like most outsiders, believed the hearts-and-minds strategy was the right one for creating a durable state, it was impossible for the affiliates to know for sure whether it was the correct policy because of one confounding variable: Global jihadists provoke powerful foreign countries to attack them. Recall that old-school global jihadists like Bin Laden wanted to drive the Western infidels from Muslim lands and win popular Muslim support before trying to set up their own governments. But when al-Qaeda's affiliates went "glocal"[118] by prioritizing state building, they still threatened the West in word or deed and so invited a powerful response. No government, especially after 9/11, wanted to take the chance that the glocal jihadists were just bluffing. So when the foreign governments attacked and defeated them, the jihadists could never say for sure how well they would have done had they been left alone. The coming civil war in Syria would give them a few years to find out what would happen if the international community let them do as they pleased.

FLYING THE FLAG IN THE ARAB SPRING

Although al-Qaeda's branches attempted and failed to establish Islamic governments from 2006 to 2012, al-Qaeda's online fanboys around the world continued to pine for them. On jihadist discussion forums, members adopted the flag of the Islamic State in Iraq as their avatars, and forum administrators set up clocks counting the days since the Islamic State in Iraq had announced its establishment. Other al-Qaeda flags were rare, and no one set up a clock to count the number of days since al-Qaeda's establishment. The idea of the Islamic State was spreading virally even as the group was on life support in Iraq and its bannermen suffered setbacks in Yemen, Mali, and Somalia.

Some jihadists were confused when al-Qaeda's affiliates flew the Islamic State's flag, wrongly assuming those affiliates had joined the Islamic State. "The whole world has pledged allegiance to the Islamic State," exclaimed a jihadist forum member in 2010. As evidence, he posted videos of the Islamic State's flag waved by jihadists in Indonesia, Somalia, and Yemen.[119]

The onset of the Arab Spring confused the flag's meaning further. In the chaos following the revolutions, jihadists formed new groups with the word "Ansar" ("Supporters") in their names. The groups shared al-Qaeda's global jihadist ideology but had no formal ties to the organization. Nevertheless, many of their members began flying the black flag of the Islamic State in Iraq, which was still an affiliate of al-Qaeda at the time. In Mali, Ansar al-Din raised the Islamic State's flag over the north in 2012.[120] Leaders of the Tunisian group Ansar al-Shari'a frequently stood in front of the flag spewing vitriol at the government.[121] Supporters of a different Ansar al-Shari'a group in Libya flew the flag whenever they talked to the press.[122]

Individuals also got into the act. Jihadists flooded their online discussion forums with pictures of the Islamic State flag popping up across the Arab world. Between May and November 2011, members of the Shumukh forum snapped photos of it at a protest in Gaza, along the Lebanese–Israeli border, at a gathering in Rabat, at a mosque in Egypt, and elsewhere.[123]

The flag made its most startling appearance in September 11, 2012. Responding to a film produced by a Christian living in California that insulted the Prophet, protestors gathered at U.S. embassies in the Middle East to display their displeasure. Some flew the Islamic State's flag, and one even managed to hoist it above the U.S. embassy in Egypt.

Many of those flying the flag during the protests were undoubtedly jihadists, Ayman al-Zawahiri's brother Muhammad among them. But non-jihadists also waved the flag. Some were unaware of its source, taking it as a simple reproduction of the Prophet's standard. Others knew its source and relished the provocative meaning attached to it. Demonstrators in Cairo who flew the flag told a reporter "they were not Al-Qaeda supporters, but were using it to protest against America and support Islam." A nearby vendor selling the flag corroborated their sentiment: "They are buying it for Islam and to show America they are wrong."[124] In the same spirit, the refrain "Obama, all of us are Osama" was chanted frequently and scrawled on walls of the U.S. embassy in Cairo.[125] The flag had transcended its origins to become a symbol of political protest. But the group that had designed the flag was about to remind the world of its original meaning.

FOUR
RESURRECTION AND TRIBULATION

Despite the success to come, the auguries boded ill for Abu Bakr al-Baghdadi when he assumed leadership of the Islamic State in May 2010. American and Iraqi troops had killed his predecessor while he was at home, which meant the Islamic State had been penetrated by its enemies. Many of the group's leaders had met similar fates at American hands. In response, the Islamic State shifted to a strategy of clandestine terrorism to cope with the setbacks but longed to fight in the open again as an insurgent group.[1] An Islamic state is nothing if it has no land.

Baghdadi was an unlikely executive. He had no bureaucratic or military training. And he was young, born Ibrahim Awwad Ibrahim al-Badri on July 1, 1971, to a lower middle-class farming family in Samarra, Iraq.[2] Despite his humble origins, though, Ibrahim had connections. Two of his uncles served in Saddam's security apparatus,[3] and one of his brothers was an officer in Saddam's army.[4] Another brother died in the army when Ibrahim was young, a casualty of the Iran–Iraq war.[5] Ibrahim himself would never serve in the military because of his poor eyesight.[6]

The city Ibrahim grew up in was famed for the golden-domed shrine containing the remains of the tenth Shi'i imam and his son. Although Ibrahim, a Sunni, would become rabidly anti-Shi'a later in life, he claimed descent from the tenth imam.[7] Through him, Ibrahim traced his lineage all the way back to the first imam, Ali, and his father-in-law, the Prophet. The man who would one day wage a war against the Shi'a was steeped in their mythology and claimed to descend from their leaders.

Neighbors, friends, and detractors remember Ibrahim's family for its piety but differ over its brand of Sunni Islam. Today, Ibrahim's Salafi-jihadist followers say the family was Salafi, an ultra-conservative form of Sunni Islam like the kind practiced in Saudi Arabia.[8] Others say Ibrahim was raised a Sufi and didn't become a Salafi until college.[9] Sufism is a mystical strain of Sunni Islam despised by the Salafis. Whatever the case, friends and neighbors uniformly describe him as "quiet," "introverted," and deeply devout.[10] Ibrahim's brother says he was a "stern" child who chided his siblings for minor religious infractions.[11] His nickname in the neighborhood was "the believer."[12]

In high school, Ibrahim has a middling student. He was excellent at math, so-so at Arabic, and terrible at English, barely passing the subject in his second try at the national exam in 1991.[13] Because of his average scores, Ibrahim couldn't study law at the University of Baghdad as he had hoped. So he enrolled in the university's College of Islamic Sciences, where he first studied the Shari'a and then switched to Qur'anic studies.[14]

Upon completing his bachelor's degree in 1996,[15] Ibrahim enrolled at Saddam University for Islamic Studies as a graduate student. (It was renamed the Islamic University after the Americans invaded in 2003.) Saddam had founded the university in 1989, and it soon became an integral part of his effort to patronize Islamic studies to offset the growth of ultraconservative Salafism, which he viewed as a threat to his rule.[16] For his master's thesis, Ibrahim edited a medieval book on Qur'anic recitation.[17] It took him more years to graduate than he would have liked because one of his advisors died and another moved to Yemen.[18] In other words, Ibrahim underwent the normal travails of a graduate student.

In the mid-1990s, Ibrahim joined the Muslim Brotherhood, a fraternal order that seeks to establish Islamic governments. Most Muslim Brotherhood branches peacefully pursue their goal, working within the local political system. Its members are intellectually diverse because the group doesn't have a fixed theological creed other than being vaguely Sunni. There are liberal members and conservative members. Ibrahim fell in with the ultraconservative Salafi members of the group in Baghdad.

After finishing his master's degree in 1999, Ibrahim was accepted into the university's doctoral program. Academically, he continued to study his favorite subject, the recitation of the Qur'an. Intellectually, he moved rapidly to the right, embracing revolutionary jihadist Salafism by 2000, three years before the American invasion of Iraq.[19] "My group does not embrace me" he told a leader of the Muslim Brotherhood when he left the organization.[20]

On June 30, 2004, a year after the Americans invaded Iraq, one of Ibrahim's professors filed a "Follow-Up Form for Students of Graduate Studies." "He has not attended my class," he noted. "Arrested."[21]

Ibrahim was sitting in Camp Bucca, a sprawling American detention center in the Shi'i south that held 24,000 inmates.[22] He had been picked up in February 2004 while visiting a friend in Fallujah whom the Americans were hunting.[23] U.S. government records show Ibrahim was held for ten months as a "civilian detainee," which means the Americans had no evidence he was in an insurgent group. His picture attached to the records shows a man with close-cropped hair and a trimmed mustache sporting a long black beard and large, silver-rimmed glasses beneath dark, bushy brows.[24]

Whether or not Ibrahim had joined the insurgency before landing in Bucca,[25] he certainly did afterward. The prison was known as the "Academy" because it brought together so many jihadists and former members of Saddam's military and security services.[26] "We could never have all got together like this in Baghdad, or anywhere else," remembered Abu Ahmed, a prisoner who knew Ibrahim. "It would have been impossibly dangerous. Here, we were not only safe, but we were only a few hundred metres away from the entire al-Qaida leadership."[27]

Abu Ahmed recalled that Ibrahim held "himself apart from the other inmates, who saw him as aloof and opaque." But the prison guards viewed Ibrahim as a leader who was able to calm disputes between factions.[28] Ibrahim befriended former members of Saddam's military and intelligence services, as well as future members of al-Qaeda in Iraq.[29] The men would meet again outside the wire and rise with Ibrahim through the ranks of the Islamic State after its senior leaders were killed or captured.

Ibrahim didn't join al-Qaeda until 2006, when his militia enlisted in al-Qaeda's umbrella organization, Majlis Shura al-Mujahidin. When the Islamic State declared itself later that year, Ibrahim was made the head of all the Shari'a committees in the group's Iraqi "provinces."[30]

Ibrahim was a multitasker. Despite the weight of his new responsibilities, he successfully defended his Ph.D. dissertation in March 2007.[31] The aspiring scholar had edited part of a medieval commentary on an Arabic poem about how to recite the Qur'an.[32] His advisor, a professor in Tikrit, could not come to Ibrahim's dissertation defense in Baghdad because travel was dangerous so he sent along his comments to the committee.[33] "The study the student wrote is good but it contained some errors which I noted on the pages of the thesis." The professor points out typographical and spelling mistakes and gives advice on how to make a critical edition from conflicting manuscripts. It was the mild criticism of a pleased professor. Ibrahim was awarded a grade of "very good" for his efforts.[34]

Meanwhile, Ibrahim was navigating the Islamic State's internal politics. The connections he had made in Camp Bucca served him well, as did his experience at negotiating between the prison factions. The Iraqis in the Islamic State chafed at the power of the foreign Arab faction headed by Abu Ayyub al-Masri, an Egyptian.[35] The Iraqis rallied around Abu Umar al-Baghdadi, the Iraqi who was nominally in charge of the Islamic State. Although he still played second fiddle to Masri, Abu Umar's stature among younger jihadists had grown,[36] perhaps because of the aura of mystery that surrounded him. Ibrahim managed to win over both Abu Umar and Masri.[37] According to one insider account, Ibrahim served as one of Abu Umar's three couriers, which meant he enjoyed the emir's trust. Some of the emir's letters to Bin Laden were supposedly drafted by Ibrahim, and "their journey always started with him."[38] But another insider portrays Ibrahim as a mere pass-through for correspondence; he never knew "the sender and the receiver."[39]

Whatever the case, Ibrahim's discretion and secrecy kept him alive.[40] When the Islamic State's commander in Baghdad was arrested, he named two couriers who carried messages to the State's leaders. The Americans tracked the couriers to the hideout of Abu Umar and Masri, who didn't survive the encounter.[41] The third courier, Ibrahim, lived to die another day.[42]

Upon the death of their leaders, the eleven members of the Islamic State's Shura Council deliberated on a new emir.[43] Bin Laden's chief of staff, Atiyya Abd al-Rahman, wrote them to suggest a procedure for selecting one:

> We suggest the noble brethren in the leadership appoint a temporary leadership to manage affairs until the consultation is complete. We believe it is best that they delay—as long as there is not an impediment or a strong preference for . . . hastening an official permanent appointment—until they send us suggested names and a report about each of them (the name, background information, qualifications, etc.) that we can send to Shaykh Osama so he can advise you.[44]

The procedure was not followed by the Islamic State, either because no one saw the letter in time or because its recipients ignored it. Clandestine communication makes it hard to run a militia from afar.

But slowness and the vagaries of clandestine communication can also create opportunities. The Islamic State's Shura Council couldn't meet in conclave for security reasons, so its members had to correspond separately.[45] The head of the Islamic State's military council, a former colonel in Saddam's army named Hajji Bakr,[46] saw a way to turn the situation to his advantage. Hajji Bakr wrote each member individually, saying the others had agreed that Ibrahim should take charge.[47] Ibrahim was one of the youngest candidates considered, but he had a lot going for him. He claimed descent from Muhammad; he was a member of the Shura Council and close to the previous emir;[48] and he had ties to other powerful members.[49] It also mattered that members of Ibrahim's tribe had been early supporters of the Islamic State.[50] His tribal connections could help the group make a comeback. Nine of the eleven Shura Council members voted for Ibrahim, now taking the nom de guerre Abu Bakr al-Baghdadi, commander of the faithful.

Al-Qaeda's leaders heard about Abu Bakr al-Baghdadi's appointment in May after everyone else did.[51] Distrustful of the new leadership, in July Bin Laden asked his chief of staff for information about Baghdadi and his deputies. "Ask several sources among our brothers there, whom you trust, about them so that the matter becomes clear to us."[52] Several days later, Atiyya promised he would do so.[53] But he was apparently unsuccessful because he wrote the Islamic State's Ministry of Media in September: "The shaykhs [in al-Qaeda] ask you for an introductory paper about your shaykhs in the new leadership." Better yet, "perhaps they can write and introduce themselves."[54]

A representative for the Islamic State's Shura Council wrote back on October 9. He claimed the Islamic State had received al-Qaeda's instructions to select a temporary emir after it had already announced Baghdadi's appointment. Nevertheless, the representative affirmed Baghdadi's loyalty to al-Qaeda and his consent to be a temporary leader. If al-Qaeda had a better candidate to lead, the Islamic State would "hear and obey."[55]

When Bin Laden died a few months later, Baghdadi made a public statement assuring the new head of al-Qaeda, Ayman al-Zawahiri, that the men of the Islamic State were "faithful" to him and al-Qaeda.[56] In a private letter on May 23, 2011, the Islamic State asked if Zawahiri wanted Baghdadi to make a more explicit public pledge of allegiance to him.[57] The al-Qaeda chief apparently declined.

While Baghdadi stalled for time with his leaders in al-Qaeda, he consolidated his hold on power in the Islamic State. At his right hand was the man who had helped him take the throne, Hajji Bakr. Those who knew the bald, white-bearded Hajji Bakr described him as the "prince of the shadows" and Baghdadi's "private minister."[58] According to insiders, the first order of business for the prince of shadows was to purge the Islamic State of leaders he suspected of disloyalty; those who didn't leave their posts willingly were killed. He and his boss replaced them with their Iraqi allies, many of whom had served as officers in Saddam's military and intelligence services.[59] Saddam, who had conducted a similar purge when he came to power, would have been pleased.

His throne secure, Baghdadi set about reviving the Islamic State's flagging fortunes.

BLUEPRINT

On the new emir's desk was a plan to turn things around. Between December 2009 and January 2010, Iraqi jihadists had circulated a "Strategic Plan for Reinforcing the Political Position of the Islamic State of Iraq."[60] The document has the look and feel of a DC think tank report, with analysis and recommendations for policy makers. Think pieces and after-action reports are common in the jihadist movement, but it was unusual to see jihadists openly criticize the Islamic State. The criticism was evidence of how far the group had fallen. The tempo of the Islamic State's attacks was nowhere near its height in early 2007, and the group held no land.

The strategy paper blamed the Islamic State's fall on a "dirty war" waged by its American adversaries, who used "awakened" Sunni tribes against it. "When the Islamic State was at the pinnacle of its power and influence, [the Americans] bombed markets, public places, and mosques, and they killed the opponents of the State, so that the mujahids were blamed. On account of things like this, we saw the influence of the Islamic State fade and disappear and the apostate Awakenings spread."[61]

The delusions continued. The authors of the paper spun online videos of Americans trying to disarm improvised explosive devices (IEDs) as videos of Americans planting the devices and inadvertently blowing themselves up. The Islamic State did not provoke the Sunni tribes by oppressing them;[62] rather, the jihadists' enemies cleverly turned tribal leaders against the jihadists. Young men in the tribes supported the Americans only for money and for pride, styling themselves as defenders of their people.

The Islamic State has fallen, the authors acknowledged, but it will return just as the Taliban returned in Afghanistan after its defeat at the hands of the Americans.[63] The American withdrawal from Iraq would be the time to act. "When the Americans withdraw within two years . . . the situation will be strongest politically and militarily for the Islamic plan to prepare to completely seize the reins of control over all Iraq."[64] But the authors recognized that other factions in Iraq were preparing to do the same.

The authors recommended several ways to overcome the other factions and control Iraq. Uniting them behind the "jihadist program" of the Islamic State was at the top of their list. "It is not about names and titles the Muslims would strive for. Aiding [the program] is a victory for the people of Islam and not a victory for a group, or a title, or a name." Merely fighting the other factions without a goal would be "stupid."[65]

Militarily, the authors contended it would be a waste of time to focus on attacking the American forces in Iraq since they were leaving; rather, the jihadists should train their fire on the Iraqi military and police, whom the Americans hoped would continue to pacify the country for them once they left. By targeting them, the jihadists would instill fear in the hearts of potential recruits.[66] They should focus in particular on the very few units that were capable of fighting against the jihadists.[67] Attacking government troops would also force them to abandon their bases in regions of the country where they were weak. That would open up security vacuums and drain the government's resources when it fought to protect its remaining bases. The jihadists could exploit these vacuums by seizing the territory and any equipment or infrastructure that was left behind.[68] "Make them always preoccupied with internal problems," wrote the authors, quoting ancient China's preeminent military strategist Sun Tzu.

Readers might find it odd that religious zealots who hate nonbelievers would quote Sun Tzu. But the practice is common, evidence of a pragmatic streak among some jihadists. In the early 2000s, for example, jihadists celebrated the strategic insight of Abu Ubayd al-Qurashi, an anonymous author who quoted dozens of non-Muslim strategists in his magazine column, "Strategic Studies." Among others, Qurashi cited Robert Taber's history of guerrilla campaigns, *War of the Flea;* William Lind's writings on fourth-generation warfare; the Prussian military theorist Carl von Clausewitz; and the Communist revolutionary Mao Zedong.[69] The authors of the "Strategic Plan" were carrying on that tradition.

The authors assumed guerrilla tactics would weaken the Iraqi government. But they also believed the jihadists could not establish their own state without co-opting the Sunni tribes. To do so, the authors advised the Islamic State to copy what the United States had done: give money and weapons to Sunni tribal leaders who were angry with the Islamic State. Doing so had reinforced the tribal leaders' authority and bought the temporary allegiance of their young men. The authors admitted that "the idea to recruit the tribes to eliminate the mujahids was a clever, bold idea and will be used by any occupier in the future because they make hard work easy for the occupier, just as they provide protection against the attacks of the mujahids." But the authors were sure the tribes would rather receive money and weapons from fellow Muslims than from foreign occupiers who disrespected their religion or promoted thugs as tribal leaders.[70] The mujahids should follow the American blueprint of creating tribal councils and militias they can work with, but do it better. The mujahids would be more respectful of local religious practice and power structures, and they could finance the endeavor with captured booty.[71] As we will see, the jihadists' respect for religious sensitivities and power structures was sometimes more theory than practice.

Uniting the jihadists behind a single program, intimidating Iraqi security forces, and co-opting the Sunni tribes would not be enough, asserted the authors. The jihadists also needed a "political symbol" or "avatar." Several things go into the making of such a symbol: the greatness of his sacrifices, his high morals, and his evenhandedness.[72] The head of the Islamic State at the time, Abu Umar al-Baghdadi, had achieved symbolic status. But the authors worried that none of his deputies was high profile enough to fill his symbolic shoes if he died (which happened a few months later).

In concluding their think piece, the authors stressed that jihadists have to instill confidence in those whom they rule. They could do this by protecting the people in lands they control and making them prosper, seeing to the needs of local governors and soldiers, selecting good executives and judges, ruling by Islamic law, implementing the *hudud* punishments stipulated in Islamic scripture, and distributing money from the treasury.[73] Since the international media is biased against the jihadists, they said, the jihadists would need a media strategy to make sure their good works were known.[74] The jihadists should also consider allying themselves with their opponents when they face a common enemy, just as the Prophet allied with the Jews against the pagans when they attacked him in Medina.[75]

The "Strategic Plan" has a lot in common with *The Management of Savagery*, a book released online by an al-Qaeda franchise in 2004, two years before the Islamic State's founding. The book explains how to take control of territory, establish a nascent state, and develop into the caliphate.[76]

The author of *The Management of Savagery* went by the nom de guerre Abu Bakr Naji. We do not know for certain who Naji was in real life, but he was probably from North Africa, based on certain turns of phrase he uses and his frame of reference. No one wrote under that name after 2004, so he is either dead[77] or started writing under a different name.[78]

Naji argued that terrorist groups should carry out "vexation operations" against sensitive enemy targets, such as oil pipelines and tourist sites vital to the nation's wealth.[79] To protect these sensitive targets, local governments would pull in their security personnel, which would open up security vacuums or "regions of savagery" in the periphery of the state. Jihadists would then move into the volatile regions, provide basic security and public goods to win over the population, and establish "Shari'a justice."[80] Securing the support of the tribes in the area would be crucial because the lack of tribal support would doom the jihadists' efforts. Bribes can go a long way, but the jihadists should also try to indoctrinate the tribes.[81] The jihadists should work with other Muslims regardless of their theology, provided they did not oppose the jihadists' program.[82] After the jihadists had established a network of these "administrations of savagery," they should coalesce into an Islamic state and then a caliphate.

Naji did not sugarcoat what it takes to conquer and control these lands: ceaseless, uncompromising violence. "Those who study only jihad as it is written on paper," Naji observed, "will never grasp this point well." The youngsters in particular "no longer understand the nature of wars." Veterans of previous jihads know "it is naught but violence, crudeness, terrorism, frightening others, and massacres." Those who are soft are better off "sitting in their homes." "If not, failure will be their lot and they will suffer shock afterwards." Even if jihadists wanted to act mercifully toward their enemies, their enemies will "not be merciful to us if they seize us." "Thus, it behooves us to make them think one thousand times before attacking us."[83] Even the enemy's women and children can be targeted, he said, as long as it deters the enemy from doing the same[84]—a principle that contradicts the Prophet's prohibition against killing women and children.[85]

Despite Naji's insistence that jihadists are constrained by Islamic scripture, the "Islamic" principles he enunciated override the Prophet's strictures on violence.[86] Maximum latitude for maximum violence is the real interpretive framework for Naji and his acolytes. To Naji's mind, anything less would make the jihadists ineffective insurgents.

Throughout his book, Naji was at pains to convince his jihadist readers that they could learn from the writings and example of non-Muslim insurgents, military strategists, and political theorists. One of the very first people he quoted was not the Prophet but Paul Kennedy, the American historian who wrote about the dangers of military overreach: "If America expands the use of its military power and strategically extends more than necessary, this will lead to its downfall."[87] Naji used the quote as the bedrock of his entire strategy for provoking the United States to overextend itself militarily. Universal laws of insurgency, argued Naji, are usually compatible with Shari'a laws.[88]

Naji's book is popular in jihadist circles. In 2008, Saudi authorities arrested seven hundred people whom they accused of plotting attacks inside the kingdom. According to the authorities, those arrested were consulting the book to help them "revive criminal activities in all regions of the Kingdom in an attempt to change the internal security situation into a stage that resembles the situation in other unsettled regions."[89] A friend with contacts in al-Shabab, the Somali branch of al-Qaeda, related to me in 2010 that members of the group used the book as a blueprint to take over Somalia.[90]

Today, seasoned jihadists in the Islamic State study Naji's book in their camps.[91] Online Islamic State fanboys also celebrate the manual, often sharing links on Twitter where followers can download the text. One such tweet from November 2014 with the hashtag "The Islamic State is coming" touted the book as "the first resource for mujahids in managing their areas of influence."[92] Another tweet going back to September 2012 promoted a PDF of the book, saying "There is no better book, I highly recommend downloading it from the net, reading it, and then burning it so no one from the state finds it among your things."[93] Other tweets quote sections of the book. One from February 2014 has a picture of a passage providing advice on dealing with jihadists who deviate from the norms of the movement, above which he tweets "a lesson from Abu Bakr in his book #TheManagementofSavagery."[94]

Blueprint in hand, the Islamic State was prepared for a comeback.

GAINING GROUND

When the Islamic State decided to set up shop in Syria, it already had a network in place. Syrian president Bashar al-Assad had funneled hundreds of jihadists into Iraq to fight against the United States. According to the U.S. government, in 2007, 85 to 90 percent of the foreign fighters in Iraq had come through Syria.[95] The Islamic State had received many of those fighters[96] and had maintained its facilitation network in Syria after the end of the Iraq war.[97]

When Syrians began peacefully protesting against their government in 2011, the Assad regime released an unknown number of jihadists from prison.[98] The release was calculated to foster violence among the protestors and give Assad a pretext for a brutal crackdown. It worked. As a Syrian intelligence officer would later reveal, "The regime did not just open the door to the prisons and let these extremists out, it facilitated them in their work, in their creation of armed brigades."[99]

Taking advantage of the volatility and the release of prisoners, al-Qaeda leader Ayman al-Zawahiri ordered the Islamic State to "form a group and send it to [Syria]."[100] The Islamic State's emir, Abu Bakr al-Baghdadi, dispatched one of his senior Syrian operatives, Abu Muhammad al-Jawlani, to oversee the effort.

The new group initially behaved like its parent, wantonly disregarding civilian casualties. In December 23, 2011, the group that would soon call itself Nusra Front (Jabhat al-Nusra) carried out a huge suicide attack in Damascus, killing dozens. The next six months were more of the same, which raised the ire of other Sunnis rebelling against Assad.[101] In August 2012, Nusra had only about two hundred operatives in Syria.[102]

But then things began to change. Nusra expanded in the north, becoming an insurgent group rather than a clandestine terrorist organization. The development made the group more sensitive to the need for popular support. It began avoiding suicide attacks on civilians and collaborated with the other Sunni insurgent groups. When the United States designated Nusra a terrorist organization on December 11, 2012, and accused it of operating under the umbrella of the Islamic State, Syria's Sunni rebels responded: "We are all the Nusra Front."[103]

Nusra's change in strategy may also have been prompted by the growing influence of Syrian jihadist Abu Khalid al-Suri. Abu Khalid, who was reportedly released from a Syrian prison in late 2011, had long ties to al-Qaeda and its new chief, Ayman al-Zawahiri. The two had met when Abu Khalid was in Pakistan in the early 1990s,[104] although Zawahiri had lost touch with Abu Khalid after his capture in Pakistan in May 2005. The Pakistanis turned Abu Khalid over to the Syrians, who transferred him to the Saydnaya military prison in Syria. The prison held many of Syria's political prisoners, including the jihadists Assad would later release. When the Assad regime freed Abu Khalid, Zawahiri quickly reestablished contact. "He was to me and my brothers such a great advisor," Zawahiri would later remark.[105]

Zawahiri and Abu Khalid were of similar mind about how to conduct an insurgency: The insurgents should win the hearts and minds of the locals. The common insurgent creed had been given a jihadist flavor by Abu Khalid's longtime comrade Abu Mus'ab al-Suri, the apocalypticist and strategist we met earlier, whom Zawahiri called the "professor of the mujahideen."[106]

In the early 1980s, Suri had participated in the Syrian Muslim Brotherhood's revolt against President Hafez al-Assad, Bashar al-Assad's father. The revolt ended in the deaths of tens of thousands of Syrians and ruin for the Brotherhood, forcing Suri into exile and a life of itinerant jihadism. He would spend the next two decades thinking and writing about what went wrong in Syria and in the other failed jihads he observed.[107]

Suri was an early booster of the 1990s jihad in Algeria, which began when the Algerian military cancelled parliamentary elections after Islamists succeeded in an early round of voting. Suri watched in dismay from London as the jihadists in Algeria became more extreme, which turned the public against them.

Suri went on to Afghanistan, where he served on the consultative council advising al-Qaeda. Suri and his comrade Abu Khalid were independent thinkers and differed frequently from al-Qaeda's leader, Bin Laden. In a 1999 email, they reprimanded Bin Laden for violating a pledge to the "commander of the faithful," Mullah Omar. The Taliban leader had asked Bin Laden to stop making media appearances and antagonizing the Western powers, a request Bin Laden ignored despite his oath of allegiance to the mullah. "You should apologize for any inconvenience or pressure you have caused," the two Syrians wrote, "and commit to the wishes and orders of the Leader of the Faithful on matters that concern his circumstances here."[108]

For Suri, 9/11 was the ultimate act of disrespect to one's host because it provoked the United States to destroy the Taliban. "The outcome, as I see it, was to put a catastrophic end to the jihadist current, an end to the period which started back in the beginning of the 1960s of the past century and has lasted up until September 11th. The jihadist current entered the tribulations of the current maelstrom which swallowed most of its cadres over the subsequent three years."[109]

Chastened by two decades of failure, Suri published a massive tome online, *The Call of the Global Islamic Resistance*, explaining where the jihadist movement had gone wrong and how to put it right again. The 1,600-page book came out around the same time Naji published his *Management of Savagery*. The two books are similar in many ways but whereas Naji emphasized conquering territory and brutally defending it, Suri promoted popular revolt. "The Islamic movement can only establish the Muslim society through a popular jihad."[110]

Suri's hearts-and-minds strategy was promulgated by Abu Khalid among the jihadists in Syria and was soon championed by Nusra's leaders. Tweets written by Sami al-Urraydi, a Nusra religious advisor,[111] showcased the "pearls"[112] he had gleaned from Suri's writings. Many of them are veiled criticisms of the excesses of the Islamic State. Urraydi quoted Suri as saying that "[t]he Algerian experience confirmed to me and others that the greatest failing of the entire jihadist experience without exception" is the lack of religious education

among jihadists, which leads to violent excess among the youth.[113]
In another tweet, Uraydi listed nineteen admonitions from Suri's
writings that all jihadists should heed. Among them is Suri's caution
against excommunicating Muslims and targeting neutral people.[114]
Both were tenets the Islamic State ignored.

Nusra itself ignored parts of Suri's advice. The strategist doubted
jihadists could overthrow Muslim rulers as long as the United States
dominated the Middle East. The American-led crusader-Zionist alliance was too powerful to be ignored; it must first be resisted and
repulsed from the Muslim countries before Muslims could contemplate establishing a truly Islamic state. According to Suri,

> The goal of the call of resistance is resisting the aggression of
> the Crusader-Zionist campaigns led by America and its Jewish
> and Crusader allies among the foreign forces of unbelief, and
> the local forces of apostasy and hypocrisy cooperating with it.
> The old strategic goal of confronting governments [in the re-
> gion] has changed. . . . No one should take from this that the
> goals of the call of resistance is anything other than establish-
> ing the rule of the law of God. . . . But we consider this the
> final goal that will result from the success of the resistance in
> repelling these campaigns and bringing about the downfall of
> the greatest power, America.[115]

Nusra, in contrast, believed a popular front against a Muslim ruler in
Syria could succeed, perhaps because the United States was not backing the regime. The group recruited heavily among Syria's Sunnis[116]
and involved locals in governing the areas they seized.[117] Nusra collaborated with other rebel groups as long as they weren't too closely
aligned with the United States (especially after the United States began bombing Nusra in late 2014). After taking a city, Nusra participated in joint "Shari'a committees" with other rebel groups to settle
disputes, provide basic services, and distribute food and medicine.[118]

In contrast, the Islamic State sought to dominate rather than
collaborate whenever it could.[119] When it had sufficient manpower,

the group preferred to govern alone and to terrify locals who questioned its writ. When the Islamic State's soldiers murdered members of other rebel groups, it refused to submit to arbitration, claiming a mere group cannot hold a state accountable. "The State is the State," wrote Islamic State scholar Turki ibn Mubarak al-Bin'ali. "Have you ever heard of the Prophet's state, or the Rightly Guiding Caliphs' state, or the Umayyad state, or the Abbasid state submitting to the judgment of an independent person? . . . We are a state, so how could you compel us to submit to the judgment of an independent court? . . . Don't you know that an independent court means a different state?"[120]

To get a sense of how these differences played out, consider reported incidents of Nusra and the Islamic State abusing Syrian Sunnis or attacking other rebel groups: From August to December 2013, the Islamic State behaved badly 43 times, Nusra, 4.[121] Put pseudoscientifically, that is a "badness factor" of ten.

The Islamic State's rule in the Syrian town of al-Bab is a case in point. When the Islamic State first arrived in late 2013, it fixed roads and cleaned up the town. But as its power grew, the State imposed harsh restrictions on women, forbade smoking, and forced people on the street to pray at the designated times. Torture and kidnapping kept the locals in line, but resentment grew.[122]

Still, not everyone resented the Islamic State's authoritarianism. Some citizens supported the State's diktat, considering it a welcome change from the abuses and arbitrary rule of other rebel groups. The Islamic State might be brutal, but it cracked down on bandits, drove out corrupt rival groups, and made decisions quickly. In contrast, Nusra often collaborated with those rebel groups, which made it hard to govern and to curb abuses.[123] As Plato observes in the *Republic*, the tyrant "sprouts from a protectorate root."[124]

FALLING OUT

Given their different strategic orientations,[125] it is little wonder that the Islamic State was soon at odds with its branch in Syria. The State wanted to carve out a domain in the Arab hinterland between Syria and Iraq. Nusra wanted to embed itself in the Syrian opposition and overthrow the Assad regime.

Nusra and the Islamic State also disagreed over the control of resources, especially oil. Selling oil on the black market ensured a steady stream of millions for funding operations and attracting recruits. As the American journalist Theo Padnos gleaned from his time as a Nusra hostage from 2012 to 2014, "The real issue between the Nusra Front and the Islamic State was that their commanders, former friends from Iraq, were unable to agree on how to share the revenue from the oil fields in eastern Syria that the Nusra Front had conquered."[126]

The spat over oil was enmeshed in tribal politics. Nusra had the strong support of conservative tribesmen in the town of Shuhail in Deir Ezzor Province bordering Iraq. But after a senior Nusra member from a rival tribe defected to the Islamic State, the latter was able to capture a Conoco gas plant in the area. The move touched off fighting between the rival tribes, which finally ended with a truce. The Shuhailis kicked out the Islamic State, but it later returned and defeated the tribe, which also meant the defeat of Nusra in eastern Syria.[127]

Jealousy also played a role in the conflict between the Islamic State and Nusra. Baghdadi suspected Nusra's fighters were more loyal to their leader, Abu Muhammad al-Jawlani, than to him, the commander of the faithful. Baghdadi reportedly sent a private letter to Jawlani, telling him to announce that Nusra was part of the Islamic State. Jawlani refused because it "would not be beneficial to the Syrian revolution." Baghdadi's consigliere, Hajji Bakr, dispatched spies to watch Jawlani in Syria. Unhappy with the slow trickle of information, Hajji Bakr and Baghdadi went to Syria themselves in March 2013.[128]

Baghdadi met with Jawlani directly and again argued that the ties between Nusra and the Islamic State should be made public. Jawlani refused once more, contending that Nusra was in Syria at the request of Zawahiri and would not answer to the Islamic State. Jawlani reminded Baghdadi that al-Qaeda had expressly forbidden the Islamic State from "announcing any official presence of al-Qaeda" in

Syria[129] because it would destroy Nusra's popular support. Changing tack, the emir praised Jawlani for his efforts. But after Jawlani left, Baghdadi met separately with each Nusra leader, trying to turn them against him.[130] Although Baghdadi was unsuccessful, fans of the antihero Frank Underwood in the television series *House of Cards* will appreciate the maneuver for what it was: cunning politicking.

Two days later, on April 9, 2013, Baghdadi publicly revealed that Nusra was a branch of the Islamic State and announced it would be absorbed into a new entity, the Islamic State of Iraq and al-Sham (the Levant). In his statement, Baghdadi disclosed that when the conflict began in Syria, he had deputized Jawlani to lead a contingent into the country. Baghdadi instructed him to work with Islamic State cells already active there to establish a branch of the State. The Islamic State gave the group its marching orders, paid its salaries, and supplied it with men. Baghdadi explained that he had delayed announcing his control of Nusra for security reasons and to avoid tarring the new venture with the bad reputation of the Islamic State. But the time for secrecy had come to an end.[131]

Jawlani responded the next day[132] by declaring Nusra's independence from the Islamic State and pledging an oath of allegiance directly to Zawahiri as leader of al-Qaeda.[133]

Baghdadi, still nominally under al-Qaeda's authority, immediately fired off a private message to Zawahiri, threatening bloodshed and *fitna*, or schism, if Zawahiri didn't rule in his favor:

> It has just now reached me that al-Jawlani has released an audio message announcing his direct oath of allegiance to you. This is what was planned for him to protect himself and those with him from the consequences of the mistakes and disasters he committed. This poor servant [Baghdadi] and those brothers with him here in al-Sham believe it is up to our shaykhs in Khorasan [Afghanistan and Pakistan] to announce a clear, unambiguous position in order to bury this conspiracy before it causes blood to flow and we [*sic*] become the reason for a new calamity for the *umma*.

We believe that any support for what this traitor has done, even tacitly, will lead to a great *fitna*, which will thwart the program for which the blood of Muslims has been shed. Delaying the announcement of the correct position will lead to making the current circumstance the reality, splitting the ranks of the Muslims and diminishing the prestige of the group such that there will be no healthy cure afterward except by shedding more blood.[134]

Zawahiri was exasperated. "We have neither been asked for authorization or advice, nor have we been notified of what had occurred between both sides," he wrote in a private letter to both men.[135] "Regrettably, we have heard the news from the media." Like a parent scolding siblings for fighting, Zawahiri blamed both parties. Baghdadi "was wrong when he announced the Islamic State in Iraq and the Levant without asking permission or receiving advice from us and even without notifying us." Jawlani erred "by announcing his rejection of the Islamic State in Iraq and the Levant, and by showing his links to al-Qaeda without having our permission or advice, even without notifying us." The Islamic State was to renounce its claim on Syria and go back to Iraq. Nusra should continue its fight in Syria but as an al-Qaeda affiliate in its own right. Both men would be subject to review after one year by the "general command" of al-Qaeda. Zawahiri appointed his trusted friend, Abu Khalid, to arbitrate between Nusra and the Islamic State should subsequent differences arise.

Despite the scolding, Nusra had gotten what it wanted. It would no longer answer to the Islamic State and was now al-Qaeda's official affiliate in Syria.

Incensed, Baghdadi publicly rejected Zawahiri's ruling. "I have chosen the command of my Lord over the command in the message that contradicts it." Baghdadi explained his decision privately in a letter dated July 29, 2013, referring to the "muhajirs," or foreign fighters, in the Islamic State: "It became clear to us that obeying our emir was an act of disobedience to God and ruinous for the mujahids

with us, especially the muhajirs. So we obeyed our Lord and preferred his good-pleasure over the good-pleasure of the emir. . . . You
do not say someone sinned because he disobeyed a command from
an emir that he believes is ruinous for the mujahids and an act of
disobedience to God the exalted."[136]

Baghdadi was alluding to a tradition from the Prophet: "No obedience in sin but rather obedience to what is right."[137] The tradition
circulated in the early years of Islam to justify revolt against Muslim
rulers.

Days after Baghdadi rebuffed Zawahiri, the Islamic State's
spokesman, Abu Muhammad al-Adnani, publicly explained Baghdadi's decision. Zawahiri erred when he tried to partition the Islamic
State according to borders drawn by colonialists. The ruling would
only embolden secessionists in the Islamic State's ranks. Clearly, Zawahiri was a biased judge who had not properly listened to the State's
complaints.[138]

Al-Qaeda had faced unruly affiliates in the past, especially the
Islamic State. But the spats had never been public, which would have
represented a direct challenge to al-Qaeda's leaders. Doubtless worried about setting a bad precedent, Zawahiri decided to kick the Islamic State out of al-Qaeda. Thus, on February 2, 2014, al-Qaeda
publicly renounced any "tie" or "connection" with the group.[139]

The Islamic State's spokesman, Adnani, shot back, arguing that
the State had never really been part of al-Qaeda. In Adnani's telling, al-Qaeda in Iraq had dissolved itself when the Islamic State was
declared in 2006. "The Mujahidin came out from the restrictiveness
of the organizations to the emancipation of the State," said Adnani,
giving the impression that the Islamic State had never answered to
Bin Laden and al-Qaeda's other leaders.[140] Al-Qaeda could not dis-
own what it no longer possessed.

Partisans of the Islamic State on Twitter repeated the talking
points. "The best news I've heard," quipped one, "is that the State
has no ties to you all. Let us reply to the deserters and liars that are
saying Baghdadi disobeyed Zawahiri."[141] When Nusra spiritual advisor Sami al-Uraydi chided Baghdadi on Twitter for his hubris, an

Islamic State fan responded, "Our shaykh Osama himself called for joining up with the State."[142] Others shared YouTube videos presenting proof that supposedly exonerated Baghdadi from the charge of disobedience.[143]

Annoyed, Zawahiri issued a statement on May 2, 2014, to clarify the nature of the historical relationship between al-Qaeda and the Islamic State.[144] Zawahiri admitted that the Islamic State had been established in 2006 without consulting al-Qaeda's leaders. But its founder, Abu Ayyub al-Masri, had sent a letter after the fact justifying the State's establishment and affirming its loyalty to al-Qaeda. Masri related that the first emir of the Islamic State, Abu Umar al-Baghdadi, had pledged his loyalty to Bin Laden in front of other Islamic State leaders, but they did not broadcast the news due to "political considerations."[145] According to Zawahiri, the same considerations kept Abu Umar's successor, Abu Bakr al-Baghdadi, from publicly pledging allegiance to Bin Laden and then to Zawahiri after Bin Laden's death. To prove his point, Zawahiri cited internal al-Qaeda memos, even those the United States had captured and declassified. Many of the memos have been presented in this book.

Flustered by Zawahiri's document dump, the Islamic State spokesman Adnani could no longer insinuate that the State had never been under al-Qaeda's authority. Changing course, he claimed the Islamic State had bent the knee to al-Qaeda's commanders only on matters outside of Iraq. The State obeyed al-Qaeda's orders not to undertake attacks outside the country, even though its rank and file demanded them in Saudi Arabia, Egypt, Libya, Tunisia, and finally Iran, where al-Qaeda's leaders wanted to "protect [the organization's] interests and its supply lines." As for attacks inside Iraq, the Islamic State's spokesman claimed that the organization ignored al-Qaeda's "repeated request" to stop targeting the Shi'a. In his telling, al-Qaeda never issued a direct order to the Islamic State or asked its leaders about the disposition of their forces inside Iraq.[146]

Here the Islamic State's spokesman is engaging in a bit of historical revisionism. It is true that the State often ignored al-Qaeda's orders for operations inside Iraq, but al-Qaeda was neither deferential nor disinterested. In private letters from 2007–2008, al-Qaeda sent directives to the group and asked about the disposition of its forces.[147]

Regardless, the crucial question was whether al-Qaeda had authority over the Islamic State for matters outside Iraq. By admitting that the Islamic State deferred to al-Qaeda for foreign operations, the spokesman had acknowledged al-Qaeda's writ outside Iraq. Clearly, the Islamic State had defied that authority, as Baghdadi himself had said privately.

The man Zawahiri had chosen to heal the rift between the Islamic State and Nusra, Abu Khalid, was disgusted by the Islamic State's duplicity. "The State group is excommunicating everyone who opposes them or differs with them, spilling their blood with impunity as if they own Islam." Such wanton disregard for life and loyalty, he sniped, could only mean the Islamic State was working for an intelligence agency to destroy the Syrian rebellion.[148] In response, the Islamic State threatened to send five suicide bombers to pay Abu Khalid a visit.[149]

FITNA

Baghdadi's disobedience divided the jihadist community. "With great regret," wrote the administrators of the most popular jihadist discussion forum, "the brothers have split into three camps because of these events":[150] Team Islamic State, Team Nusra, and the mushy middle.

Jihadists in the thousands, many of them young, took to their favorite social media platforms to voice their views. Gone were the days when disagreements among jihadists were confined to private discussion boards, silenced by moderators. The rest of the world could watch the melee in real time, keeping score by tabulating retweets and "likes." The biggest split ever in the global jihadist community happened just when people could use new forms of social media to quickly sort themselves into rival camps. The two phenomena are probably related.

From the Olympian heights, jihadist scholars traded blows that reverberated throughout the community. Influential graybeards like

Abu Qatada al-Filistini and Abu Muhammad al-Maqdisi sided with Nusra. Abu Qatada blasted the Islamic State for "trespasses in . . . cooperating with their brothers and opposing them" and for behaving as if it were an actual state rather than an insurgent group like the rest. Baghdadi should take his organization back to Iraq, Abu Qatada counseled, just as Zawahiri ordered.[151]

Maqdisi, the don of jihadist scholarship, mocked the Islamic State's claims that its jihadist opponents were part of a Western-backed conspiracy against it. The idea that jihadists should treat Baghdadi as the head of an actual Islamic state, much less a caliphate, was absurd.[152]

Maqdisi was particularly annoyed that some of his protégés had backed the Islamic State. "I hope my anger reaches them," he reportedly said.[153] The criticism stung. One of them lashed out: "O you who have made war on the [Islamic] State with your fatwas," he said, "you have created this state of division [*fitna*]."[154]

Online fans of both camps also got in on the action, tweeting support for their side and denigrating the other. A prominent Islamic State cheerleader calling himself Shami Witness led the charge for his team on Twitter. "Nusra is over," he tweeted confidently a few weeks after Nusra seceded from the Islamic State. Its "approach of collaboration with and appeasement of non-jihadi grps [*sic*]" had ruined the organization.[155] "LOL why are all these Nusra fanboys attacking me at once?" he taunted. "That insecure eh?"[156]

The barbs were not just traded online. In early January 2014, Islamic State members in Aleppo killed a popular commander in a powerful Salafi militia, Ahrar al-Sham, after weeks of skirmishes with other Sunni rebels in Syria. The rebels demanded the Islamic State submit to arbitration to settle the conflict, but the State refused because it would "infringe on the right of the Muslim sovereign and his state."[157] Various jihadists tried to mediate between the two groups, but the effort went nowhere due to the Islamic State's intransigence. When other rebel groups attacked the State for similar transgressions, Ahrar al-Sham reluctantly joined the fight.

Organizing the fight for Ahrar al-Sham was Abu Khalid, Zawahiri's representative who commanded the group's forces in Aleppo Province in northern Syria. On January 17, 2014, Abu Khalid issued a statement condemning the Islamic State, saying it had broken all the rules of Islamic warfare, attacked its fellow jihadists, and violated the tenets of insurgency put forward by Abu Mus'ab al-Suri, Zawahiri, and Bin Laden. Its method was as "far as possible from the proper method." The Islamic State's war on its brothers would only help Syrian president Bashar al-Assad, who stood to gain the most from rebels fighting one another instead of him.[158]

In response, the Islamic State decided to make good on its earlier threat to kill Abu Khalid with suicide bombers.

FULFILLING A PROMISE

The man charged with carrying out the Islamic State's order was Ahmad Lulu, a thirty-five-year-old native of Aleppo who worked for a relief organization, Syria Khayr. Lulu enjoyed close ties with Ahrar al-Sham's members, particularly people in the group's humanitarian aid office.[159] His job took him to the old crusader city of Antakya (Antioch), Turkey, where licit and illicit aid flowed across the border with Syria. There Lulu met Abu Hurayra, an Islamic State fighter convalescing away from the battlefront. The two men struck up a friendship, which deepened when they returned to Syria.

At Abu Hurayra's prompting, Lulu soon joined the Islamic State. "In the organization, they knew I worked in the relief field," Lulu later explained. "They left me to complete my work in this field, in addition to working with them to spy and gather information."

When fighting broke out between Ahrar al-Sham and the Islamic State, Lulu was summoned by a State security official. "The task . . . was to 'purge the leadership of Ahrar al-Sham.'" Because of the difficulty and sensitive nature of the operation, only a few of the Islamic State's senior leaders knew of it, including Baghdadi and his spokesman, Abu Muhammad al-Adnani.

Lulu was introduced to Abu Maryam al-Iraqi, an Islamic State operative who would assist him. Lulu recounted that he and Abu Maryam "agreed on the details" and planned to meet after Friday prayers. Abu Maryam showed up with three men and a van. Lulu stowed the men in a house, after which he and Abu Maryam went to case one of Ahrar al-Sham's offices in the al-Halak district of Aleppo.

On the third day, February 23, 2014, Lulu was present when some of Ahrar al-Sham's senior leaders, including Abu Khalid, showed up for a meeting. Lulu "left and informed Abu Maryam in precise language." Abu Maryam responded: "Do it and don't wait." Lulu secreted two of the three would-be assassins in a nearby village. "Then I went and confirmed that the leadership [of Ahrar al-Sham] was still present." It was. Lulu returned to the two men. "Go!"

Local activists reported that armed men charged into the meeting, firing their weapons until one of the gunmen detonated a bomb.[160] The explosion killed six, Abu Khalid among them.

Soon after Abu Khalid's death, the rebel offensive against the Islamic State stalled. The rebels had reached the limit of their power and stretched themselves too thin. Over the ensuing months, the Islamic State consolidated its hold over eastern Syria, becoming its undisputed master. Its strategy of going it alone to capture and control territory may have alienated everyone, but it had paid off.

The Islamic State now had a vast war chest from captured oil fields, taxes, and loot, and it ruled its territory unchallenged. Its Sunni opponents were weakened, and President Assad had turned a blind eye, happy to let the Islamic State threaten his domestic and foreign enemies as long as it didn't threaten him; 90 percent of all Syrian air assaults against the rebels fell on the Islamic State's competitors.[161]

Thousands of fighters left Nusra and the other rebel groups to join the Islamic State. Some wanted to play for the winning team, some believed it was doing God's work, some saw it as the Sunnis' only hope, some had no choice, and some just wanted to make a little money.[162] Then there were the foreigners who had come to fight in the final battles of the apocalypse and usher in the caliphate reborn. The Islamic State welcomed them all.

FIVE
SECTARIAN APOCALYPSE

The chaos unleashed by the Arab Spring revolts prompted many Arab Muslims to wonder whether the end of the world was nigh. Even when the protests were peaceful, the sudden churn of Arab politics after decades of stagnation fired the apocalyptic imagination. Theories circulated online that Hosni Mubarak, the deposed president of Egypt, had really been the Antichrist prophesied in early Islamic scripture. Others swore they had seen End-Time heroes moving among the demonstrators in Egypt and Tunisia.[1] Half the Arabs polled in 2012 believed the Mahdi, the Muslim savior, would appear any day.[2] The mounting violence in Syria, or al-Sham, the land of the eastern Mediterranean mentioned in Islamic prophecies as the site of the final battles of the apocalypse, made the doomsday interpretation of events hard to resist.

Musa Cerantonio, an Australian convert to Islam, watched the events unfolding with glee. "There is a reason why Syria, or Sham more specifically, is special for the believers," he told a Melbourne audience in 2012. "It holds a very specific, special, and strategic place in the future" of the Muslim community. God had revealed its future to Muhammad, Cerantonio said, so the Muslims could prepare themselves for battle. That future had arrived.[3]

Sunni prophecies attributed to Muhammad laud the region of al-Sham as the gathering place for the final battle against the infidels. "Go to Sham . . . and those who are not able to go to Sham should go to Yemen," says one Sunni prophecy credited to Muhammad.[4] "Al-Sham is the land of gathering" for the Day of Judgment, according to another.[5]

Although Sham encompasses the entire eastern Mediterranean, jihadists often equate it with modern Syria. It helps that many of the important apocalyptic sites mentioned in the prophecies are located around Damascus. "The Muslims' place of assembly on the day of the Great Battle will be in Ghouta near a city called Damascus, one of the best cities in al-Sham," says one.[6] Ghouta is where the Assad regime killed hundreds with sarin gas in 2013. "A group in my community will continue fighting at the gates of Damascus and its environs and at the gates of Jerusalem and its environs," says another prophecy.[7]

Their relevance to the current conflict is heightened by the fact that these prophecies mention the same places that are the scenes of today's battles, which makes them useful for jihadist recruitment pitches. "O youth of Islam!" declared Abu Bakr al-Baghdadi. "Go forth to the blessed land of Sham!" "Come to your State to raise its edifice. Come . . . for the Great Battles are about to transpire."[8] The apocalyptic pitch "always works," confided an Islamic State fighter to a reporter.[9]

Musa Cerantonio often quoted the Sham prophecies to persuade young Muslims to fight in Syria under the banner of the Islamic State. Cerantonio himself claimed to join them in July 2014, tweeting: "I have arrived in the land of . . . Ash-Sham!" Cerantonio was actually in the Philippines, where he had been living since February of that year. He was arrested a week after his tweet because the Australians had cancelled his passport.[10]

THE STRANGERS

Jihadists, especially foreigners who travel to fight in distant lands, call themselves "strangers." They are strange, they claim, because they adhere to the true Islam that most Muslims neglect. They are strange because they have abandoned their countries for foreign lands to fight the final battles against the infidels.

"Islam began as something strange," the Prophet told his companions, "and it will return to being something strange as it first began, so glad tidings to the strangers." "Who are the strangers?" someone asked. "Those who break off from their tribes," the Prophet replied.[11]

For jihadists, leaving their tribes means leaving their homelands and emigrating to fight elsewhere, just as the Prophet's companions, "the emigrants," did. In Arabic, the word for "stranger" is *gharib*. The plural is *ghuraba'*. The word can also mean "foreigner," which is apt for the foreign jihadists who volunteer to fight in distant lands. *Ghuraba'* is often the name of the camps they set up, and it's the title of a popular hymn they chant. When Abu Mus'ab al-Zarqawi left for Afghanistan in the late 1980s, he called himself al-Gharib, "the Stranger."[12]

Most of the prophecies about the strangers are found in a medieval compendium of the Prophet's words and deeds. In a section titled *The Book of Tribulations*, End-Time prophecies intermingle with descriptions of the strangers, giving them an apocalyptic hue.[13] These prophecies are of a piece with others of a "saved group" of Muslims who will fight the infidels until the Day of Judgment.

Jihadists of all stripes, not just Islamic State followers, have been stirred by the promise of fighting in the final battles preceding the Day of Judgment. "If you think all these mujahideen came from across the world to fight Assad, you're mistaken," said a jihadist fighting in Aleppo. "They are all here as promised by the Prophet. This is the war he promised—it is the Grand Battle." Another fighter in northern Syria believed the same. "We have here mujahideen from Russia, America, the Philippines, China, Germany, Belgium, Sudan, India and Yemen and other places. They are here because this [is] what the Prophet said and promised, the Grand Battle is happening."[14] God "chooses the best of people to come" to Sham, asserted Abu Muthanna, a Yemeni from Britain. "You see where the muhajirin are," he said, using the Arabic term for "emigrants." "This is the biggest evidence that they are upon the haqq," or truth.[15]

Many of the emigrants or strangers have flocked to the Islamic State's banner. A popular gray-bearded Tunisian commander goes by the nom de guerre "Father of the Strangers" (Abu al-Ghuraba'). The Strangers Media Foundation produces propaganda supporting the Islamic State and criticizing its jihadist detractors.[16] A YouTube video titled "Strangers—Islamic State in Iraq and Sham—Pictures from the Land of the Great Battles" depicts fighters from around the world.[17] A Jordanian blogger collects Islamic State propaganda on his website, *Strangers of the Lands of Sham*.[18] The strangers have found their home in the Islamic State.

DABIQ

The meadow outside the small village of Dabiq north of Aleppo, Syria, is an unlikely setting for one of the final battles of the Islamic apocalypse. Although close to the Turkish border, "Dabiq is not important militarily," observed a leader in the Syrian opposition.[19] And yet the Islamic State fought ferociously to capture the village in the summer of 2014. Its members believed the great battle between infidels and Muslims would take place there as part of the final drama preceding the Day of Judgment.

Abu Mus'ab al-Zarqawi himself had stirred apocalyptic expectations by citing a prophecy about Dabiq.[20] In it, the Prophet predicts the Day of Judgment will come after the Muslims defeat Rome at al-A'maq or Dabiq, two places close to the Syrian border with Turkey:

> The Hour will not come until the Romans land at al-A'maq or in Dabiq. An army of the best people on earth at that time will come from Medina against them. When they arrange themselves in ranks, the Romans will say: "Do not stand between us and those [Muslims] who took prisoners from amongst us. Let us fight with them." The Muslims will say: "Nay, by God,

how can we withdraw between you and our brothers. They will then fight and a third [part] of the army will run away, whom God will never forgive. A third [part of the army], which will be constituted of excellent martyrs in the eye of God, will be killed and the third who will never be put to trial will win and they will be conquerors of Constantinople.[21]

For Zarqawi, Dabiq was the ultimate destination of the fire that had "been lit here in Iraq" by the "strangers"; they need only persist in their fight.[22] The Islamic State's first commander of the faithful, Abu Umar al-Baghdadi, quoted the Dabiq prophecy too, reminding Muslims what his followers were fighting for.[23]

The Dabiq prophecy probably first circulated in the early eighth century AD when the Umayyads attempted to conquer Constantinople, the seat of the eastern Roman (or Byzantine) Empire. There the Umayyad caliph Sulayman (Arabic for "Solomon"), stirred by a prophecy that someone bearing the name of a prophet would conquer Constantinople (Soloman is considered a prophet in Islam),[24] prepared for an assault on the city in 716. Too sick to lead the campaign himself, Sulayman handed command to his brother, who led the caliph's troops in a failed siege on the "Roman" capital. Sulayman died waiting for the victory that never came.[25]

Despite early mentions of Dabiq in Islamic State propaganda, the group's statements did not really focus on the village until 2014. In April, an Islamic State spokesman mentioned the ill-fated village as one of several places prophesied to fall to the jihadists. "You were promised Baghdad, Damascus, Jerusalem, Mecca, and Medina. You were promised Dabiq, Ghouta, and Rome."[26] In July, the Islamic State released an English-language magazine named *Dabiq*. The editors, calling themselves the Dabiq team, explained why they adopted the name: "The area will play a historical role in the battles leading up to the conquests of Constantinople, then Rome." But first the Islamic State had to "purify Dabiq" from the "treachery" of the other Sunni rebels who held it and raise the flag of the caliphate over its land.[27]

A few weeks later, Islamic State fighters took the village from Sunni rebels, killing forty and capturing dozens. The State lost twelve of its own men.[28] Setting up snipers and heavy machine guns on the hill overlooking Dabiq, they repelled an attempt by the Free Syrian Army to retake the area.[29] Islamic State supporters were jubilant, tweeting pictures of their flag from the hilltop together with quotes from the prophecy. "Dabiq is the most important village in all of Syria for them . . . especially the foreign fighters," explained one of the Muslim rebels who fought the Islamic State advance.[30] In October, the State released a video of European jihadist fighters sitting on the same hilltop, daring the infidel West to intervene. "We are waiting for you in Dabiq," challenged Abu Abdullah from Britain. "Try, try to come and we will kill every single soldier." Abdul Wadoud from France quoted the Dabiq prophecy and another predicting that the infidel forces will gather under eighty flags.[31] He assured his listeners that the Islamic State will defeat the infidel enemies allied against it because the prophecies say so.[32]

Jihadist tweets about Dabiq spiked again in September, when the United States began to consider military action against the Islamic State in Syria. Supporters of the State counted the number of nations that had signed up for "Rome's" coalition against it. "Thirty states remain to complete the number of eighty flags that will gather in Dabiq and begin the battle" tweeted one.[33] After Turkey's parliament approved military operations against the Islamic State in Syria and Iraq, the jihadist Twittersphere applauded. "Turkey's entry into the war will permit the foreign invasion of northern Syria, meaning from the plain of Dabiq. The battles [of the End Times] have grown near."[34] "In Dabiq the crusade will end" tweeted another.[35]

The last time the Turks invaded Dabiq, things didn't go well for the Arabs. The Turkish Ottoman sultan, Selim I, defeated the slave armies of the Mamluk Sultanate on the plain of Dabiq in 1516, which gave the Ottoman sultan control of the eastern Mediterranean and eventually Egypt and the Hijaz in western Arabia. The conquest inaugurated five hundred years of Ottoman rule over the Arabs and strengthened the Ottoman claim to the title of caliph.

Selim I's grandfather, Mehmed II, had conquered Constantinople from the Byzantine Empire in 1453.

The fact that Turkish Muslims, not infidel Romans, control Constantinople, or Istanbul, today and are working with the infidel West against the Islamic State makes the Dabiq prophecy a poor fit for contemporary events. The inevitable defeat of the State at Dabiq, should it ever confront "Rome," would also argue against the prophecy's applicability. But in the apocalyptic imagination, inconvenient facts rarely impede the glorious march to the end of the world.

Islamic State fighters pray to God to "protect the Islamic State and support it until its army fights the crusaders near Dabiq."[36] An essay on Dabiq was written by a woman claiming to be the mother of Adam Karim al-Mejjati, a child killed with his father who worked for al-Qaeda's branch in Saudi Arabia. Speaking of U.S. President Barack Obama, Adam's mother sneered: "The Creator lures the runaway slave and his dismal procession of evil creatures to the meadow of Dabiq in fulfillment of the Beloved's prophecy and as a lesson to all created things." When a masked British member of the Islamic State beheaded a U.S. aid worker in November 2014, he growled, "Here we are, burying the first American Crusader in Dabiq, eagerly waiting for the remainder of your armies to arrive."[37]

Somewhere nearby, the tomb of the Umayyad caliph Sulayman lay in ruin, destroyed by Islamic State members who consider ornate graves idolatrous. The resting place of the man who wanted to fulfill prophecy by conquering Constantinople did not survive the zealotry of his modern heirs.[38]

CHRIST AND ANTICHRIST

"You have seen us on the hills of al-Sham and on Dabiq's plain chopping off the heads that have been carrying the cross for a long time," proclaimed a camouflaged Islamic State narrator standing on Libya's Mediterranean coast in a video released in February 2015. A row of fourteen Egyptian Christians in orange jumpsuits kneeled before him and his black-clad brothers, members of the State's branch in

Libya. Now, announced the narrator, the world would watch as they beheaded the Christians as part of a war with Christianity that will last until Jesus descends from heaven.[39]

Anticipating Jesus's descent and executing his followers probably strikes most readers as odd. The Qur'an portrays Jesus as a messenger of God and his followers as those "nearest in love to the believers" (5:82). But the prophecies attributed to Muhammad outside the Qur'an foresee Jesus returning to fight alongside the Muslims against the infidels. As in the Bible, the appearance of Jesus heralds the Last Days. But instead of gathering the faithful up to heaven, he will lead the Muslims in a war against the Jews, who will fight on behalf of the Antichrist, called the Deceiving Messiah. Jesus will "shatter the crucifix, kill the swine, abolish the protection tax, and make wealth to flow until no one needs any more," says one prophecy attributed to Muhammad and quoted by the first emir of the Islamic State.[40]

According to another prophecy imputed to Muhammad, God will send Jesus the Messiah when the Antichrist appears. He will "descend at the white minaret at the east of Damascus,"[41] which popular legend locates in the Umayyad Mosque. Afterward, Jesus will defeat the Antichrist. In February 2013, the Islamic State's spokesman proclaimed, "We will not lay down this flag until we present it to Jesus, the son of Maryam, and the last of us fights the Deceiver."[42] "We will remain, by the permission of God, until the arrival of the Hour and the last of us fight the Deceiver," he vowed in another statement.[43]

Islamic prophecies about the Antichrist give hints about his identity. In most accounts, he is a one-eyed Jew of grotesque appearance. He is either tall with a receding hairline or short with curly hair. His arms are hairy, and one hand is longer than the other.[44] With such vivid clues to work with, Islamic State fans let their imaginations run wild. Most recently, the Antichrist is the blind Grand Mufti in Saudi Arabia,[45] a baby born with one eye,[46] or a Zionist.[47]

Others interpret the prophecy figuratively. "The West is the one-eyed Deceiver," tweeted an Islamic State supporter after the January 2015 attack on the *Charlie Hebdo* newspaper office in Paris.

"When we criticize them, we are anti-Semitic. When they insult our sacred things, it is freedom of expression. Bombing us is a fight against extremism. When we respond, we are terrorists."[48]

There is one prophecy about the Antichrist that the Islamic State and its fans have studiously avoided, even though it is in a collection of prophecies they revere: The Antichrist will "appear in the empty area between Sham and Iraq."[49] That, of course, is precisely where the Islamic State is located.

THE SUFYANI

Despite fighting bitterly against each other in Iraq and Syria, many of the Sunni and Shi'i militants drawn to the battlefield were motivated by a common apocalyptic belief that they fight in the vanguard of the Mahdi. "I was waiting for the day when I will fight in Syria. Thank God he chose me to be one of the Imam's soldiers," confided twenty-four-year-old Abbas, a Shi'i from Iraq who, like other Shi'a, believes the Mahdi is the twelfth imam, or leader descended from Muhammad.[50] "With every passing day we know that we are living the days that the Prophet talked about," asserted Mussab, a Sunni fighting for al-Qaeda's branch in Syria, the Nusra Front.[51]

Readers might puzzle at the incongruity of Muslims killing one another somehow fulfilling a prophecy of Muslims defeating infidels. But the early Islamic apocalyptic prophecies are intrinsically sectarian because they arose from similar sectarian conflicts waged at the time in Iraq and the Levant. As such, they resonate powerfully with today's sectarian civil wars.

Soon after the death of Muhammad in AD 632, civil wars, or *fitan* ("tribulations"), consumed the nascent Islamic empire as Muhammad's companions battled one another for political supremacy. The contest was framed in religious terms, which was unavoidable given that Muhammad and his immediate successors, the caliphs, wielded both spiritual and temporal authority. Before and after each tribulation, partisans on both sides circulated prophecies in the name of the Prophet to support their champion. With time, the context was forgotten but the prophecies remained. The word used for the upheavals of the apocalyptic Last Days, "tribulations," was the same word used for the early sectarian civil wars.

To understand the sectarian dimension of Islamic apocalyptic prophecies, consider the example of the enigmatic figure known as the Sufyani. According to the prophecies, the Sufyani descends from Abu Sufyan, the leader of Muhammad's tribe in Mecca who persecuted the Prophet and his early followers. Although Abu Sufyan and his family converted to Islam before the death of the Prophet, Abu Sufyan's son Mu'awiya later fought Muhammad's son-in-law Ali for control of the Islamic empire. Mu'awiya eventually became caliph, establishing the Umayyad dynasty that ruled for nearly a century.

As one might expect, the partisans of the losing side, called the Shi'a of Ali (Partisans of Ali and later just the Shi'a), began circulating words of the Prophet prophesying the new dynasty's downfall at the hands of the Mahdi, the "Rightly-Guided One." The Mahdi would be a member of the Prophet's family who would defeat the dynasty's champion, the Sufyani, in the Levant. "When the Sufyani reaches Kufa [a city in Iraq] and kills the supporters of the family of Muhammad, the Mahdi will come," according to one early prophecy.[52]

Many Shi'a today believe the Sufyani's appearance is imminent, but they do not welcome it because of his antagonistic role in the apocalyptic drama. "All of us believe the Sufyani will fight the Imam [Mahdi], and the Prophet will kill him in the land of al-Sham," asserted a former leader of Kata'ib Hizballah, a Shi'i militia in Iraq. "We want to stress that what is happening in al-Sham is the beginning of the tribulation and is the beginning of the appearance of the army of the Sufyani, which is now called the Free Army."[53] The "Free Army" is the Free Syrian Army fighting against Shi'i Iran's ally in Syria, Bashar al-Assad.

In contrast, Sunnis are more ambivalent about the Sufyani. Though most Sunni prophecies about him are negative, a few are positive because some Sunnis do not believe the Sufyani's kin, the Umayyads, were wrong to seize the caliphate from the Prophet's family. The Sufyani reconciles with the Mahdi in some prophecies and either swears allegiance to him[54] or hands over the caliphate to him.[55] In early Islam, Syrians were particularly partial to the Sufyani because his kin, the Umayyads, had ruled the caliphate from Damascus. A descendent of Abu Sufyan was proclaimed the Sufyani by his Syrian followers when he unwisely rebelled in Damascus against scions of the Prophet's family to restore the Umayyad dynasty around 750. As the ninth-century Iranian historian al-Tabari records, forty thousand rebels "proselytized on his behalf and said, 'He is the Sufyani who has been mentioned.'" The government killed him soon after.[56]

Several decades later, another "Sufyani" rebelled in Aleppo.[57] In 811, Umayyad supporters circulated prophecies of the Sufyani's imminent return, hinting that all signs pointed to an octogenarian descendent of the Umayyad dynasty named Abu al-Amaytar.[58] The "Sufyani" managed to capture and hold Damascus for two years before his defeat at the hands of the same descendants of the Prophet's family who had defeated his Sufyani predecessors.[59]

As in the ninth century, the Sufyani is a national hero for some Sunnis today, especially those in Syria. "God willing, all of us will be in the army of the Sufyani, who will appear in [Syria] by the permission of God," prayed Adnan al-Ar'ur, a popular Syrian Salafi cleric and supporter of the rebellion who currently lives in Saudi Arabia.[60]

The sectarian wrangling over the identity of the Sufyani suggests an important difference between Islamic and Christian End-Time prophecies. Although both envision a fight between good and evil, the Islamic prophecies foretell a period of intracommunal fighting before the Day of Judgment. "The sword of vengeance will fall upon hypocrites before being turned against infidels," observes a scholar of Muslim apocalypticism.[61] Syria and Iraq, ground zero for the final apocalypse, are also ground zero for the sectarian conflict that must precede it.

YELLOW FLAGS, BLACK FLAGS

Early Islamic prophecies of the End Times resonated with the conflicts in Syria and Iraq not only because of their geographical setting;

even the colors of the belligerents' flags—yellow for Hizballah, black for al-Qaeda and the Islamic State—seemed to match. "If the black banners and the yellow banners meet in the center of al-Sham," a companion of the Prophet prophesied, "the bowels of the earth will be better than its surface."[62]

Some Shi'a identified the yellow flag with Hizballah and the black flag with the Sunni jihadists. "When those who carry the yellow flag engage in a conflict with anti-Shi'a elements in Damascus and Iranian forces join them, this is a sign and a prelude to the coming of his holiness [the Mahdi]," stated Ruhollah Hosseinian, a member of Iran's parliament and the former deputy intelligence minister. "We see that [now] the masters of the yellow flag, meaning Hizballah of Lebanon, are engaged with anti-Shi'a groups in Damascus. Perhaps this is the event that promises the appearance of his holiness, and we must prepare ourselves."[63]

Sunni jihadists saw it the same way. "The [prophecy] of the black banners and the yellow banners is playing out in al-Sham," asserted a Sunni tweeter. "The mujahids have the black flags and Hizb al-Shaytan has the yellow flags."[64] Hizb al-Shaytan, or the Party of Satan, is the jihadist put-down of Hizballah, the Party of God.

When Shi'a and Sunnis assign the yellow banners to Shi'i Hizballah and the black banners to al-Qaeda or the Islamic State, they miss two historical ironies: First, the black flags were originally associated with the Shi'a and others who wanted to restore the caliphate to the Prophet's family, as described in an earlier chapter.

Second, the people who first inspired the yellow flag prophecies were quite anti-Shi'a and lived in North Africa, far from Hizballah's home base in Lebanon. The yellow flag prophecies date to the time of the Berbers' revolt against the Umayyad and then Abbasid governors of the Maghrib, or North Africa, in the 740s and 750s. In one instance, Berbers plundered Kairouan (in present-day Tunisia) in 757 and massacred its inhabitants. They were cheered on by the extreme "yellow" (Sufri) Kharijites, an Islamic sect whose founders had excommunicated and assassinated their enemies, including the first Shi'i imam, Ali.

The Umayyads and their successors, the Abbasids, feared the Berbers would sweep farther east, a fear documented in numerous prophecies of yellow flags invading the Levant from North Africa.[65] According to one prophecy, "the Berbers will come forth to the center of Syria, that will be the sign for the emergence of the Mahdi."[66] Another predicted "a tremor in Syria in which a hundred thousand will be killed and which God will make an [act of] mercy for the faithful and a punishment for the infidels. When that will happen, look out for the men with the grey nags and the yellow flags advancing from the Maghrib until they descend in Syria."[67]

One might expect that the recent entry of infidel armies into Iraq and Syria would lessen the internecine tone of the modern-day prophesying and focus attention on the Mahdi's battle with the infidels. But it has only heightened the sectarian apocalyptic fervor as each sect vies to destroy the other for the privilege of destroying the infidels. Little wonder such a heady enactment of the End-Time drama on the original stage where it was first rehearsed has drawn an unprecedented number of Sunni and Shi'i foreign fighters to the theater. In early 2015, the number of Sunni foreign fighters in Syria and Iraq had reached twenty thousand, most of whom had joined the Islamic State.[68] The number on the Shi'i side was comparable.[69] In the sectarian apocalypse, everyone has a role to play in a script written over a thousand years ago. No one wants to miss the show.

SATAN'S SLAVES

Not all early Islamic prophecies map onto the current conflict so easily. In some cases, the Islamic State has gone out of its way to explain its actions as a fulfillment of prophecy.

Consider the Yazidis, a religious minority in Iraq. Many Muslims wrongly accuse them of devil worship because Yazidis believe the devil was a fallen angel who eventually repented.[70] Many Yazidis live around the Sinjar Mountains close to the Syrian border and the territory held by the Islamic State, which besieged the area in August 2014. Before attacking the Yazidis, the State asked its own scholars if they could be enslaved. The scholars answered affirmatively, arguing that Islamic law permitted the enslavement of Yazidi women on the grounds that they are *mushrik*s (polytheists) and not members of any protected religion mentioned in the Qur'an. "This large-scale enslavement of mushrik families is probably the first since the abandonment of this Shari'ah law," glowed the author of an article explaining the decision in the Islamic State's online magazine.[71]

Although the Qur'an sanctions slavery, Muslim countries formally forbade the practice in the nineteenth and twentieth centuries. In 1981, Mauritania became the last Muslim-majority country to abolish slavery, though it continues informally there and in a few other Muslim countries.[72] In the fall of 2014, the Islamic State proudly celebrated the return of the practice to public view and distributed captured Yazidi "virgins" as sex slaves to its members.[73]

The Islamic State not only cheered the revival of slavery as a major step in the return of Islamic law, which the group wants to impose in its totality; it also hailed slavery's renewal as "one of the signs of the Hour," or Day of Judgment. According to a prophecy attributed to Muhammad, the Prophet foretold the Hour would be close when "the slave girl shall give birth to her master."[74] The prophecy's wording is not clear about the return of slavery, but the Islamic State argued its import was obvious: Slavery is prohibited today, so a slave girl giving birth to her master must mean slavery will return.[75]

As further proof that its interpretation of the prophecy was correct, an Islamic State author cited the Dabiq prophecy. According to that prophecy, the Romans will line up against the Muslims near the small town of Dabiq, Syria, and say, "Leave us and those who were enslaved from amongst us so we can fight them."[76]

The Islamic State sold some of its Yazidi slaves in markets. In a 2014 video, State fighters laughed at how much their captured women would fetch. "Who wants to sell?" a man asks. "I will sell her for a Glock (pistol)," a fighter replies. "The price differs if she has blue eyes," chuckles another.[77] The slaves were bought by jihadists and human traffickers, who reportedly shipped them to homes and brothels across the Middle East.[78]

Yazidi children are not shielded from the sexual advances of the Islamic State's fighters. "Is it permissible to have intercourse with a female slave who has not reached puberty?" asked a pamphlet distributed by the fighters in mosques throughout Mosul. "Yes, if she can have intercourse. If she cannot have intercourse, then one should enjoy her without intercourse."[79]

Many of the Yazidi women were shipped to the Islamic State's stronghold in Raqqa, Syria, where they were forced to provide sex on demand for the Islamic State's soldiers.[80] The women's jailers were other women, many of them European Muslims in their teens or early twenties. They were members of the Khansa Brigade in Raqqa, where they roam the streets with guns and grenades policing "un-Islamic" behavior.[81] They offer women who flout the strict dress code a choice between flogging and the "biter." "I did not know what a 'biter' was," recalled one woman. "I thought it is a reduced sentence, I was afraid of whipping, so I chose the 'biter.'" The Khansa women pressed a "sharp object that has a lot of teeth" to her breast. "I screamed from pain and I was badly injured. They later took me to the hospital." "I felt then," she recalled, "that my femininity has been destroyed completely."[82]

The Khansa Brigade is named for a pagan poetess who converted to Islam in the time of Muhammad. "You are the greatest poet among those who have breasts," Khansa was once told by the caliph Umar. "I am the greatest poet among those who have testicles too," she replied.[83]

The European women who have joined the brigade share Khansa's pride, but in service of the Islamic State's men, who do the fighting. "The primary role of the woman who has emigrated here is supporting her husband and his jihad" tweeted a woman calling herself Khansa.[84] A twenty-year-old Scottish woman leading the Khansa Brigade, Aqsa Mahmood, encouraged other women to immigrate to the Islamic State and advised them on how to find a husband.[85] Islamic State fangirls on Twitter mooned over the group's hirsute warriors.[86] Marriage brings status; the death of a husband brings more, as well as financial compensation.[87]

Status is not the only reason young women join the Islamic State. They share many of the men's motives: seeking adventure, wanting to be part of something larger than themselves, indignation at the suffering of their coreligionists, a chance to rebuild the caliphate, or a belief that they are living in the Last Days.[88] And they are no less bloodthirsty. "So many beheadings at the same time, Allahu Akbar, this video is beautiful," exclaimed one after watching the Islamic State's men behead eighteen Syrian hostages and the American aid worker and Muslim convert Peter Kassig in November 2014.[89]

The women of the Islamic State gleefully abide by and enforce the group's strictures on women. They stand guard as the State's men rape their captured sex slaves. "Here I can really be free," a teenage Austrian recruit texted. "I can practise my religion." The United Nations worries she may now be dead.[90]

THE TWELVE CALIPHS

In April 2014, the Islamic State's spokesman hinted that the group was about to make a major announcement. "O God! A state of Islam rules by your Book and by the tradition of your Prophet and fights your enemies. So reinforce it, honor it, aid it, and establish it in the land. Make it a caliphate in accordance with the prophetic method."[91]

The last line alludes to a prophesy of the caliphate's return. "Prophethood will be among you as long as God intends, and then God will take it away when He so wills," Muhammad purportedly told his followers. His prophetic office would be followed by an Islamic empire governed by the Prophet's "successors," or caliphs.[92] They would each rule as the spiritual and temporal head of the Muslim community as the Prophet had. After them, "There will be a mordacious monarchy. It will be among you as long as God intends, and then God will take it away when He so wills. Then there will be a tyrannical monarchy. It will be among you as long as God intends, and then God will take it away when He so wills. Then there will be a caliphate in accordance with the prophetic method."

Afterward, the Prophet "fell silent."

Some Sunni Muslims today interpret the Prophet's silence to mean the world will end soon after the reestablishment of the caliphate.[93] Among them are those who believe the real caliphate hasn't existed since the early days of the Islamic empire. Others think the last real caliphate was abolished by the secular Turkish leader Mustafa Kemal Atatürk in 1924 after the defeat and dismemberment of the Ottoman Empire in World War I. Either way, the caliphate is destined to return.

Jihadists frequently cite the prophecy because they are fighting to restore the caliphate. But most jihadists see it as a distant goal that will be reached after the Muslims unite and regain their former glory. In 2013, for example, al-Qaeda's chief Ayman al-Zawahiri counseled jihadists to focus on unifying the Muslim world. Then they could consider "the establishment of the caliphate in accordance with the prophetic method."[94]

The Islamic State was impatient. Why wait for the fractious Muslim world to unite when the State already controlled so much land? Why pine for a caliphate later when they could have a caliphate now? The Islamic State knew there were skeptics, most of all among the jihadists, who would say the time wasn't right or the State wasn't qualified. But prophecy demands to be fulfilled.

To make the case, the Islamic State turned to its ablest apologist, twenty-nine-year-old Turki ibn Mubarak al-Bin'ali. A young firebrand from Bahrain, in his early twenties Bin'ali was already running afoul of the authorities. While studying religious subjects at a college in Dubai, he was arrested for "extremist ideas" in 2005. Returning to Bahrain, he tried teaching at a school but was kicked out for proselytizing his jihadist beliefs. Bin'ali's next gig as an imam at a mosque didn't work out either: He was fired for hanging up a jihadist fatwa. When the Syrian civil war started, Bin'ali traveled to Syria for relief work and to spread his message in missionary camps. In March 2013, he announced that he had joined the Islamic State.[95]

Bin'ali quickly became one of its most prominent apologists, reportedly overseeing its powerful Shari'a committee.

Two weeks after the Islamic State hinted that it was going to fulfill Muhammad's prophecy of a "caliphate in accordance with the prophetic method," Bin'ali wrote a treatise on the subject.[96] He had to establish, first, that the caliphate would return; second, that the Islamic State merited the title; and third, that Abu Bakr al-Baghdadi deserved the job of caliph.

To establish that the caliphate would return, Bin'ali quoted another Islamic prophecy that there will be "twelve caliphs" from the Quraysh, the tribe of Muhammad.[97] Of course, there had already been far more than twelve caliphs descended from the Quraysh tribe, so Bin'ali sided with those who interpreted the prophecy as requiring twelve *just* caliphs. There had already been five, six, or seven, so only a handful more were destined to appear.[98] Bin'ali cited another prophecy indicating that, in the future, the final caliphs would be direct descendants of Muhammad's son-in-law Ali. The last one either would pave the way for the Muslim savior, the Mahdi, or would be the Mahdi himself.[99]

As for whether the Islamic State should be considered the caliphate, Bin'ali contended the State was already the "nucleus of the anticipated rightly-guiding caliphate."[100] The caliphate requires "power, authority, and control of territory," he noted, which the Islamic State possessed. Bin'ali disputed the idea that the caliphate should extend over all Muslim lands before it is declared or that all Muslims had to select the caliph.[101] The first caliph, Abu Bakr, he pointed out, lost almost all of the Muslims' territory only to regain it later.[102] Many Muslims rejected the fourth caliph, Muhammad's son-in-law Ali, in favor of a rival claimant. Ali's son Hasan controlled even less territory when he was briefly proclaimed caliph; his brother Husayn controlled nothing at all.[103] The later Abbasid insurgents who overthrew the Umayyad caliphs and proclaimed their own caliphate were also afraid to publicly declare their allegiance to their imam at first. The overthrown Umayyad caliphs went to Andalusia (modern Spain) and proclaimed a new caliphate.[104] Muhammad himself controlled only a small amount of territory when he established a state, and his followers pledged themselves to him long before that. Even when Muhammad began establishing his state, he had not subdued every faction within it.[105]

Bin'ali's case that Abu Bakr al-Baghdadi should get the job of caliph is found in a separate treatise.[106] As we have seen, Bin'ali reckoned that a "caliphate according to the prophetic method" would be reestablished by a direct descendent of Ali, Muhammad's son-in-law. So Bin'ali traced Baghdadi's lineage to Ali through a brother of the eleventh Shi'i imam, a startling pedigree for the man hell-bent on eradicating the Shi'a.[107] Conveniently for Baghdadi, the brother of the eleventh imam had denied the existence of the twelfth imam, whom the Shi'a believe went into hiding and will return at the end of time as the Mahdi. (Never mind that Baghdadi's forefather instead claimed the title of twelfth imam for himself.)[108]

Bin'ali next went about establishing Baghdadi's religious credentials. In his telling, Baghdadi obtained a bachelor's and a master's degree in Qur'anic studies and a doctorate in Islamic jurisprudence. Baghdadi even published a book on the rules of Qur'anic recitation and worked as an imam in several mosques. Some of that isn't true—Baghdadi's dissertation was on Qur'anic recitation, and it was never published—but close enough. "Thus is combined in Shaykh Abu Bakr what is separated in others," Bin'ali exclaimed. "Knowledge that ends with the Prophet, peace and blessings be upon him, and a lineage that ends with the Prophet, peace and blessings be upon him!"[109]

Having demonstrated Baghdadi's familial and intellectual bona fides, Bin'ali addressed his managerial experience. During the early days of the U.S. invasion of Iraq, Baghdadi was in positions of authority in some jihadist groups and then rose through the ranks of the Islamic State to become the chief judge. When the head of the Islamic State was killed, the State's senior officials appointed Baghdadi their new leader.[110]

Bin'ali acknowledged that other jihadists had raised doubts about Baghdadi's suitability. They say, "How can Shaykh Abu Bakr al-Baghdadi be the emir when all of the people have not pledged allegiance to him?" Bin'ali replied that Islamic law does not require unanimous agreement on an emir. Requiring everyone to agree is the evil stuff of democracy.[111] But then they say, "How can the authority of Shaykh Abu Bakr al-Baghdadi be recognized when some of the regions were conquered by force but the leaders of the community there have not given their oath of allegiance?" Bin'ali responded that Muslim scholars have ruled that people are to obey a Muslim who conquers them.[112] But "How can the pledge to Shaykh Abu Bakr al-Baghdadi be correct when he is unknown?" Bin'ali parried that he is known to the jihadists and, regardless, Islamic law does not require that every person know the emir personally, only their leaders must. Were it a requirement, the Abbasid family that clandestinely gathered oaths of allegiance before establishing Islam's mightiest caliphate would never have come to power.[113] Still, "How can the authority of Shaykh Abu Bakr al-Baghdadi be correct when he does not have full territorial control?" Not even the Prophet was held to such a high standard! Bin'ali replied.[114]

Bin'ali either knew or anticipated that the Islamic State was about to declare the caliphate with Baghdadi at its head. "The authority of his state has spread throughout Sham, which is why the shaykh became the 'Commander of the Faithful in the Islamic State in Iraq and Sham.' We beseech God to hasten the day in which we will see our shaykh seated upon the throne of the caliphate!"[115]

When Bin'ali's teacher and critic of the Islamic State Abu Muhammad al-Maqdisi read the treatise about the twelve caliphs and its title, "An Investigation into Whether Absolute Political Power Is a Prerequisite for the Caliphate," he immediately understood its implication. "They will rename their organization 'the caliphate' imminently," Maqdisi foretold. "All of us hope for the return of the caliphate," he acknowledged. But it must actually exist to merit the name. "Announcing something prematurely sets it back on account of its absence." "What concerns me greatly is . . . whether this caliphate will be a refuge for oppressed people and a haven for every

Muslim or will become a sword hanging over the Muslims who oppose it."[116]

The Islamic State had been animated by the apocalyptic abiogen-
esis of the Iraq war and invigorated by the inrush of foreign fighters
to Syria, many of them seeking a role in the End-Time drama. The
rough beast born and raised in two sectarian civil wars was about to
come of age.

SIX
CALIPHATE REBORN

In early June 2014, a thousand Islamic State fighters converged on Mosul,[1] the second-largest city in Iraq. With them were their Sunni allies—disgruntled tribesmen and former Saddam loyalists.[2] They faced little resistance. The Iraqi troops and police guarding the city fled, having seen videos of what happened to anyone who opposed the black-clad fighters.[3] Days later, the Islamic State raised its flag over the city's government buildings. It now dominated land stretching from Mosul to the outskirts of Aleppo in Syria, roughly the distance between Washington, DC, and Cleveland, Ohio. The land was once ruled by Nur al-Din Zengi,[4] the scourge of the crusaders who so inspired Zarqawi, the founder of al-Qaeda in Iraq.

Flush with victory, the Islamic State's spokesman issued a proclamation three weeks later:[5]

> The sun of jihad has risen, and the glad tidings of goodness have shone forth. Triumph looms on the horizon, and the signs of victory have appeared.
>
> Here, the flag of the Islamic State, the flag of monotheism, rises and flutters. Its shade covers land from Aleppo to Diyala. Beneath it the walls of the tyrants have been demolished, their flags have fallen, and their borders have been destroyed. . . .

It is a dream that lives in the depths of every Muslim believer. It is a hope that flutters in the heart of every mujahid monotheist. It is the caliphate. It is the caliphate—the abandoned obligation of the era. . . .

Now the caliphate has returned. We ask God the exalted to make it in accordance with the prophetic method.

With that, the caliphate was supposedly reborn and prophesy was fulfilled. All Muslims had to now bend the knee to Abu Bakr al-Baghdadi, renamed Caliph Ibrahim al-Baghdadi.[6]

There had not been a credible claimant to the office of caliph in the Middle East since the defeat of the last Ottoman sultan in World War I. In early Islam, the caliphs had wielded great political and spiritual authority over all Muslims. Although the caliph's authority waned over time, the office still carried tremendous symbolic import among Sunnis. When the founder of secular Turkey abolished the office after World War I, many conservative Sunnis were aggrieved. In their eyes, the loss of the caliphate represented the end of Muslim political power and the triumph of the West. It is no great exaggeration to say that Sunni political Islam began as an effort to restore the caliphate. Several world congresses were convened in the 1920s and 1930s to name a new caliph, but political discord led to deadlock. No Muslim country wanted to see its rivals get the office.

Of course, individual Sunnis had tried to claim the caliphate for themselves, but they were ridiculed. A Jordanian jihadist in Afghanistan proclaimed himself caliph in the 1990s. As an al-Qaeda operative later commented, the caliph and his followers foolishly "excommunicated everyone who opposed them." Making too many enemies of people with guns, the movement crumbled quickly, and the caliph had to relocate to London.[7] With no land, no government, and no followers, his claim to be caliph was silly.

All jihadists fight to restore the caliphate, but most see it as a distant goal. Either the Western nations are too powerful to allow it[8] or Muslims are too divided to see it through.[9] The caliphate will come one day, but first Muslims must become strong and united.

By aspiring to the caliphate, the Islamic State challenged the conventional wisdom among jihadists and other Sunni Muslims. You don't have to overthrow Muslim countries to make a caliphate, and you don't have to persuade them to declare one, argued the State. Conquer land and declare your own. You don't have to wait until the Muslim masses want the caliphate, and you don't have to beg them to support your caliphal project. Ignore popular opinion and establish a caliphate by force of arms. You don't have to cower in fear of the West or its allies. Defy them and defeat them.[10]

By establishing a government and declaring it a caliphate, the Islamic State threatened to overturn conventional wisdom completely. Unlike any other rebel pretenders to the caliphate in the modern Middle East, the Islamic State had the money, fighters, weapons, and land to make a plausible case that it was the caliphate reborn. It helped that its caliph had more religious training than any political leader in the Muslim world. Most Sunni Muslims may have rejected the Islamic State as a travesty and a sham, but they could not easily dismiss it as a joke when it declared itself a caliphate in 2014. The Islamic State was too powerful.

Days after the June declaration of the caliphate, the new caliph rolled up in a black SUV to the Nuri Mosque in Mosul,[11] named for Zarqawi's hero Nur al-Din Zengi, who had ordered it built in the twelfth century. Baghdadi wore a black robe and turban. His followers speculated he had donned the black either because the Prophet wore a black turban when he conquered Mecca or because Baghdadi wanted to signal his descent from the Prophet.[12] Both could be true. The Abbasid caliphs, whose memory Baghdadi was invoking, had done the same.

"God, blessed and exalted, has bestowed victory and conquest upon your mujahid brethren, and has granted them power after long years of jihad, patience, and fighting the enemies of God," proclaimed Baghdadi from the pulpit. "They rushed to announce the caliphate and appoint a leader. This is a duty incumbent on Muslims, which had been absent for centuries and lost from the face of the earth."[13] Echoing the words of the first caliph and his namesake Abu

Bakr, the new caliph embraced his office and exhorted his flock to hold him to account. "I was appointed to rule you but I am not the best among you. If you see me acting truly, then follow me. If you see me acting falsely, then advise and guide me. . . . If I disobey God, then do not obey me."[14]

The evocative dress and humble words were belied by the luxury watch the new caliph sported.[15] And the black clothes didn't help soothe the jangled nerves of Mosul's residents, whose men were threatened with lashes if they didn't attend. "We were frightened by the way he wore his black clothes. We had never seen a Sunni imam completely dressed in black clothes," said one female eyewitness. "We women were on the second floor crying, terrified that they would hear us and hurt us. We waited for an hour after the sermon, where there were armed men guarding the doors."[16]

Despite the fear of those living under the caliphate, jihadist fanboys of the Islamic State cheered its return. The announcement "will enter history" proclaimed a tweet on July 3, 2014.[17] Other Islamic State fans declared the end of Western-defined borders. In a widely retweeted example, an activist posted two maps: The first has penciled-in borders for a "Sunni-stan," "Kurdistan," "Alawi-stan," and "Druze mountain." The other shows these borders obliterated by the caliphate. The author challenged readers: "Compare the West's dream of division to Baghdadi's caliphate."[18] In a response to the tweet, an Islamic State enthusiast exclaimed, "the Islamic State has no borders, and its conquests will continue, with God's permission."[19]

In its first incarnation in 2006, the Islamic State had fired the jihadist imagination with its ambiguous audacity. It called its emir the commander of the faithful, but it wouldn't outright call him the caliph. The Islamic State's name and flag harkened back to the medieval caliphate's name and flag, but it wouldn't declare a caliphate. The group encouraged others to view it as the caliphate but would never say so itself. Until now.

The Islamic State was nearly destroyed in 2008 because it tolerated no challenge to its authority as a state. For al-Qaeda's leaders, especially Bin Laden, the State's downfall was further proof that popular support had to be secured before a state could be established, much less a caliphate.

Despite its setbacks, the Islamic State's symbol and the idea it represented lived on. The flag of the Islamic State, still an al-Qaeda affiliate, was taken up by other al-Qaeda affiliates. Its state-building enterprise was taken up as well, much to the annoyance of Bin Laden. Some of al-Qaeda's affiliates, mindful of the Islamic State's poor precedent, tried to be more lenient toward the people they ruled and more considerate of their subjects' economic welfare. But they were not considerate enough and made too many enemies, suffering defeat as a consequence.

Despite the failure of its sister affiliates, the Islamic State doubled down on its state-building strategy during the Syrian civil war. When its subordinates in the Nusra Front and its leaders in al-Qaeda objected, the Islamic State rejected both. It would persevere no matter the consequences.

Were this Iraq in 2008, the Islamic State would have been defeated again, ratifying the jihadist conventional wisdom. At that time, the Americans simply had too many troops on the ground and the Sunni tribes were too willing to cooperate with the Shi'a-dominated government in Baghdad against a common foe. But in 2014, Iraq's Sunni tribes no longer trusted Baghdad, the Americans were gone, and government troops could no longer pacify the Arab Sunni hinterland in western Iraq.

The restless hinterland extended next door into Syria, but President Assad was more worried about direct threats to his stronghold closer to the Mediterranean coast. The Sunnis on the border of Iraq could be dealt with later. Assad also found it politically expedient to leave the Islamic State alone to attack his domestic enemies, scare the hell out of his citizens, and terrify the foreign countries that opposed him. He calculated that the average Syrian, Arab, and Westerner would prefer him to the greater evil of the Islamic State.

As a consequence of Baghdad's and Damascus's policies, the restive Sunnis between Syria and Iraq were ripe for the ruling by someone who wanted to establish a state and had enough manpower, muscle, and managerial experience to do it.

The Islamic State fit the bill. Its apocalypse-laced recruiting pitch had drawn thousands of foreign fighters, as had its political theology and state-building program. That gave it enough men to subdue the towns it captured, drive off its competitors, and raise revenue. The Islamic State was used to organizing itself as a state, and it was staffed by former officers from Saddam's military and intelligence services who could run it.

The Islamic State had once been an object lesson in what *not* to do. Its critics, jihadist and non-jihadist alike, had attributed its defeat in 2008 to its brutality, zealotry, and arrogant belief that it was a state. But by 2014, those were the very qualities that made the Islamic State so successful. While other rebel groups worked together to overthrow governments, the State was busy creating its own.

BRANDING THE CALIPHATE

When the Islamic State's spokesman proclaimed the caliphate, he prayed that God would make it a "caliphate in accordance with the prophetic method" and thus fulfill prophesy. After the proclamation, the Islamic State went about making sure everyone knew God had answered affirmatively.

Across Syria and Iraq, billboards popped up at Islamic State checkpoints. On the right side, the black flag proclaimed "No god but God. Muhammad is the messenger of God." On the left: "The Islamic State: A Caliphate in Accordance with the Prophetic Method."[20] Islamic State soldiers wore patches emblazoned with the latter slogan,[21] and the group's official letterhead included the words.[22] Photos of State members baking bread in Iraq's Diyala Province circulated on Twitter with the tagline.[23] The phrase was the title of the State's very first Da'wa Gathering, a proselytizing festival held in Raqqa in autumn 2014. Pictures of the event posted on

Twitter show an outdoor venue filled with rapt attendees—including some wide-eyed boys—listening to preachers.[24]

The phrase also appeared on coins the Islamic State planned to mint. Not only were the coins meant to end the State's reliance on "dollar-linked fiat currencies;" but also to evoke the coins of the early Islamic caliphate, which are mentioned often in medieval histories of the period.[25] Never mind that there were no "Islamic" coins in the time of Muhammad, an uncomfortable fact the Islamic State acknowledged in passing.[26] Muhammad and his companions used Roman and Persian currency, which bore the images of non-Muslim emperors and religious symbols. It was not until the time of the Umayyad caliphs that Muslims began minting their own coins. (Shocking to later Sunni Muslim sensibilities, the Umayyads may have put an image of Muhammad on their coins.)[27] For a group so against religious innovation and so obsessed with creating a state on the model of the Prophet, the Islamic State sometimes ignored the Prophet's example altogether when he fell short of its exacting standards or failed to sanction something it wanted.

In the eyes of Muslims, the juxtaposition of the slogan and the Islamic State's cruelty strained its claims to represent the Prophet's method. A gate in the town of Hawija, Iraq, welcomed visitors to the "Caliphate in Accordance with the Prophetic Method." Beneath it swung eight lifeless Iraqi troops, suspended by their feet. Horrified Muslims circulated the image on Twitter with the bodies and the slogan highlighted in red.[28]

The Islamic State's personnel and sectarianism also made its slogan an object of satire. One flier circulated online read "A Caliphate in Accordance with the Ba'athist Method."[29] The Ba'ath was the socialist political party that dominated Iraq under Saddam Hussein. Many former Ba'athists now ran the Islamic State.

When Shi'i militias recaptured a town from the Islamic State after the caliphate was announced, they scaled the local water tower festooned with the Arabic slogan and added two dots. The slogan now read "The Caliphate of Ali, a Prophetic Method," alluding to the first Shi'i imam.[30]

As any business knows, brand management isn't easy. But the Islamic State didn't go out of its way to dissociate its slogan from its atrocities.

DEBATING THE CALIPHATE

The jihadist old guard scoffed at the Islamic State's announcement of the caliphate. In their lead were Abu Qatada al-Filistini and Abu Muhammad al-Maqdisi, the two most influential jihadist scholars alive.[31] Both were Palestinian Jordanians who had written some of the seminal texts in jihadist literature. They wanted the caliphate to return through violent revolution but were unimpressed with the Islamic State's claim. In their eyes, the mere trappings of a caliphate do not a caliphate make.

"There are simpletons who have deluded themselves with their announcement of the caliphate and the application of the *hudud* penalties," sneered Abu Qatada, referring to the fixed punishments mentioned in Islamic scripture. "The rational person remembers where they came from and what they have done. You see they have dedicated themselves to killing Muslims and mujahids."[32] It is a "heinous conspiracy," charged Maqdisi. How else could one explain the establishment of a state that sought to kill its jihadist opponents, destroy its scholars, shun popular support, and soak the concept of the caliphate in blood?[33]

Furious at the criticism, the Islamic State's spokesman warned darkly: "All who try to sever the ranks will have their heads severed."[34]

The mutual recriminations became so complex and heated by August 2014 that one jihadist foe of the Islamic State even compiled a series of talking points, "A Summary for Discussing the Announcement of the Caliphate."[35] To summarize the summary: The Islamic State's caliphate is illegitimate because a majority of Muslim leaders had not endorsed it. Not even a majority of jihadist leaders had endorsed it. The only people who elevated Baghdadi to caliph were senior leaders in the Islamic State itself.[36]

Unsurprisingly given its fallout with the Islamic State, al-Qaeda also condemned the group's declaration of a caliphate. "We call for the return of the rightly-guiding caliphate according to the prophetic method," declared a senior al-Qaeda leader, "not according to the method of deviating, lying, violating treaties, and breaking pledges. A caliphate based on justice and consultation, affinity and concord, not oppression, excommunication, murder of monotheists, and dividing the ranks of the mujahids."[37]

The head of al-Qaeda, Zawahiri, took a different tack. Rather than denounce the caliphate, he began to hint there was already a caliph: Mullah Omar, the head of the Taliban in Afghanistan. Bin Laden and Zawahiri had pledged their allegiance to Mullah Omar as the commander of the faithful. Although the title is usually reserved for the caliph, Zawahiri had previously taken pains to assure his followers that Mullah Omar was only the commander of the faithful in Afghanistan. "As for the commander of the believers across the world," Zawahiri said in 2008, "this is the leader of the caliphal state that we, along with every faithful Muslim, are striving to restore, God willing."[38] Zawahiri and his boss, Bin Laden, also didn't take their oath to Mullah Omar very seriously, having repeatedly defied his demand that they stop talking to the media.[39]

But after Baghdadi was proclaimed caliph, al-Qaeda began to promote Mullah Omar as a countercaliph. In July 2014, al-Qaeda's media wing released an old video of Bin Laden explaining his decision to give his oath of allegiance to Mullah Omar as commander of the faithful. A questioner asked Bin Laden if his oath implied that he considered Mullah Omar to possess "supreme leadership," the prerogative of the caliphs, which Bin Laden affirmed. Later that same month, al-Qaeda released a newsletter that began with a renewal of the oath of allegiance to the "Commander of the Faithful Mullah Muhammad Omar" and "affirm[ed] that al-Qaeda and its branches in all locales are soldiers in his army, acting under his victorious banner."[40]

In September, Zawahiri upped the ante when he announced the establishment of a new al-Qaeda affiliate, "al-Qaeda in the Indian

Subcontinent."[41] Zawahiri stressed the new group was, like al-Qaeda, under the authority of the "Islamic Emirate" ruled by the "commander of the faithful," Mullah Omar. He then proceeded to heap praise repeatedly on the "commander of the faithful."

Still, Zawahiri stopped short of proclaiming Mullah Omar the caliph. He did not explain why, but his reasons are not hard to guess. If Mullah Omar was still alive, which was unclear, he might not want the job. Claiming to rule Afghanistan is much more modest than claiming to rule the entire Muslim world, which would alienate potential allies, such as some of the Gulf states. Moreover, many jihadists had criticized Baghdadi and the Islamic State for declaring the caliphate too soon. Al-Qaeda would be subject to the same criticism if it aped the State (and Zawahiri would not even control the caliphate he declared). Better for the time being to walk the ambiguous middle way between forthrightly declaring a countercaliph and having no caliph at all.

Despite al-Qaeda's protestations, the Islamic State's declaration of the caliphate drew recruits from all over the world. "To all my brothers in Tunisia who have Jihad in their hearts," proclaimed a young Tunisian, "the Caliphate has been established . . . it is a great blessing."[42] For its admirers, the caliphate promised a place of honor for Muslim youth who felt shut out by their political systems or alienated from their societies. A popular recruitment video declared the bankruptcy of nation-states by showing Islamic State citizens ripping their passports: "[We are] tearing these passports, these identities, and . . . these borders, and we will live in one Islamic state. We will spread from the West to the East, and no one but great God will rule us. One Islamic nation, in which we are not linked with identities, cards, or passports."[43]

"We have brothers from Iraq, from Cambodia, from Australia, the UK," proclaimed British jihadists fighting for the Islamic State.[44] A future Egyptian "martyr" extolled the diversity of the group as a reason for other Arabs to join: "Why don't you emigrate? Why don't you leave your homes? Why don't you leave your home as the Prophet left his? Entire families are coming from

Uzbekistan. . . . We have families coming from Uzbekistan, from Turkey, from everywhere!"[45]

The Islamic State's momentum also drew fighters from rival rebel groups, including al-Qaeda's official Syrian arm, al-Nusra. From the outset, the two groups attracted more foreign fighters than the other rebel factions in Syria,[46] and both had received a large influx of men from the Free Syrian Army who left the flailing rebel conglomerate for the better-funded and better-organized jihadist groups.[47] But after the Islamic State and Nusra parted ways in 2013, a reported 60 percent of Nusra's foreign fighters went to its rival.[48]

THE BAGHDAD OF AL-RASHID

The Islamic State's claim to have reestablished a caliphate according to the prophetic method has misled at least one observer to conclude that the State only seeks "its inspiration from the first four caliphates" that followed Muhammad.[49] As the argument goes, not even the grandest of the caliphates, the Abbasid, is a model for the Islamic State.

This is not quite right. The Islamic State was no doubt inspired by the Prophet's model of state building, but it was not the only model that galvanized the group. Take a look at the State's propaganda, and you will see that its leaders have sought, from its founding, to restore the glory days of the Abbasid caliphate that ruled its empire from Baghdad. The State especially celebrated the era of Harun al-Rashid of *1,001 Nights* fame.[50] "Know that the Baghdad of al-Rashid is the home of the caliphate that our ancestors built" proclaimed an Islamic State spokesman in 2007. "It will not appear by our hands but by our carcasses and skulls. We will once again plant the flag of monotheism, the flag of the Islamic State, in it."[51] "Today, we are in the very home of the caliphate, the Baghdad of al-Rashid," stated the Islamic State's first ruler, the aptly named Abu Umar al-Baghdadi, the same year.[52] Even after the Islamic State established its primary base of operations in Syria's Raqqa, once a second home to Harun al-Rashid, and captured Mosul in Iraq, its spokesman still referred to "the Baghdad of the Caliphate" or "the Baghdad of al-Rashid."[53] The first caliph of the Islamic State, Abu Bakr, used the alias of al-Baghdadi, "of Baghdad," even though he hailed from Samarra.

The Islamic State's plan to revive the Abbasid caliphate in Baghdad suffers from two problems. The first is cultural: The values of Harun al-Rashid and his court are not the values of the Islamic State. One of Harun's favorite court poets, Abu Nuwas, often wrote verses glorifying wine drinking and sex with boys:

> *A boy of beckoning glances and chaste tongue . . .*
> *Proffers me wine of hope mixed with despair.*[54]

The caliph himself was frequently drunk. In one account, he ordered the death of his boon companion (some say lover), Ja'far the Barmakid, after drinking too much wine. When the assassin refused to carry out the caliph's order because he was inebriated, Harun screamed, "Bring me Ja'far's head, motherfucker!"[55]

Music was also a fixture in the Abbasid court. Although many conservative Muslims frowned on musical instruments then as they do today, Harun's nights were filled with the sounds of lutes, trumpets, and drums.[56] For ultraconservatives like those leading the Islamic State, the devil uses such instruments to entice the unwary. Better to listen to the unaccompanied voice of males singing battle hymns.

In contrast to the State's pogrom against the Shi'a, Harun's court usually got on well with them. Harun's advisors, the Barmakids, were Persian converts from Buddhism who were friendly with the Shi'a. Harun was also on good terms with the Shi'a early in his reign,[57] and his son Ma'mun even nominated a Shi'i imam to succeed him as caliph.

Pagan Greek learning and interreligious debates were celebrated in the Baghdad of Harun, also anathema to the Islamic State. Harun and his advisors funded translations of Greek tracts on science and philosophy, preserving texts that would otherwise be lost in medieval Europe.[58] Jews, Christians, Muslims, and irreligious philosophers debated in court and in private salons around Baghdad. As a British scholar put it, "The pious Muslims of Mecca and Madina who came thither were scandalized to find unbelievers invested with the highest offices at Court, and learned men of every religion holding friendly debate as to high questions of ontology and philosophy, in which, by common consent, all appeal to revealed Scripture was forbidden."[59]

The Islamic State's leaders studiously ignored Harun al-Rashid's religious shortcomings, however, celebrating instead his jihads against Christian Byzantium. But here too Harun is out of step with the State's religious sensibilities, which require constant war against the unbelievers. Harun, the Muslim ruler of North Africa and the Middle East, exchanged several diplomatic embassies with Charlemagne, the premier ruler of the Christian West. One of the gifts Harun sent was an elephant named for the first Abbasid caliph, Abu al-Abbas. The elephant, delivered by a Jew on the caliph's behalf, became an exotic fixture in Charlemagne's court.[60] It was just one of many gifts exchanged between the two rulers to cement an alliance against their mutual enemies: the Umayyad caliphate in Spain and the Christian kingdom of Byzantium.[61]

Selective memory could surmount the cultural contradictions posed by the restoration of "the Baghdad of al-Rashid" but not the demographic problem: Baghdad is a majority-Shi'a city whose inhabitants would not give up without a fight. When the Islamic State captured Mosul in June 2014, tens of thousands of armed Shi'i men marched in a show of force through the streets of Baghdad. The men belonged to the Mahdi Army, just one of several Shi'i militias in Iraq.[62] Shi'i foreign fighters streamed into Iraq too, responding to a call to arms in late 2014 by the influential but usually quietist cleric Grand Ayatollah Sistani.[63] In India, up to thirty thousand Shi'i men supposedly pledged to fight against the Islamic State in Iraq.[64]

Even if the Islamic State could overcome Iraq's Shi'i militias, it would still have to contend with Iran. Iranian special forces had funneled weapons and personnel to Iraq's Shi'a fighting against the American occupation. They did it again in Syria to save their ally Bashar al-Assad and once again in Iraq after the Islamic State stormed Mosul. Qasem Soleimani, the commander of Iran's special forces, who could have been a body double for Sean Connery in *The Hunt for Red October*, made regular appearances among the Shi'i militias battling the Islamic State. As powerful as the State was, it could not possibly take Baghdad at its current strength.

Given that, outsiders might reasonably conclude that the Islamic State would be foolish to attempt to take Baghdad rather than consolidate its gains in the Sunni-majority areas it now holds. But sometimes historical imperatives override strategic ones.

In its early days, the Islamic State was more sober when assessing its chances of restoring the caliphate of Harun al-Rashid. In 2008, the Islamic State's founder, Abu Ayyub al-Masri, chided his fellow jihadists for their great expectations. "Some of us incorrectly believe that the concept of the state that ought to be established and announced is the state of al-Rashid who spoke to a cloud in the sky, ladled gold like water, and dispatched armies that stretched all the way from Baghdad to his enemies."[65]

The proper frame of reference, argued Masri, is the Islamic state when it was first established by the Prophet. The original state was a state of sacrifice and few supporters.[66] It was located in a land with little water and filled with disease.[67] The Prophet's companions suffered from hunger and poverty.[68] His army was ragtag[69] and coped with major military setbacks, as when it was defeated at the battle of Uhud.[70]

In comparison with the first Islamic state, the Islamic State of 2008 wasn't doing too badly, Masri contended. "Has the Islamic State in Iraq met the requirements of a state with regard to territorial control, power, and extent of influence in comparison to the prophetic state after taking into account the different trials besetting them?" Absolutely, Masri concluded, especially given the power of the enemies arrayed against the State today compared to those who challenged the Prophet.[71] As we have seen, this was wishful thinking.

Nevertheless, Masri understood that running a state is nothing like a running a war. Governing makes the jihadists more vulnerable to military attack and risks angering the population. "Every monotheist knows . . . that the change from jihad to the stage of ruling—the rule of God on the earth—and the return of the Islamic caliphate is a dangerous matter."[72]

GOVERNING THE CALIPHATE

Despite being declared in 2006, the Islamic State never had a chance to govern in its first few years. Although its predecessor, al-Qaeda in Iraq, tried to govern the land it controlled, the Islamic State itself had virtually no land of its own when it was declared in 2006. Neither did it monopolize violence, try as it might, or consistently provide services. In other words, it lacked the essential characteristics of any government, modern or otherwise.

In 2014, the Islamic State had its chance. It was the unquestioned authority in many cities between Syria and Iraq. How would it govern? What had it learned from the experience of its predecessors in al-Qaeda who tried and failed to set up their own governments? Recall that Bin Laden had counseled al-Qaeda's affiliates to keep the welfare and consent of their subjects uppermost in their minds. From that dictum flowed the rest of his governing advice: Be lenient in applying Islamic punishments, focus on the economic well-being of your subjects, and seek their advice and approval.

As al-Qaeda in the Arabian Peninsula had done, the Islamic State addressed the economic needs of its subjects or at least wanted to be seen trying. It distributed videos of fighters handing out food and humanitarian relief, introduced price controls and regulations, and attempted to keep the lights on.[73] But the usual subsidies and supplies distributed by the governments of Syria and Iraq were gone, and war made commerce and agriculture difficult. It didn't help that the Islamic State was more focused on fighting than on governing. The local economies in the State suffered as a consequence.

"We used to blame [Iraqi prime minister] Maliki for everything. Now we cry and hope for the return of those days," said a Sunni living under Islamic State rule. "Before, there was some kind of security, some kind of state. It is incomparable to the current situation."[74] As Bin Laden had feared, the subjects of a jihadist government would be quick to turn against their rulers if they failed to deliver the normal meager services people were accustomed to.

Rather than distribute its wealth equitably or invest in infrastructure and jobs, the Islamic State gave money, fuel, and food to people who cooperated with it. Seeking the most *bay'a* for its buck, the State funneled its largesse to local leaders with many followers, the tribal shaykhs.[75] Tribes that cooperated could handle their own security and gain an advantage over rival tribes.[76] Tribes that didn't cooperate had their children kidnapped[77] and their members dumped in mass graves.[78] Some Sunni tribes wanted to fight back against the Islamic State, but the Shi'i governments in Damascus and Baghdad did not see it as in their interests to empower tribes that might one day fight against them.[79]

One could argue that the Islamic State hadn't done so badly, given the exigencies of war and the rough-and-tumble nature of tribal politics, especially when compared to the poor standards of governance in the region. But in the one area where it had the most freedom of action, the Islamic State had surpassed all others in authoritarian excess: the meting out of the harsh *hudud* punishments.

Today most Muslim countries refuse to apply the *hudud*. One of the few is Saudi Arabia, whose brand of ultraconservative Islam is nearly identical to that of the Islamic State. When the State needed textbooks to distribute to schoolchildren in Raqqa, it printed out copies of Saudi state textbooks found online.[80] Unsurprisingly then, most of the Islamic State's *hudud* penalties are identical to penalties for the same crimes in Saudi Arabia: death for blasphemy, homosexual acts, treason, and murder; death by stoning for adultery; one hundred lashes for sex out of wedlock; amputation of a hand for stealing; amputation of a hand and foot for bandits who steal; and death for bandits who steal and murder.[81]

But there are two ways the Islamic State distinguishes itself from Saudi Arabia, which it believes is ruled by apostates. Firstly, the State carries out its penalties in public whereas Saudi Arabia hides them because of international censure. "A man was brought to the square, blind-folded," an eyewitness recounted. "A member of ISIS read the group's judgment. Two people held the victim tightly while a third man stretched his arm over a large wooden board." A fourth man wearing latex gloves impassively watched, then calmly reached out and cut off the victim's hand. "It took a long time," recounted the eyewitness. "One of the people who was standing next to me vomited and passed out due to the horrific scene."[82] Not only would such scenes terrify those who watched them and cow them into submission; they would also attract the bloody-minded to the cause.[83]

Secondly, the Islamic State goes the extra mile in its penalties. It opts for eighty lashes for drinking and slander rather than leaving it to the judge's discretion, as in Saudi Arabia. Whereas Saudi Arabia prefers to execute people by beheading, the Islamic State does that and more, throwing people off buildings or crucifying them after shooting them in the head. When Muslims raise a hue and cry that its actions aren't Islamic, the Islamic State's jurists cite chapter and verse. It is almost as if the group does extreme things to create opportunities for demonstrating its scholarly dexterity and burnishing its ultraconservative bona fides.

Consider the immolation of the Jordanian Muslim pilot, Moath al-Kasasbeh, captured by the Islamic State and burned alive for his alleged apostasy. In Islamic scripture, the Prophet Muhammad expressly and repeatedly forbade this form of punishment for apostasy because only God could punish apostates with fire.[84] The Islamic State's scholars, however, argued that Muhammad was just being humble and not actually forbidding the punishment. For support, they cited some medieval Muslim jurists who argued the same. Not convinced? How about this: Some Islamic scriptures say that when people gouged out the eyes of Muhammad's followers, he had their eyes burned out in retaliation.[85] Therefore, if the apostate government of Jordan was going to drop bombs on the Islamic State, then the Islamic State could respond with a similar punishment against the Jordanians. Still not convinced? It doesn't matter—the Islamic State's scholars will go on and on, relishing the chance to show why they're more faithful to scripture than their detractors.

To see how the Islamic State differentiates itself from other ultra-conservatives, let's take something more mundane, like smoking tobacco. Smoking came to the Middle East at the end of the sixteenth century and quickly became popular among all classes of society regardless of gender.[86] Moralists didn't like it for the same reasons they didn't like coffee, which had also recently become popular: It gave people a buzz, which seemed akin to intoxication, and it encouraged conviviality in public places, which could lead to loose behavior.[87] Because smoking was new, Islamic scripture didn't have anything to say directly about it, which was also a mark against it in conservative eyes. The case for smoking wasn't helped by the fact that European merchants were involved in the tobacco trade, which fed paranoia about a Christian plot to subvert Muslims.[88] Playing to the conservatives or fearful of rabble-rousing in places where tobacco was smoked in public, governments in the region tried several times to ban it. We find similar attempts to ban smoking across Eurasia around the same time for some of the same reasons. But by the eighteenth century, governments in the Middle East had largely given up because smoking was so popular.[89] The last major effort to outlaw smoking in the early modern period was in eighteenth-century Arabia, where fighters in the ultraconservative Wahhabi movement and its tribal allies in the Saud family banned it in the towns they captured.[90]

Today, smoking remains popular in the Middle East, and to my knowledge no country bans it, not even Saudi Arabia. Western expats who move to the Arab world are often shocked when someone lights up in an office building or classroom. But despite its popularity, smoking is still a touchstone for religious conservatives. One's stance on smoking signals one's seriousness about religion, even though Islamic scripture doesn't touch on it directly.

Jihadists who take over a town and want to impose their authority are faced with a dilemma. On one hand, if they ban smoking, they'll demonstrate their ultraconservative religious credentials. After all, not even Saudi Arabia bans smoking anymore. On the other hand, they'll be wildly unpopular with the locals, especially smokers and shopkeepers who sell cigarettes. How jihadists fall on the issue gives you some sense of where their priorities are in the hearts-and-minds debate. Some, like the al-Qaeda affiliate in Somalia, banned smoking and imposed a fine and thirty days of jail for violators.[91] Others, like al-Qaeda's affiliate Jabhat al-Nusra in Syria, didn't. "These rules will be introduced gradually. We will advise people at first," remarked a Nusra commander to a reporter.[92]

By now, you can guess where the Islamic State came down on the issue. Some smokers had to pay fines; others received forty lashes of the whip. Repeat offenders faced jail time, severed fingers, and even death. Not even Islamic State commanders were exempt. The severed head of a State commander in Syria was found with a cigarette dangling from his mouth and a sign that read: "This is not permissible, Sheikh."[93] There are a few exceptions to the rule. Some local Islamic State commanders have lifted the ban on smoking, as happened in the Iraqi town of Hawija. Their reason for reversing the ban is telling: They wanted to shore up flagging popular support.[94] Being so strict was good for impressing puritans, but it wasn't terribly crowd pleasing.

ENDURING AND EXPANDING

In 2007, when the Islamic State was beset on all sides in Iraq, its first emir adopted a one-word slogan: "Enduring."[95] The United States and the Iraqi government had thrown everything they had at the State, but they could not destroy it. The slogan seemed silly by 2008 when the Islamic State was nearly defeated, but it took on the aura of prophecy when the State made a comeback after 2010. When the State moved into Syria, a new word was added to the slogan: "Expanding." Not only had the Islamic State survived, it was now on the march.

The Islamic State believes prophecy requires the conquest of every country on earth. "This religion will reach everywhere day and night reach" the Prophet had foretold, so the Islamic State determined to make it a reality. As its magazine proclaimed, "The shade of this blessed flag will expand until it covers all eastern and western extents of the Earth, filling the world with the truth and justice of Islam and putting an end to the falsehood and tyranny."[96] In 2014, the Islamic State set about laying the groundwork for taking over the world, beginning in Muslim-majority countries.

On November 10, 2014, the Islamic State announced it had received oaths of allegiance from jihadists in Egypt's Sinai, Libya, Yemen, Algeria, and Saudi Arabia. "Glad tidings, O Muslims," Baghdadi celebrated. "We give you good news by announcing the expansion of the Islamic State to new lands." Lands claimed in those countries were no longer independent but rather provinces in the new caliphate.[97] In accordance with prophecy, the Saudis would rid the Arabian Peninsula of non-Muslims, the Yemenis would muster for the last battles, and the Egyptians would prepare for the final assault to retake Jerusalem from the Jews.[98] (Algeria and Libya receive less apocalyptic attention because North Africa does not figure prominently in End-Time prophecies.)

Initially, reality belied the bold predictions and celebrations that supposedly greeted the announcement. The so-called Army of the Caliphate in Algeria was a small group that had split from al-Qaeda's franchise in North Africa.[99] An Islamic State "province" in Libya was just one jihadist group among several vying for control of the backwater town of Derna; its second "province" in the North would later control a few buildings in the coastal city of Sirte and briefly capture the small town of Nawfaliya.[100] The Islamic State's main booster in Yemen refused to give his oath of allegiance, and his parent organization,[101] al-Qaeda in the Arabian Peninsula, posted a rebuke of the State on its Twitter page, accusing the group of degrading the legitimacy of the global jihadist cause.[102] The Islamic State's supporters in Saudi Arabia were nobodies. Only one of the groups, the Ansar Bayt al-Maqdis in the Sinai, was actually viable. Even then, the group's faction in the Nile Valley reportedly remained loyal to al-Qaeda.[103]

But over time, the Islamic State "provinces" gained ground in the Arab countries riven by civil war. In Libya, the spiritual leader of Ansar al-Shari'a, the powerful jihadist group that attacked the U.S. consulate in Benghazi, pledged allegiance to Baghdadi; his acolytes will likely soon follow.[104] The Islamic State "province" in Yemen also grew more powerful as the country descended into civil war. In just four days in March 2015, the group killed 137 people in Yemen's capital and another 29 soldiers in the South.[105] That same month, the powerful Boko Haram group in northern Nigeria pledged allegiance to Baghdadi. The group, notorious for kidnapping and enslaving hundreds of Christian girls, controlled territory the size of Belgium.[106] In Somalia, some high-ranking members of the Shabab, an al-Qaeda affiliate, started urging the group to join the Islamic State.[107]

The accession of new "provinces" to the Islamic State is mutually beneficial. The State demonstrates that it is constantly expanding and thus succeeding in its divine mission. It also gets to draw on the human and financial resources of its new provinces, which it can call on to retaliate against its enemies. For the provinces, they get to sign up for the hottest thing going. Obscure jihadist groups all of a sudden gain notoriety for pledging allegiance, and unruly factions in al-Qaeda affiliates can circumvent their bosses. They also get the help of the Islamic State's formidable media apparatus[108] and perhaps a taste of its spoils.

As we have seen, al-Qaeda fretted endlessly about expanding the number of its affiliates. Because Bin Laden and Zawahiri worried so much about popular Muslim support, they were reluctant to sign on groups that might behave badly and tarnish the al-Qaeda brand.[109] The Islamic State didn't care about popular Muslim support, so it signed on affiliates at breakneck speed. Unlike Bin Laden, who counseled patience and care for Muslim lives, Baghdadi will only stoke his princes' worst impulses.

When the Islamic State first broke with al-Qaeda, Zawahiri tried to compete for market share in the global jihadist movement. He hinted at a countercaliph, declared a new affiliate in India, and denied the legitimacy of Baghdadi's caliphate. But he couldn't compete with the Islamic State's political success. To make matters worse, al-Qaeda's affiliates were restless and had long admired the Islamic State's ambition.

In 2015, rumors began circulating that Zawahiri would dissolve al-Qaeda.[110] If that happens, it will be little cause for celebration. The end of al-Qaeda will free its affiliates to join the Islamic State. If they do, they will dramatically augment the State's strength in the Middle East and provide operatives capable of mounting attacks in the West. With such validation of the Islamic State's slogan, "Enduring and Expanding," it's hard to imagine mere arguments to the contrary would do anything to discredit it.

THE ABSENT MAHDI

Absent from the Islamic State's plans for conquest is the Mahdi, the Muslim savior who will appear at the End of Days to lead the Muslims to victory. Whereas Islamic prophecies predict Muslim fighters will travel to Mecca and Medina to join forces with the Mahdi, he merits no mention in Islamic State propaganda about the conquest of Saudi Arabia. The State's magazine *Dabiq* predicts the flag of the caliphate "will rise over" Mecca and Medina in Saudi Arabia,[111] and Islamic State fanboys anticipate the group will invade Saudi Arabia any day now.[112] But they mention no Mahdi.

The Mahdi's absence in today's Islamic State propaganda is a major contrast with the statements released by the group's founders. Whereas Abu Ayyub al-Masri foretold that the Islamic State's fighters would hand their black flag to the Mahdi,[113] who could be anyone, today's Islamic State proclaims that their fighters will hand it to Jesus, who will be recognized when he descends from heaven.[114]

In one April 2007 statement, the first Islamic State emir, Abu Umar al-Baghdadi, hoped to lead troops from Iraq to "aid the Mahdi clinging to the curtains of the Ka'ba,"[115] the cuboid shrine in Mecca toward which Muslims pray. Abu Umar was presumably referring to a prophecy in which tribes around the Ka'ba war with one another, each believing they have the mandate of heaven. Some flee the battle and find a man who has buried his face in the Ka'ba's coverings, weeping. Because of the man's purity, they pledge allegiance to him. He refuses to lead but changes his mind after they threaten to behead him. The man turns out to be the Mahdi.[116]

The prophecy is unusual for its content—in most other prophecies, the Mahdi is not reluctant to lead. It is also unusual for its provenance. The prophecy appears in *The Book of Tribulations* by Nu'aym bin Hammad. You will recall that many jihadists and other Muslims consider the prophecies to be spurious. But because the book is the richest collection of prophecies of the End Times, some jihadists find it irresistible. That the Islamic State's first emir succumbed to its gravitational pull is a testament to the apocalyptic fervor of the State's founders.

Preference for one collection of prophecies over another does not explain why the Mahdi is absent from today's Islamic State propaganda. The Mahdi appears often in the "authentic" collections of prophecies favored by the State's current leaders, whose rhetoric is no less apocalyptic than that of their forebears. Yet they omit the Mahdi in their propaganda.

Without access to the Islamic State's internal deliberations, we can only guess why. Caliph Baghdadi watched the first incarnation of the Islamic State nearly destroy itself because its leaders made hasty strategic decisions in the belief that the Mahdi would appear any day. Perhaps chastened by the experience, he has made the caliphate the locus of the group's apocalyptic imagination rather than the Mahdi. That does not mean the Mahdi will not appear soon—only a handful of just caliphs need rule before the Mahdi arrives. But for the moment, the caliphate is a greater priority than doomsday. The shift of eschatological emphasis from the person of the Mahdi to the institution of the caliphate buys the group time to govern while sustaining the apocalyptic moment that has so captivated its supporters.[117] It is not an easy balance to strike.

One of the Islamic State's few recent references to the Mahdi is found in its magazine, *Dabiq*. On the last page of the fifth issue, there is a prophecy attributed to Muhammad: "If there were not left except a day from the world, God would lengthen that day to send forth on it a man from my family whose name matches my name and whose father's name matches my father's name. He will fill the Earth with justice and fairness as it was filled with oppression and tyranny."[118]

The prophecy is given without written commentary, foregrounding a picture of the sons of Islamic State fighters dressed in battle fatigues. We are meant to infer that a Mahdi born of the Islamic State's dark imagination will one day lead their murderous ranks.

CONCLUSION

APOCALYPSE THEN AND NOW

The French scholar of Muslim apocalypticism, Jean-Pierre Filiu, has argued that most modern Sunni Muslims viewed apocalyptic thinking with suspicion before the United States invaded Iraq in 2003. It was something the Shi'a or the conspiracy-addled fringe obsessed over, not right-thinking Sunnis.[1] Sure, the Sunni fringe wrote books about the fulfillment of Islamic prophecies. They mixed Muslim apocalyptic villains in with UFOs, the Bermuda triangle, Nostradamus, and the prognostications of evangelical Christians, all to reveal the hidden hand of the international Jew, the Antichrist, who cunningly shaped world events.[2] But the books were commercial duds.

The U.S. invasion of Iraq and the stupendous violence that followed dramatically increased the Sunni public's appetite for apocalyptic explanations of a world turned upside down. A spate of bestsellers put the United States at the center of the End-Times drama, a new "Rome" careering throughout the region in a murderous stampede to prevent violence on its own shores. The main antagonists of the End of Days, the Jews, were now merely supporting actors.[3] Even conservative Sunni clerics who had previously tried to tamp down messianic fervor couldn't help but conclude that "the triple union constituted by the Antichrist, the Jews, and the new Crusaders" had joined forces "to destroy the Muslims."[4]

The Iraq war also changed apocalyptic discourse in the global jihadist movement. The languid apocalypticism of Osama bin Laden and Ayman al-Zawahiri now had to contend with the urgent apocalypticism of Abu Mus'ab al-Zarqawi, the founder of al-Qaeda in Iraq, and his immediate successors. Iraq, the site of a prophesied bloodbath between true Muslims and false, was engulfed in a sectarian civil war. As Zarqawi saw it, the Shi'a had united with the Jews and Christians under the banner of the Antichrist to fight against the Sunnis. The Final Hour must be approaching, to be heralded by the rebirth of the caliphate, the Islamic empire that had disappeared and whose return was prophesied.

Because of the impending Final Hour, Zarqawi's successor, Abu Ayyub al-Masri, had rushed to establish the Islamic State in 2006 and declare a commander of the faithful, the traditional title of the caliph, supreme religious and political ruler of the early Islamic empire. The Islamic State was meant to be a caliphate in all but name. Masri believed the caliphate had to be in place to fight for the Mahdi, the Muslim savior, who would appear any day. The actual person of the caliph was an afterthought, someone practically plucked off the street. The world wouldn't be around long enough for it to matter.

Chastened by his failed predictions that first year, Masri's messianic ardor cooled. At the same time, the person of the Islamic State's first commander of the faithful, Abu Umar al-Baghdadi, became more substantial. Iraqis in the Islamic State were unhappy with the power amassed by Masri, an Egyptian, and the other Arab foreign fighters. They gravitated toward Abu Umar, a fellow Iraqi, which enhanced his standing in the organization. As his stature grew, so did the power of his office.

When Masri and Abu Umar were killed, the new commander of the faithful, Abu Bakr al-Baghadi, brought even greater substance to the office. Also an Iraqi, Baghdadi was supposedly descended from the Prophet and had scholarly credentials his predecessor lacked. Rather than declare Baghdadi the Mahdi, the Islamic State's scholars argued he was one of the prophesied handful of just caliphs who would rule before the end of the world. The immediacy of the Mahdi's return and the apocalypse to follow was attenuated in favor of building the institution of the caliphate. Messiah gave way to management. It was a clever way to prolong the apocalyptic expectations of the Islamic State's followers while focusing them on the immediate task of state building.

Earlier messianic caliphates had done the same. The Islamic State's medieval heroes, the Abbasids, had swept to power on a wave of apocalyptic fervor, and many of the early Abbasid caliphs had adopted apocalyptic titles like Mahdi. But the Final Hour never quite came. The same happened to the Almohads in Spain and North Africa and the Fatimids in Egypt, a Sunni caliphate and a Shi'i caliphate that had both announced a Mahdi only to downplay the apocalypse once in power.

Although the messianic fervor has cooled in the Islamic State's leadership, the group's apocalyptic rhetoric has intensified. References to the End Times fill Islamic State propaganda. It's a big selling point with foreign fighters, who want to travel to the lands where the final battles of the apocalypse will take place. The civil wars raging in those countries today lend credibility to the prophecies.

The Islamic State has stoked the apocalyptic fire. Its fighters died to capture the militarily unimportant town of Dabiq, Syria, because it's mentioned in the prophecies. The Islamic State's English-language magazine is named after the place. European fighters in the State have filmed themselves from the hillside overlooking the town, explaining to other Europeans that they are living in the End Times.

For Bin Laden's generation, the apocalypse wasn't a great recruiting pitch. Governments in the Middle East two decades ago were more stable, and sectarianism was more subdued. It was better to recruit by calling to arms against corruption and tyranny than against the Antichrist. Today, though, the apocalyptic recruiting pitch makes more sense. Titanic upheavals convulse the region in the very places mentioned in the prophecies. Sunnis and Shi'a are at war, both appealing to their own versions of prophecies to justify their politics.

This is not Bin Laden's apocalypse.

HEARTS AND MINDS

The Islamic State has defied conventional thinking about how to conduct a successful insurgency. Most people, al-Qaeda's leaders among them, can't imagine that political success could come from enraging the masses rather than charming them. The Western theory of counterinsurgency so popular over the past decade is predicated on the idea that governments and insurgents compete for the hearts and minds of the locals. Those who win them over win the conflict. Recall what Ayman al-Zawahiri, the leader of al-Qaeda today, wrote to the bloody-minded Zarqawi: "we shouldn't stir questions in the hearts and minds of the people about the benefit of our actions . . . we are in a media battle in a race for the hearts and minds of our [Muslim] community."[5]

But the Islamic State has deliberately provoked the anger of Muslims and non-Muslims alike with its online videos of outrageous and carefully choreographed violence. It showcases the beheading of prisoners—something Zawahiri had expressly warned against—and dumps enemy soldiers in mass graves while the camera is rolling. The State revels in gore and wants everyone to know it. And yet it has been remarkably successful at recruiting fighters, capturing land, subduing its subjects, and creating a state. Why?

Because violence and gore work. We forget that this terrifying approach to state building has an impressive track record. The pagan Mongols used it to great effect in the thirteenth century to conquer land stretching from the Pacific to the Mediterranean. They were far more brutal than the Islamic State, massacring entire towns that refused to surrender in order to discourage anyone else from resisting.[6] The Bible says the ancient Israelites did the same in their conquest of Canaan.[7] More brutal too was the Saud family and its ultraconservative Wahhabi allies, who came to power three times between 1744 and 1926, when the third and last Saudi state was established. A Spanish traveler who saw firsthand the rise of the Wahhabis in their second incarnation describes the scene when their fighters stormed the Shi'i holy city of Karbala in 1801: "The inhabitants made but a feeble resistance; and the conqueror put to the sword all the men and male children of every age. Whilst they executed this horrible butchery, a Wehhabite [*sic*] doctor cried from the top of a tower, 'Kill, strangle all the infidels who give companions to God.'"[8] A contemporary Wahhabi historian wrote, "We took Karbala and slaughtered and took its people [as slaves], then praise be to Allah, Lord of the Worlds, and we do not apologize for that and say: 'And to the unbelievers: the same treatment.'"[9] It was one massacre of many,[10] and locals thought twice before resisting.

More recently, the Sunni Taliban came to power in the 1990s in Afghanistan by murdering thousands of unarmed civilians, often Shi'a or ethnic minorities. After capturing cities and villages that resisted, they would line up and gun down the locals, including women and children. According to a report on the Taliban's recapture of Bamian in 1999, "Hundreds of men and some women and children were separated from their families, taken away, and executed; all of them were noncombatants. In addition, houses were razed to the ground, and some detainees were used for forced labor."[11]

All these groups were savvy at working with local tribes with whom they had ethnic and religious ties. Some tribes joined for political advantage over their rivals or because they wanted a share in the spoils. Others saw the fight as a religious duty. Still others didn't want to resist for fear of what would follow.[12] But allying with local tribes is quite different from appealing to the general public. Playing nice with a tribal leader whose followers have guns is not the same thing as trying to win over your average citizen to the cause.

This is not to say that the softer approach can't work. America's own revolution is a case in point, especially when compared to the French Revolution a few years later. The American rebels warred with British troops and avoided deliberate attacks on civilians;[13] in contrast, the French revolutionaries executed an ever-widening circle of "enemies of the revolution" to subdue the public in what the revolutionaries enthusiastically called "The Terror," from which we get the term "terrorism."

The point is that extreme brutality is not incompatible with establishing a new state. It may not be the wisest course of action, and it probably won't create a state many people would want to live in. But that doesn't mean it won't work.

Just as most people can't imagine that brutality would be a winning political strategy, they also can't imagine that any religious scripture would justify such a thing. Muslims and non-Muslims are equally baffled as to how anyone could commit atrocities in the name of God. To explain it, some either assume the perpetrators use scripture cynically or that they are ignorant of its nuances.

To be sure, many of the Islamic State's foot soldiers are ignorant of their own scriptures. Islamic scripture is vast, encompassing not only the Qur'an but also the *ahadith*, the words and deeds attributed to Muhammad by his followers. Collections of *ahadith* run into the hundreds of volumes, and that's just the Sunni variety. The Shi'a have their own collections, adding more volumes to the pile. Want to find passages justifying peace and concord? They're in there. Want to find passages justifying violence? They're in there too. Medieval Muslim scholars spent their whole careers trying to reconcile the contradictions between them. It's extremely difficult to do, which is why early Muslims called the effort *ijtihad*, or "hard work." People chuckled at the news of two men buying a copy of *Islam for Dummies* on their way to join the Islamic State.[14] But having spent two decades studying the intricacies of Islamic scripture, I empathized with their bewilderment.

Although the Islamic State's soldiers might not know Islamic scripture very well, some of its leaders do. The caliph has a Ph.D. in the study of the Qur'an, and his top scholars are conversant in the *ahadith* and the ways medieval scholars interpreted it. There are many stupid thugs in the Islamic State, but these guys are not among them.

As to whether the Islamic State uses scripture cynically to justify whatever it wants to do, that's harder to know. It's certainly the case that the State's scholars pick and choose scripture to suit their biases and desires. But anyone who reads and acts on scripture does that.

The better question to ask is where those biases and desires come from.

First, the Islamic State's biases: The Islamic State's theology and method of engaging with scripture is nearly identical to Wahhabism, the ultraconservative form of Islam found in Saudi Arabia. It's very different from the kind of Islam you find in other parts of the world. In Wahhabism, religious innovation is bad; medieval scholarly authorities are respected but disregarded if need be; outside cultural influences should be expunged; and the definition of a good believer is very narrow. Wahhabi scholars might reach different conclusions from Islamic State scholars, but they start at much the same place.

Second, the Islamic State's desires: The Islamic State's politics differ profoundly from that of most Wahhabis, who view the Saudi kingdom as a legitimate Islamic government. As the State sees things, no Muslim-majority state in the world deserves to call itself Islamic, which is why it set up its own state and declared a caliphate. To achieve that end, the Islamic State had to wage an insurgency, which it justified with scripture.

Still, brutal insurgency doesn't necessarily follow from Islamic scripture. Bin Laden and other jihadists found plenty of scriptural support for waging a hearts-and-minds campaign in the Muslim world. The Islamic State's scholars acknowledge these passages of scripture but look for ways around them or find other passages that fit their views. Thus, the Islamic State's disagreement with al-Qaeda's leadership isn't scriptural; it's strategic. The State doesn't believe a hearts-and-minds strategy is effective, and for the past few years it has been proven right.

This is not Bin Laden's insurgency.

A GOVERNMENT FEARED BY THE PEOPLE

The Islamic State defied another bit of conventional jihadist wisdom when it declared itself a caliphate without the support of the Sunni masses. Al-Qaeda's leaders had advised patient coalition building before declaring an Islamic state, much less a caliphate. They looked upon the defeat of the Islamic State in 2008 as an object lesson in what not to do. But even when the Islamic State was nearly destroyed, its idea of immediately establishing Islamic governments without popular consent caught fire among the jihadist rank and file. When the Arab Spring uprisings in 2011 created political instability, several al-Qaeda groups leapt at the chance to establish governments even though Bin Laden warned them not to. The Islamic State also tried again and was far more successful the second time around, parting company with al-Qaeda to realize its ambition.

Part of the State's success had to do with its style of governing. There were carrots: It tried to provide public services, such as fixing potholes, running post offices, and distributing food. It even had a campaign to vaccinate its subjects against polio.[15] Several of the Islamic State's former sister affiliates in al-Qaeda had attempted the same.

The State also rewarded tribal allies with a share of the spoils to buy their support. As one Islamic State commander wrote to Baghdadi, "We have focused on bribing tribesmen and encouraging them to support the mujahids."[16] In dealing with the Sunni tribes, the State benefited a great deal from the tribes' anger toward the central governments in Damascus and Baghdad.

Bin Laden would have approved of the Islamic State's carrots, but he would have objected to its sticks. The al-Qaeda leader had counseled his affiliates to be lenient in their application of the *hudud*, the harsh fixed punishments mentioned in Islamic scripture. To do otherwise would only alienate the locals. The Islamic State ignored this counsel, either out of religious conviction or to convince other ultraconservatives of its conviction. The hands of thieves were severed, adulterers were stoned, bandits were shot and crucified, all in full public view. The Islamic State's harsh punishments subdued the locals as effectively as massacring its enemies had. Religious convictions and political benefit are not always antithetical.

Bin Laden had also advised his affiliates against attacking tribes that didn't want to cooperate. He worried it would start a cycle of blood feuds. And yet the Islamic State killed hundreds of tribal members when their leaders refused to bend the knee. Rather than inaugurating blood feuds, the massacres silenced dissent because the tribesmen could find no support from their governments or from foreign nations.

That brings us to the major reason why the Islamic State was so successful from 2013 to 2014: It was left alone. Whereas other Sunni rebels in Syria tried to overthrow their government, the State focused on making its own government in the Sunni hinterland. It filled its leadership with ex-Ba'athists from Saddam's military and intelligence services who had been fighting an insurgency for a decade and were accustomed to running an authoritarian government. The Islamic State also replenished its foot soldiers with thousands of foreigners, more than any other rebel group attracted, by using a propaganda mix of apocalypticism, puritanism, sectarianism, ultraviolence, and promises of a caliphate. The head of the National Counterterrorism Center in the United States testified in February 2015 that the rate of influx of foreign fighters to Syria "is unprecedented," exceeding "the rate of travelers who went to Afghanistan and Pakistan, Iraq, Yemen or Somalia at any point in the last 20 years."[17] The government in Baghdad couldn't stop the Islamic State and the government in Syria didn't want to, preferring to keep it around as a boogeyman to antagonize President Assad's enemies and scare his subjects. Better to focus the firepower of the Syrian state on other rebel groups that posed an immediate threat to his rule.

Bolstered by a combination of government neglect, careful planning, brutal tactics, and clever recruitment, the Islamic State had the manpower, money, and territory to make a credible claim to be a state. Whether the Islamic State is actually a caliphate is something for Muslims to decide. But judging purely by political criteria, the Islamic State is the only insurgent group in the Middle East to have made a plausible claim to the office since the fall of the Ottoman caliphate in the early twentieth century. And it did it by defying the common wisdom about how to govern properly.

This is not Bin Laden's caliphate.

RECONCILING THE CONTRADICTIONS

The Islamic State today is full of contradictions, which make its actions hard to explain. Apocalyptic language suffuses its propaganda, yet the group is careful in its planning and cunning in its execution, qualities that we do not often associate with apocalypticists. The State subscribes to a puritanical religious ideology, yet it is willing to collaborate with the self-interested leaders of local tribes and with former and current members of Saddam's secularist Ba'ath party. The Islamic State believes it is better to be feared than to be loved and deliberately stokes the anger of international onlookers, but the group also tries to provide government services to its subjects.

One explanation is that these are just criminals or cynics who'll say and do whatever it takes so long as they can seize and hold power. Their apocalyptic and puritanical religious rhetoric is designed to appeal to people who are interested in that sort of thing, but the Islamic State's leaders don't really believe it themselves. They'll dress their actions up in prophecy and adopt the trappings of an austere Islamic caliphate but it's not from conviction. They see religious symbols and laws as useful vehicles for realizing their ambitions, which is not an irrational viewpoint, as I've argued above.

But there's another way to reconcile the contradictions: The group is devoted to establishing an ultraconservative Islamic state at all costs, so it modifies its religious and political doctrines when they get in the way of that goal. The early Islamic State nearly destroyed itself because of the messianic beliefs of its founder. So the State modified its apocalyptic doctrine to focus on institution building rather than on the imminent appearance of a savior. The Islamic State's narrow definition of a good Muslim would make it impossible to collaborate with many of its coreligionists, which would hamper the group's ability to win an insurgency. So the State makes allowances for working with others as long as they do not get in the way of its project. The State's brutality risks turning its subjects against it in large numbers, which would make it impossible for a state to function. So the group sees to the economic well-being of its subjects so it can maintain a low level of support and a tax base to fund its project.

In this interpretation, we'd need to modify our own understanding of what political behaviors follow from a group or state described as "apocalyptic," "religious," or "totalitarian." Apocalypticism does not necessarily demand rash and irrational behavior. A severe religious theology is not incompatible with practical considerations. And using the stick to discipline a population is not incongruous with giving it some carrots.

Whatever one makes of the true motivations of the Islamic State's leaders, the political impact is the same: the founding of a brutal government at war with its neighbors. But the Islamic State's expansionary policy puts at risk what its leaders hold most dear: the continued existence of its state. Perhaps the Islamic State will modify its doctrine as it has modified others in the interest of self-preservation. Or perhaps this is the one doctrine it can't let go because it believes it is destined to be a world-encompassing state. If the latter, it would go against the argument that these are mere thugs who want power. Criminal gangs aren't suicidal.

Either way, the world can't afford to wait and find out.

WHAT TO DO

From 2012 to 2014, the wait-and-see approach of the international community emboldened the Islamic State and filled its ranks, making it a real threat to vital U.S. interests in the Middle East. The United States could have decided those interests weren't worth defending, but it was not willing to chance the possible consequences of further inaction: refugees in the region numbering in the tens of millions, repeated shocks to world energy prices, and an everexpanding proving ground for future militants. The United States' allies were divided and lacked the ability to organize and lead an effective counteroffensive on their own. The Islamic State was also expanding to other hot spots, like Afghanistan, Libya, Yemen, and

Egypt, which would inevitably poison the politics of those already tumultuous countries and create further instability in a restless Middle East.

Some of the usual methods for dealing with jihadist statelets might have worked early on in Syria and Iraq. But the Islamic State is too entrenched now for quick solutions. Defeating its government is going to take time. Disrupting the Islamic State's finances will be difficult because the group does not rely much on outside funding. Attacking from the air will degrade the Islamic State but will not destroy it. Its soldiers are in urban areas where they are hard to target without killing thousands of civilians.

Some methods will help only at the margins. Stanching the flow of foreign fighters is very difficult, given Syria's porous borders and the excitement the Islamic State generates among Muslim radicals. Reducing the mass appeal of the State is pointless, given that it doesn't have mass appeal[18] and isn't trying to cultivate it. What little appeal the Islamic State has rests on its ability to endure and expand. Take away either of those and you erode its legitimacy. In this case, the ideological fight is an actual fight.

Some methods work well but have a lot of downsides. Arming the Sunni tribes against the Islamic State doesn't guarantee they'll fight against it. They don't trust the Shi'i governments in Damascus and Baghdad and could just as easily decide to support the Islamic State or sit out the fight.

Arming Arab Sunni rebel groups to fight the Islamic State is no guarantee they'll get the job done either. They're focused on fighting their respective governments in Syria and Iraq and reluctant to tangle with a powerful rival. Furthermore, a number of those groups are religiously extreme and won't contribute to building a pluralistic future in either country.

Arming the Kurds is attractive because they're more pluralistic, but they won't be able to do much against the Islamic State in its Sunni Arab stronghold. The Kurds are an ethnic minority in Syria and Iraq, and they won't take and hold Arab territory far from their homeland. Plus, the Kurds might use the weapons to fight for their own independence, which would create further instability.

Building the capacity of the governments in Iraq and Syria to deal with the Islamic State is also fraught with problems. Bolstering the Shi'a-dominated government in Baghdad might further reinforce the country's sectarian politics that alienated its Sunnis in the first place. It's an even more dangerous policy in Syria because of its leader, who has let the Islamic State flourish to make his bloody methods appear less repugnant and to destroy his opposition from the inside.

The last option, sending in a large contingent of American troops, would enflame public opinion at home and abroad, ensuring that the United States will not be able to see its mission through. It would also absolve local governments of making the tough political choices required to end the Sunni disenfranchisement that fuels the insurgency.

Until the Shi'i governments in Syria and Iraq reach an accommodation with their Sunni citizens, the international coalition against the Islamic State can only constrain its growth. The coalition should continue using air power to diminish the State's ability to raise money and wage war. It shouldn't work with President Assad in Syria because he has deliberately fueled the rise of the Islamic State and probably won't stop. The government in Baghdad hasn't deliberately helped the State come to power, but its anti-Sunni policies have contributed to the State's success. So the coalition should give the government in Baghdad all the intelligence and logistical support it needs to fight against the Islamic State, but it should be wary of supplying more heavy weapons than are necessary to prosecute the war. The weapons could end up in the State's hands, as happened when Iraq's soldiers fled Mosul; but perhaps more important, giving the government whatever it wants discourages it from making the hard political compromises with the Sunnis that will sap the Islamic State's base of support.

The international coalition can also support proxies to fight against the Islamic State, but the support must be carefully calibrated so as to avoid creating more long-term political problems. The coalition should provide air cover and intelligence to Sunni tribal militias and rebel groups that fight against the Islamic State, whether Arab or Kurd. If it looks like the groups are in the fight for the long haul, then the coalition should consider arming them with light weaponry if they need it. Working with the Shi'i militias against the Islamic State is unnecessary, given that they already have a powerful state sponsor in Tehran.

If you think all of that sounds a lot like the coalition's current military strategy, you're right. It's not a great plan, but it's the best option at the moment.

I'm confident that the Islamic State's government in Syria and Iraq will crumble. No modern jihadist statelet has provoked international intervention and survived. But the disappearance of a jihadist statelet doesn't mean the disappearance of the jihadists. They will continue to wage insurgencies, taking advantage of the political instability and social unrest that gave rise to their statelets in the first place. The Islamic State stuck around after its defeat in 2008. So did al-Qaeda's affiliates in Mali, Yemen, and Somalia after they tried and failed to create states.

The question is, how will the jihadists evaluate the demise of the Islamic State? Will it prove to them that Bin Laden was right? Or will it prove that the State just needed to double down on its strategy? As I argued in chapter three, there's no obvious answer to the question because foreign powers always end the experiment prematurely. Even if a government established by global jihadists isn't serious about its rhetorical attacks on foreign nations, those nations won't wait long to find out.

The current political conditions in the Arab world all but ensure that some jihadists will follow the Islamic State's playbook, especially the group's growing number of affiliates or "provinces." Large-scale violence heightens the appeal of apocalyptic narratives, particularly in areas mentioned in the prophecies, and it creates the political vacuums in which armed groups can flourish. Of course, the Islamic State copycats can be defeated using some of the same methods the international coalition is using against the State in Iraq and Syria. But the Islamic State has demonstrated that a modern caliphate is possible, that doomsday pronouncements and extreme violence attract bloodthirsty recruits, and that cutting out the hearts and minds of a population can subdue them faster than trying to win them over. This may not be Bin Laden's jihad, but it's a formula future jihadists will find hard to resist.

SUNNI ISLAMIC PROPHECIES OF THE END TIMES

To give readers a fuller appreciation of the prophecies cited by the Islamic State and celebrated by its followers, I have translated some of them in the following appendices.[1] The prophecies come from early collections of words and deeds attributed to the Prophet Muhammad. Conservative Sunni Muslims consider most or all of the following prophecies to be authentic, which means they have the status of scripture second only to the Qur'an.

Modern Muslim authors have collected the prophecies and arranged them according to theme or chronology. I used the arrangements found in three books: The first two are from books available on the premier jihadist website, *Tawhed.ws*. For the sake of comparison with a more mainstream Islamist group, the third arrangement is from a book by a well-known Hamas activist. The final appendix is the first half of a treatise about the return of the caliphate written by the Islamic State's main scholar.

Readers should bear in mind the historical background of these prophecies I gave in the preceding pages. Readers should also know that many Muslims don't know these prophecies, don't care about them, or deny their authenticity altogether. If you're familiar with arguments about prophecies in your own religious tradition, you'll appreciate the range of views on the topic in the Muslim community.

THE FINAL DAYS

I have translated several of Muhammad's supposed prophecies of the End Times based on the original sources, arranging them in the chronological order found in The Final Days (al-Ayyam al-Akhira), *a book written by Adnan Taha that was published in 1997 by a Jordanian press. The jihadist website* Tawhed.ws *digitally republished its own edition of the book. I have used some of Taha's section headings but relied on the original sources for the Arabic text of the prophecies, which he either cites or reproduces differently with editorial comment. For the passages from the Qur'an, I have modified Arberry's translation.*[1]

THE FULL EMERGENCE OF THE RELIGION AND THE PRESENT REALITY

Verily, God knit together the earth for me. I beheld its easts and its wests. Truly, my community will rule everything that was knit together for me. (*Sahih Muslim*)

This cause [Islam] will reach everywhere night and day reach. God will leave no house of clay or camel skin without this religion by strengthening the strong and abasing the abased, with which God strengthens Islam and abases unbelief. (*Sahih Ibn Hibban*)

While I was sleeping, the keys of the treasuries of the earth were brought to me and put in my hand. (*Sahih Muslim*)

"Prophethood is among you as long as God wills it to be. Then God will take it away when He so wills. Then there will be a caliphate in accordance with the prophetic method. It will be among you as long as God intends, and then God will take it away when He so wills. Then there will be a mordacious monarchy. It will be among you as long as God intends, and then God will take it away when He so wills. Then there will be a tyrannical monarchy. It will be among you as long as God intends, and then God will take it away when He so wills. Then there will be a caliphate in accordance with the prophetic method." Then he [the Prophet] fell silent. (*Musnad Ahmad*)

A part of my community will continue fighting for the truth until the Hour comes and until the promise of God is fulfilled. God will cause the hearts of the people to deviate and he will bestow their possessions upon the group until the [Final] Hour arises. (*Sunan al-Nasa'i*)

After me the ground will collapse in the east, in the west, and in the Arab Peninsula. (*al-Mu'jam al-Awsat li-l-Tabarani*)

Iraq will withhold its dirhams and its measure of *qafiz* [a measure for grain]. Sham will withhold its dinars and its measure of *mudi* [a measure for grain]. Egypt will withhold its dinars and its measure of *irdab* [a measure for grain]. You will return from whence you began. (*Sahih Muslim*)

THE STAGE BEFORE THE MAHDI

The Hour will not come until a man of the Qahtan tribe appears, driving the people with his stick. (*Sahih al-Bukhari*)

Day and night will not end until a man called al-Jahjah rules. (*Sahih Muslim*)

The Hour will not come until the Euphrates lays bare a mountain of gold. The people will fight over it, and ninety-nine out of every hundred will be slain. Every man among them will say, 'Perhaps I am the one who will be saved.' (*Sahih al-Bukhari*)

The Euphrates will uncover a treasure of gold. The one who finds it should take none of it. (*Sahih Muslim*)

THE APPEARANCE OF THE MAHDI

Three people will fight for your treasure, each of them the son of a caliph, but none of them shall gain it. Then the black banners will come from the east and they will kill you in a manner no people have been killed before. . . . If you see him, pledge him allegiance even if you have to crawl over snow. For verily, he is the caliph of God, the Mahdi. (*Sunan Ibn Majah*)

At the end of my community will be a caliph who scatters wealth like dust that cannot be counted. (*Sahih Muslim*)

The earth will neither perish nor end until a man of my house whose name is my name rules the Arabs. (*Musnad Ahmad*)

The Mahdi will appear at the end of my community. God will send down rain for him and the earth will give forth its plants. He will distribute the wealth equitably . . . and livestock will multiply and the community will flourish. He will live seven or eight . . . pilgrimage seasons.[2] (*Mustadrak al-Hakim*)

I give you tidings of earthquakes and the Mahdi who will be sent to all people. He will fill the earth with fairness and justice as it was filled with injustice and oppression. The denizens of heaven and earth will be pleased with him. He will distribute wealth equitably. (*Musnad Ahmad*)

The Mahdi has a broader brow than I have and a nose more curved. He will fill the earth with fairness and justice as it was filled with injustice and oppression. He will rule seven years. (*Sunan Abi Dawud*)

A people who have no power, great numbers, or weapons will seek refuge in my House, meaning the Ka'ba. An army will be sent against them that the earth will swallow when they reach the desert. (*Sahih Muslim*)

Strange that a group of people from my community would go to the House with a man from the Quraysh tribe who sought shelter at the House. When they reached the desert, the earth swallowed them. (*Sahih Muslim*)

FIGHTING ROME

You will offer Rome a treaty of security. You will attack them because they are enemies behind you. Then you will arrive at a meadow with hills. A man from Rome will come bearing the cross saying 'The Cross has been victorious.' A man among the Muslims will stand against him and kill him. Rome will betray you and there will be great battles, and they will mass against you. They will come against you with eighty flags, and under each flag will be ten thousand. (*Sunan Abi Dawud*)

The Hour will not come until the Romans would land at al-A'maq or in Dabiq. An army consisting of the best of the people of the earth at that time will come from Medina. When they will arrange themselves in ranks, the Romans will say: Do not stand between us and those [Muslims] who took prisoners from amongst us. Let us fight with them." The Muslims will say: "Nay, by God, how can we withdraw between you and our brothers? They will then fight and a third [part] of the army would run away, whom God will never forgive. A third [part of the army], which would be constituted of excellent martyrs in God's eye, will be killed and the third who will never be put to trial will win and they will be conquerors of Constantinople. (*Sahih Muslim*)

The Muslims' place of assembly on the day of the Battle will be in al-Ghutah near a city called Damascus, one of the best cities in al-Sham. (*Sunan Abi Dawud*)

CONQUEST OF CONSTANTINOPLE

You have heard of a city on one side of which is land and on the other the sea. . . . The Hour will not come until seventy thousand of the tribe of Isaac attack it. When they reach it, they will disembark. They will not fight with weapons or shoot arrows. They will say, "There is no God but God, God is most great!" One of its two sides will collapse. . . . They will say a second time, "There is no God but God, God is most great." Then the other side will collapse. They will say a third time, "There is no God but God, God is most great." A breach will open for them and they will enter and gather the spoils, distributing it among themselves. Thereupon they would hear a cry, "Verily the Deceiver has appeared." They will abandon everything and return whence they came. (*Sahih Muslim*)

CONQUEST OF ROME

When the Messenger of God was asked which of the two cities will be conquered first, Constantinople or Rome, he said, "The city of Heraclius is first, meaning Constantinople." (*Musnad Ahmad*)

THE DECEIVER

The cry will reach them that the Deceiver is behind them at their homes. They will drop what is in their hands and turn back, sending ten horsemen in the vanguard. The Prophet said, "I know their names, the names of their fathers, and the colors of their horses. They will be the best horsemen on the face of the earth on that day or among the best of horsemen on the face of the earth that day." (*Sahih Muslim*)

While I slept, I saw myself circumambulating the Ka'ba. There was a man with brown skin and long straight hair between two men. Water trickled from his head or was poured over his head. I said, 'Who is this?' They said, 'This is the son of Mary.' Then I went and saw a corpulent man of red complexion, frizzy hair, and blind in one eye, which was swollen like a grape. I said, 'Who is this?' They said, 'The Deceiver.' (*Sahih al-Bukhari*)

The Deceiving Messiah is a short man with bowed legs, frizzy hair, and blind in one eye that neither protrudes nor sinks in its socket. (*Sunan Abi Dawud*)

Between his eyes is written 'Infidel.' . . . Every Muslim can read it. (*Sahih al-Bukhari*)

WHERE HE WILL APPEAR

"He is not in the sea of al-Sham or in the sea of Yemen. Rather, he is in the east, he is in the east." Then he pointed with his hand to the east. (*Sahih Muslim*)

The Deceiver will appear from the land in the east called Khorasan. (*Jami' al-Tirmidhi*)

The Deceiver will appear among the Jews of Isfahan. Seventy thousand Jews will be with him. (*al-Fath al-rabbani li-tartib Musnad Ahmad*)

Seventy thousand Jews from Isfahan wearing shawls will follow the Deceiver. (*Sahih Muslim*)

Verily, he will appear in the empty land between al-Sham and Iraq, wreaking havoc left and right. (*Sahih Muslim*)

I know what the Deceiver will have with him. He will have two rivers running. The eye perceives one of them to be white and the other flaming fire. If anyone sees that, let him go to the river that appears to be fire, close his eyes, lower his head, and drink from it, for it is cool water. (*Sahih Muslim*)

I will tell you of the Deceiver what no prophet has told his people. He will be blind in one eye. He will bring the semblance of paradise and hellfire with him. What he calls paradise will be hellfire. (*Sunan Ibn Majah*)

We said, "O Messenger of God, how long will he remain on earth." He said, "Forty days. One day like a year, one day like a month, one day like a week, and the remaining days like your days." We said, "O Messenger of God, how quickly will he move on earth." He said, "Like the rain driven by the wind. . . . He will command the sky, and it will rain and the earth will bloom. . . . The treasures will be gathered for him. He will call to a man filled with youth and strike him with the sword, cutting him into two pieces at a distance of an archer from his target. He will then call the man, who will approach with gleaming face and laughing." (*Sahih Muslim*)

The Deceiver will come but he will be forbidden from entering the rugged pass of Medina. He will camp at one of the salt flats around Medina. A man will go out to him on that day who is the best of the people or one of the best. He will say, 'I bear witness that you are the Deceiver of whom the Messenger of God (peace and blessings be upon him) spoke.' The Deceiver will say, 'If I kill this man and bring him back to life, will you doubt my claim?' They will say no. Then the Deceiver will kill the man and bring him back to life. The man will say, 'By God, what I have seen today has convinced me.' The Deceiver wanted to kill him again but he was not given the authority to do so. (*Sahih al-Bukhari*)

Medina will be shaken with its people three times. No male or female hypocrites will remain for they will all go out to him. The city will be cleansed of impurity just as the bellows purifies the iron of dross. (*Sunan Ibn Majah*)

DESCENT OF JESUS (PEACE BE UPON HIM)

God will send the Messiah son of Mary who will descend at the white minaret in the eastern side of Damascus wearing two garments dyed with saffron and placing each hand on the wing of two angels. When he lowers his head, drops of water fall, and when he raises his head, beads like pearls trickle down. Every infidel who catches a scent of his breath can only die, and his breath will reach far away. (*Sahih Muslim*)

A group from my community will continue fighting for the truth and conquering until the Day of Resurrection. . . . Jesus the son of Mary (peace be upon him) will descend. Their leader will say, "Come pray for us." He will say, "No, some of you are leaders over others as a blessing of God for this community." (*Sahih Muslim*)

FIGHTING THE JEWS

The Hour will not come until the Muslims fight the Jews. The Muslims will kill them until the Jews hide behind rocks and trees. The rocks and trees will say, "O Muslim! O servant of God! This is a Jew behind me so come and kill him." Except for the Gharqad, which is a tree of the Jews. (*Sahih Muslim*)

On that day the Arabs will be few, and most of them will be in Jerusalem. Their leader will be a righteous man. When he steps forward to lead them in morning prayer, Jesus son of Mary will descend upon them. Their leader will step back to allow Jesus to lead the people in prayer. Jesus will put his hand between his shoulder blades and say, 'Go to the front and pray, for the call to prayer was given in your name.' He will lead them in prayer. After he finishes, Jesus will say, 'Open the gate.' So they will open it, and behind it will be the Deceiver with seventy thousand Jews, each with an ornate sword and green cloak. When the Deceiver gazes upon [Jesus], [the Deceiver] will melt like salt melts in water. He will start to run away, and Jesus (upon him be peace) will say, 'I have one blow for you that you cannot escape.' He will overtake him at the eastern gate of Lod and slay him. Then God will defeat the Jews. There will be no thing created by God for the Jews to hide behind without God causing it to speak and say, 'O Muslim servant of God, this is a Jew, come kill him!'—neither rock, nor tree, nor wall, nor beast—except the Gharqad tree. (*Sunan Ibn Majah*)

THE APPEARANCE OF GOG AND MAGOG

They will question you about the Man with Two Horns. Say: 'I will recite to you a story of him. We established him in the land, and We gave him a path to everything; and he followed a path until, when he reached the setting of the sun, he found it setting in a muddy spring, and he found nearby a people. We said, "O Man with Two Horns, either you will inflict pain upon them, or you will take towards them a way of kindness." He said, "As for the oppressor, we will inflict pain upon him, then he will return to his Lord Who will inflict horrible pain upon him. But as for him who believes, and does righteousness, he shall receive as recompense the reward most fair, and we shall speak to him, of our command, easiness." Then he followed a path until, when he reached the rising of the sun, he found it rising upon a people for whom We had not appointed any veil to shade them from it. And so, We encompassed in knowledge what was with him. Then he followed a path until, when he reached between the two barriers, he found on this side of them a people scarcely able to understand speech. They said, "O Man with Two Horns, behold, Gog and Magog are doing corruption in the earth; so shall we assign to thee a tribute, against your setting up a barrier between us and between them?" He said, "That wherein my Lord has established me is better; so aid me forcefully, and I will set up a rampart between you and between them. Bring me ingots of iron!" Until, when he had made all level between the two cliffs, he said, "Blow!" Until, when he had made it a fire, he said, "Bring me, that I may pour molten brass on it." So they were unable either to scale it or pierce it. He said, "This is a mercy from my Lord. But when the promise of my Lord comes to pass, He will make it into powder; and my Lord's promise is ever true." Upon that day We will leave them surging on one another, and the Trumpet will be blown, and We will gather them together. (*Qur'an* 18:83–99)

There is a ban upon any city that We have destroyed; they shall not return until Gog and Magog are loosed, and they swarm down out of every slope, and nigh has drawn the true promise, and behold, the eyes of the unbelievers staring: "Alas for us! We were ignorant of this; nay, we were evildoers." (*Qur'an* 21:75–77)

You will continue to fight an enemy until Gog and Magog come, broad of face, small of eye, and covered with hair, coming from every direction, their faces as wide as shields and as thick as a hammer. (*Musnad Ahmad*)

God revealed to Jesus, "I have brought forth my servants whom none will be able to fight. So take my servants to Mt. Sinai." Then God will loose Gog and Magog, who swarm down every slope. The first of them will pass the Sea of Galilee and drink from it. When the last of them pass, they will say, "There was once water here." They will encircle the prophet of God Jesus and his companions until the head of the bull will be better for one of them than a hundred dinars for one of you today. The prophet of God Jesus and his companions will supplicate God, and God will afflict their enemies' necks with myiasis. In the morning they will die as if one body. Then the prophet of God Jesus and his companions will go down the mountain, where they will find no place on earth that is not filled with their stench and smell. The prophet of God Jesus and his companions will supplicate God and God will send birds with necks like Bactrian camels that will take the bodies and dispose of them where God wills. (*Sahih Muslim*)

By Him in Whose hand is my soul, the son of Mary (peace and blessings be upon him) will descend among you as a fair ruler. He will break the cross, kill the swine, abolish the protection tax, and pour forth so much wealth that no one will accept it. (*Sahih Muslim*)

DEATH OF THE BELIEVERS AND DESTRUCTION OF MECCA AND MEDINA

At that time Allah will send a pleasant wind that will even reach their armpits. It will take the life of every believer and every Muslim. Only the wicked will survive, committing adultery like asses until the Last Hour would come to them. No one will remain on earth saying, "God, God." (*Sahih Muslim*)

God will send a perfumed breeze by which everyone who has in their heart even a mustard grain of faith will die. Those who remain will have no goodness in them, and they will revert to the religion of their forefathers. (*Sahih Muslim*)

"Medina will be left in the best way that it is until a dog or wolf enters it and urinates on one of the pillars of the mosque or on the minaret." They asked, "Messenger of God! Who will have the fruit at that time?" He said, "Animals seeking prey, birds and wild beasts." (*Muwatta' Malik*)

The thin-legged man from Abyssinia will destroy the Ka'ba. He will then plunder its finery and remove its cover. It is as if I am seeing him now, bald and bow-legged, beating on it with his plane and pick. (*Musnad Ahmad*)

Afterward no one ever rebuilt it. (*Musnad Ahmad*)

THE GREAT UNIVERSAL SIGNS

The Hour will not come until the sun rises from the West. When it rises, the people will see it and all believe. But by then, no soul will benefit from its belief. (*Sahih al-Bukhari*)[3]

When the Word falls on them, We will bring forth for them a beast from the earth who will speak to them: "People had no faith in Our signs." (*Qur'an* 27:82)

The first sign is the rising of the sun in the West and the appearance of the beast to the people in the forenoon. Whichever happens first, the other is soon to follow. (*Sahih Muslim*)

At the end, fire will blaze from Yemen, driving the people to their place of assembly. (*Sahih Muslim*)

"There you will assemble, there you will assemble, there you will assemble . . . riding and walking and on your faces." He pointed with his hand to al-Sham. "There you will assemble." (*Musnad Ahmad*)

THE VICTORIOUS GROUP

In 1993, jihadist author Abu Basir al-Tartusi wrote a book about the characteristics of the "victorious group" of Muslims prophesied to fight in the final battles leading up to the Day of Judgment. In it, he provides a brief chronology of the End Times based on a few of Muhammad's prophecies. (I have preserved his subject headings.) Note that Tartusi, a strong critic of the Islamic State, places the reestablishment of the caliphate after the fight against the Romans and the Jews.

1—THE CONQUEST OF ROME, THE CAPITAL OF ITALY

When the Messenger of God was asked which of the two cities will be conquered first, Constantinople or Rome, he said, 'The city of Heraclius is first, meaning Constantinople.' (*Musnad Ahmad*)

2—THE CONQUEST OF CONSTANTINOPLE A SECOND TIME

The Hour will not come until the Romans would land at al-A'maq or in Dabiq. An army consisting of the best [soldiers] of the people of the earth at that time will come from Medina [to counteract them]. When they will arrange themselves in ranks, the Romans will say: "Do not stand between us and those [Muslims] who took prisoners from amongst us. Let us fight with them." The Muslims will say: "Nay, by God, how can we withdraw between you and our brothers?" They will then fight and a third [part] of the army will run away, whom God will never forgive. A third [part of the army], which will be constituted of excellent martyrs in God's eye, will be killed and the third who will never be put to trial will win and they would be conquerors of Constantinople. (*Sahih Muslim*)

3—FIGHTING THE JEWS AND VICTORY OVER THEM

The Hour will not come until the Muslims fight the Jews. The Muslims will kill them until the Jews hide behind rocks and trees. The rocks and trees will say, 'O Muslim! O servant of God! This is a Jew behind me so come and kill him.' Except for the Gharqad, which is a tree of the Jews. (*Sahih Muslim*)

4—THE INVASION OF INDIA

God will safeguard two groups from my community from hellfire: a group that invades India and a group with Jesus the son of Mary. (*Musnad Ahmad*)

5—ESTABLISHING THE RIGHTLY GUIDING CALIPHATE IN ACCORDANCE WITH THE PROPHETIC METHOD

"Prophethood is among you as long as God wills it to be. Then God will take it away when He so wills. Then there will be a caliphate in accordance with the prophetic method. It will be among you as long as God intends, and then God will take it away when He so wills. Then there will be a mordacious monarchy. It will be among you as long as God intends, and then God will take it away when He so wills. Then there will be a tyrannical monarchy. It will be among you as long as God intends, and then God will take it away when He so wills. Then there will be a caliphate in accordance with the prophetic method." Then he [the Prophet] fell silent. (*Musnad Ahmad*)

6—THE PENETRATION OF ISLAM INTO EVERY HOUSE IN THE WORLD

Verily, God knit together the earth for me. I beheld its easts and its wests. Truly, my community will rule everything that was knit together for me. (*Sahih Muslim*)

This cause will reach everywhere night and day reach. God will leave no house of clay or camel skin without this religion by strengthening the strong and abasing the abased, with which God strengthens Islam and abases unbelief. (*Sahih Ibn Hibban*)

While I was sleeping, the keys of the treasuries of the earth were brought to me and put in my hand. (*Sahih Muslim*)

7—THE DESCENT OF JESUS (PEACE BE UPON HIM) TO THE EARTH

There is no prophet between me and him, meaning Jesus. Verily, he will descend. When you see him you will recognize him as a man of medium height, reddish to fair, wearing two light yellow garments. His head will appear to be dripping though it is not wet. He will fight the people for Islam, breaking the cross, killing the swine, and abolishing the poll tax. In his time, God will destroy every religious community except Islam. He will destroy the Deceiving Messiah. He will dwell on earth for forty years. When he dies, the Muslims will pray for him. (*Sunan Abi Dawud*)

THE MAHDI IS PRECEDED BY AN ISLAMIC STATE

In 2009, Jawad Bahr al-Natsha, a Hamas activist, published a book titled The Mahdi Is Preceded by an Islamic State.[1] *Below I have translated his proof texts and section titles.*

SECTION ONE: EXPLICIT PROOF TEXTS THAT THE MAHDI IS PRECEDED BY AN ISLAMIC CALIPHATE

Differences will occur at the death of a caliph. A man will emerge among the people of Medina, fleeing to Mecca. Some of the people of Mecca will come to him. They will bring him forward against his will and swear allegiance to him between the corner and the *maqam*.[2] An army will be sent against him from Sham, which will be swallowed up in the desert between Mecca and Medina. When the people see the righteous of Sham and the troops of the people of Iraq coming to him, they will pledge allegiance to him between the corner and the *maqam*. Then there will arise a man of the Quraysh tribe whose maternal uncles belong to the Kalb tribe. He will send an army from the Kalb tribe against them, which will prevail. Those who do not witness the booty of the Kalb will be disappointed. He will divide the wealth and treat the people according to the practice of their Prophet (peace and blessings be upon him). He will apply himself to establishing Islam on the earth. He will remain seven years then die. The Muslims will pray over him. (*Sunan Abi Dawud*)

Three people will fight for your treasure, each of them the son of a caliph, but none of them shall gain it. Then the black banners will come from the East and they will kill you in a manner no people have been killed before. . . . If you see him, pledge him allegiance even if you have to crawl over snow. For verily, he is the caliph of God, the Mahdi. (*Sahih Ibn Majah*)

SECTION TWO: IMPLICIT PROOF TEXTS

"Prophethood is among you as long as God wills it to be. Then God will take it away when He so wills. Then there will be a caliphate in accordance with the prophetic method. It will be among you as long as God intends, and then God will take it away when He so wills. Then there will be a mordacious monarchy. It will be among you as long as God intends, and then God will take it away when He so wills. Then there will be a tyrannical monarchy. It will be among you as long as God intends, and then God will take it away when He so wills. Then there will be a caliphate in accordance with the prophetic method." Then he [the Prophet] fell silent. (*Musnad Ahmad*)

The caliphate will be in my community thirty years, then there will be monarchy after that. (*Jami' al-Tirmidhi*)

No house of clay or camel skin will remain on the face of the earth but that God has made the word of Islam enter it by strengthening the strong and abasing the abased, whether God . . . strengthens them and makes them among its people or abases them and they bow to it. (*Musnad Ahmad*)

TWELVE CALIPHS

Before the Islamic State declared itself the caliphate, Turki al-Bin'ali, its young schol-
arly apologist and now head of its powerful Shari'a Committee, wrote a short treatise
on why the time was right to do so.[1] Below is a translation of the portion on the rightly
guiding caliphs who will appear before the Mahdi. The bolded and underlined portions
are Bin'ali's doing.

The Messenger of God (peace and blessings be upon him) said:

> "Prophethood is among you as long as God wills it to be. Then God
> will take it away when He so wills. Then there will be a caliphate in
> accordance with the prophetic method. It will be among you as long
> as God intends, and then God will take it away when He so wills.
> Then there will be a mordacious monarchy. It will be among you as
> long as God intends, and then God will take it away when He so wills.
> Then there will be a tyrannical monarchy. It will be among you as
> long as God intends, and then God will take it away when He so wills.
> **Then there will be a caliphate in accordance with the prophetic**
> **method." Then he fell silent.**

The learned Ibn Khaldun (may God bless him) said:

> It is mentioned in the *Sahih* that [the Prophet] said, "This cause will
> abide until the Hour comes **or there are twelve caliphs of the**
> **Quraysh tribe over you.**"[2]

The Prophet made known that some of them will be in the beginning of Islam and some will be at its end. [The Prophet] said, "The caliphate after me will be thirty,[3] thirty-one, or thirty-six years." It ends in the caliphate of al-Hasan and the beginning of Mu'awiya's rule. The beginning of Mu'awiya's rule is a caliphate in the original meaning of the word. He is the sixth caliph. As for the seventh caliph, it is Umar b. Abd al-Aziz.

The other five are of the People of the House [members of the Prophet's family] descended from Ali, which is supported by [the Prophet's] statement: "You are the possessor of two epochs," meaning the community has you [Ali] as a caliph in its beginning and your progeny as caliphs at its end.

Imam Ibn Kathir (may God bless him) said after mentioning the *hadith* [of Safina], "The prophetic caliphate will last thirty years then God will give His kingdom to whomever He wills":

This hadith is an explicit rebuttal of the rejectionists [the Shi'a] who denied the three caliphates and a refutation of the hateful among the Umayyad tribe and their followers in Sham who denied the caliphate of Ali b. Abi Talib. So how does one reconcile this *hadith* of Safina and the *hadith* of Jabir b. Samura found in *Sahih Muslim:* "**The religion will abide until the Hour comes or there are twelve caliphs over you, each of them from the Quraysh tribe**"?

The answer is that some people say the religion continued until twelve caliphs ruled, then it collapsed after them in the time of the Umayyad tribe. **Others say this hadith is a prophecy of twelve just caliphs from the Quraysh tribe, even if they have not yet come to power. Rather, it is consistent with the fall of the caliphate in the thirty years that followed the prophetic period. After that, there were rightly guiding caliphs, including Umar b. Abd al-Aziz b. Marwan b. al-Hakim the Umayyad, may God be pleased with him.** More than one of the imams has endorsed his caliphate, his justice, and his being counted among the rightly guiding caliphs. Even Ahmad b. Hanbal (may God be pleased with him) said about him, "The words of any among the generation that came after [Muhammad's Companions] have no standing except those of Umar b. Abd al-Aziz." Also among those they mentioned is al-Mahdi bi-l-Amr Allah, the Abbasid, and the Mahdi prophesied at the end of time by

virtue of his being one of the People of the House and his name being
Muhammad b. Abd Allah. He is not the person awaited in the cellar
of Samarra, who absolutely does not exist even if the ignorant among
the rejectionists [the Shi'a] wait for him."

Therefore, the caliphate is a prophetic promise foretold by [the Prophet]. The
just caliphs are twelve in number as mentioned in the two *Sahihs*, even though
they are not consecutive. Rather, five of them appeared in the early period.
Some say six, some say seven. The last of them will pave the way for the Mahdi
with the help of God, the exalted.

With patience and certitude, the community from east to west anticipates
the return of the rightly guiding caliphate and hopes to live in the age of the
remaining rightly guiding caliphs!

However, few in the expectant community work for the return of that
rightly guiding caliphate. Among those few are many who commit deviant acts
of unbelief or sin for the sake of a "lofty and noble purpose." So some of them
nominate themselves for presidential elections to gradually apply the Shari'a
until the caliphate returns, as they claim!

The least of their evils is having political parties and societies calling for
the return of the caliphate through leaflets and posters!

A the minority in the small group working for the return of the caliphate
are those who have been successful in their method of returning the rightly
guiding caliphate, the method of speech and spear. As the Shaykh of Islam
Ibn Taymiyya says (may God bless him): **"Religion is invigorated with a
book that guides and a sword that assists, and your Lord is sufficient as
guide and helper."** He also said, **"Religion was invigorated with sword and
scripture."** Moreover, **"Everyone must strive to be in conformity with the
Qur'an and with God's iron [the sword]. He must ask what he has that can
be of service to God. When that happens, the world will serve religion."**

That small minority arose to establish Islamic emirates here and there—
which are sometimes strong and sometimes in retreat in the face of the fierce
global campaigns against them!—until God the exalted favored the establishment of the Islamic State in Iraq and Sham to be the nucleus of the anticipated
rightly guiding caliphate, by the aid of God, the exalted.

NOTES

PREFACE TO THE 2016 EDITION

1. Dabiq, issue 12, 2.
2. http://www.mirror.co.uk/news/uk-news/hero-paris-attack-brave-brit-6835535.
3. http://www.prophetictimes.tv/forum/here-is-isis-s-statement-claiming-responsibility-for-the-paris-at.
4. http://www.nytimes.com/2015/11/23/world/europe/paris-attacks-isis-threatens-west.html?_r=0.
5. http://english.alarabiya.net/en/perspective/analysis/2015/11/22/-ISIS-s-criminal-mind-chemical-arms-ambitions-pose-as-risk-.html.
6. http://www.thedailybeast.com/articles/2015/03/18/is-isis-building-a-drone-army.html
7. http://www.nbcnews.com/storyline/paris-terror-attacks/terror-shoestring-paris-attacks-likely-cost-10-000-or-less-n465711.
8. Dabiq, issue 12, 2, 50.
9. http://www.nytimes.com/2015/12/08/world/middleeast/us-strategy-seeks-to-avoid-isis-prophecy.html?_r=1.
10. http://www.thedailybeast.com/articles/2015/11/15/confessions-of-an-isis-spy.html.

CHAPTER 1

1. Marc Leibowitz (@Marc_Leibowitz), Twitter post, August 12, 2014, https://twitter.com/Marc_Leibowitz/status/499230249063043075.
2. Jessica Remo, "Garwood Man Says Home's Flag Represents Islam, Not ISIS, Is Not Anti-American," *NJ.com*, August 13, 2014, http://www.nj.com/union/index.ssf/2014/08/garwood_resident_removes_isis_flag.html; Abby Phillip, "How the Violent Islamic State Extremists Got Their Signature Flag," *Washington Post*, August 15, 2014, http://www.washingtonpost.com/blogs/worldviews/wp/2014/08/15/how-the-violent-islamic-state-extremists-got-their-signature-flag/.
3. Michael Weiss and Hassan Hassan, *ISIS: Inside the Army of Terror* [Google edition] (New York: Regan Arts, 2015), 18.

4. For Zarqawi's biography, see Bruce Riedel, *The Search for Al Qaeda* (Washington, DC: Brookings Institution Press, 2008), 85–115; Weiss and Hassan, *ISIS*, 14–30.

5. Not much is known about Sayf, and he is frequently misidentified. The best synthesis of what we know can be found in Clint Watts, Jacob Shapiro, and Vahid Brown, *Al-Qa'ida's (Mis)adventures in the Horn of Africa*, Harmony Program, Combating Terrorism Center at West Point, July 2, 2007, 119–129, https://www.ctc.usma.edu/posts/al-qaidas -misadventures-in-the-horn-of-africa.

6. The following account is based on Sayf's brief memoir of his time with Zarqawi. Sayf had known of Zarqawi before they met because details of Zarqawi's trial in Jordan had made the rounds in jihadist circles. See Sayf al-Adl, "Tajrubati ma'a Abi Mus'ab al-Zarqawi," *Minbar al-Tawhid wa-l-Jihad*, May 2005, http://www.tawhed.ws/dl?i=ttofom6f.

7. Steve Coll, *The Bin Ladens: An Arabian Family in the American Century* (New York: Penguin Press, 2009), 75.

8. Adl, "Tajrubati," 3–6. Zarqawi's mentor, Abu Muhammad al-Maqdisi, said Zarqawi refused to join al-Qaeda in Afghanistan because he could not reconcile his extreme views with Bin Laden's. See Cole Bunzel, "From Paper State to Caliphate: The Ideology of the Islamic State," The Brookings Project on U.S. Relations with the Islamic World, Analysis Paper No. 19 (March 2015): 13, http://www.brookings.edu/~/media/research /files/papers/2015/03/ideology-of-islamic-state-bunzel/the-ideology-of -the-islamic-state.pdf.

9. Adl, "Tajrubati," 12.

10. Thomas Asbridge, *The Crusades: The War for the Holy Land* (London: Simon & Schuster, 2012), 1138–1139.

11. S. J. Allen and Emilie Amt, eds., *The Crusades: A Reader*, 2nd ed., *Readings in Medieval Civilizations and Cultures: VIII*, series ed., Paul Edward Dutton (Toronto: University of Toronto Press, 2014), 122.

12. Adl, "Tajrubati," 13.

13. For example, Bin Laden uses both terms interchangeably when discussing what to name the Shabab's government in Somalia. See Osama bin Laden, "Letter from Osama bin Laden to Mukhtar Abu al-Zubayr [English translation]," personal correspondence to Abu al-Zubayr (aka Ahmed Abdi Godane), SOCOM-2012-0000005, Harmony Program, Combating Terrorism Center at West Point, August 7, 2010, available at Jihadica, http://www.jihadica.com/wp-content/uploads/2012/05/SOCOM-2012 -0000005-Trans.pdf. Original Arabic version available at http://www .jihadica.com/wp-content/uploads/2012/05/SOCOM-2012-0000005 -Orig.pdf.

14. Ibid., 20.

15. Ibid., 25.

16. Ibid., 18.

17. Craig Whitlock, "Zarqawi Building His Own Terror Network," *Washington Post*, October 3, 2004, http://old.post-gazette.com/pg/04277/388966. stm; "Report of the Select Committee on Intelligence on Postwar Findings About Iraq's WMD Programs and Links to Terrorism and How They Compare with Prewar Assessments," U.S. Senate Select Committee on Intelligence, 109th Congress, 2nd session, September 8, 2006, 109, http://www.intelligence.senate.gov/phaseiiaccuracy.pdf.

18. Weiss and Hassan, *ISIS*, 36–37.

19. Abu Mus'ab al-Zarqawi, "A-yanqus al-din wa-ana hayy," *Kalimat mudi'a: al-Kitab al-jami' li-khutab wa-kalimat al-shaykh al-mu'taz bi-dinihi*, June 10, 2006, 303, http://e-prism.org/images/AMZ-Ver1.doc.

20. Abu Mus'ab al-Zarqawi, "Zarqawi Letter [English translation]," personal correspondence to Osama bin Laden and Ayman al-Zawahiri, February 2004, U.S. Department of State Archive, http://2001-2009.state.gov/p/nea/rls/31694.htm. Portions of the original are in "Risala min Abi Mus'ab al-Zarqawi ila al-Shaykh Usama bin Ladin," *Kalimat mudi'a*, February 15, 2004, 56–73.

21. Ibid., modified translation.

22. Ibid., modified translation.

23. See Thomas Hegghammer, *Jihad in Saudi Arabia: Violence and Pan-Islamism since 1979* (New York: Cambridge University Press, 2010); Sami Yousafzai, "Terror Broker," *Newsweek*, April 10, 2005, http://www.newsweek.com/terror-broker-116359.

24. The anonymous Islamic State insider "Abu Ahmad" said Zarqawi hoped al-Qaeda would augment his group's money and give him access to its network of funders in the Gulf; "al-Haqa'iq al-mukhfa hawla dawlat al-Baghdadi," *al-Durar al-Shamiyya*, April 5, 2014, http://eldorar.com/node/45368.

25. Zarqawi, "al-Bay'a li-tanzim al-Qa'ida bi-qiyadat al-Shaykh Usama bin Ladin," *Kalimat mudi'a*, October 17, 2004, 171. Prior to his oath of allegiance, Zarqawi had stated frequently that his group in Iraq was fighting to establish an Islamic state. See Bunzel, "Ideology," 15–16.

26. Ayman al-Zawahiri, "Zawahiri's Letter to Zarqawi [English translation]," personal correspondence to Abu Mus'ab al-Zarqawi, Harmony Program, Combating Terrorism Center at West Point, July 9, 2005, https://www.ctc.usma.edu/posts/zawahiris-letter-to-zarqawi-english-translation-2. Original Arabic version available at https://www.ctc.usma.edu/v2/wp-content/uploads/2013/10/Zawahiris-Letter-to-Zarqawi-Original.pdf.

27. Ibid.

28. Ibid., modified translation.

29. Atiyya Abd al-Rahman, "'Atiyah's Letter to Zarqawi [English translation]," personal correspondence to Abu Mus'ab al-Zarqawi, Harmony Program, Combating Terrorism Center at West Point, December 12, 2005, https://www.ctc.usma.edu/posts/atiyahs-letter-to-zarqawi-english-translation-2. Original Arabic version available at https://www.ctc.usma.edu/v2/wp-content/uploads/2013/10/Atiyahs-Letter-to-Zarqawi-Original.pdf.

30. Ibid.

31. Craig Whitlock and Munir Ladaa, "Atiyah Abd al-Rahman, Liaison to Iraq and Algeria," *Washington Post*, 2006, http://www.washingtonpost.com/wp-srv/world/specials/terror/rahman.html.

32. Abd al-Rahman, "'Atiyah's Letter to Zarqawi."

33. Ibid.

34. Ibid.

35. Ibid.

36. Quoted in "Limadha nujahid? Liqa' Mu'assasat al-Furqan ma'a al-Shaykh Abi Mus'ab al-Zarqawi," *Majmu' kalimat qadat Dawlat al-'Iraq al-Islamiyya*, July 17, 2010, http://up1430.com/central-guide/pencil/elit

/the_sum/the_sum_3/pages/authority/14/index.php. The video featuring the original interview appears to have been released posthumously on June 12, 2006. See "Hadiyyat Mu'assasat al-Furqan hiwar ma'a al-Shaykh Abi Mus'ab al-Zarqawi 'rahimahu Allah,'" *Shabakat Ana al-Muslim li-l-Hiwar al-Islami*, June 12, 2006, http://www.muslm.org/vb/archive/index .php/t-190782.html.

37. Zarqawi, "Hadha balagh li-l-nas," *Kalimat mudi'a*, April 24, 2006, 511.

38. The statement comes from a fuller version of the video that was captured by U.S. forces in May 2006. See Bunzel, "Ideology," 16. Not all of al-Qaeda's leaders urged Zarqawi to be cautious. Sayf al-Adl advised Zarqawi in May 2005 to quickly "announce the state" because "the affairs and circumstances . . . are ripe and favorable." See Adl, "Tajrubati," 22.

39. "'Majlis Shura al-Mujahidin' yu'lin ta'sis imara Islamiyya fi al-'Iraq," *Al Arabiya*, October 15, 2006, http://www.alarabiya.net/articles/2006/10 /15/28296.html.

40. The title of this section is taken from my *Foreign Affairs* article, "State of Confusion," September 10, 2014, http://www.foreignaffairs.com/art icles/141976/william-mccants/state-of-confusion.

41. On the Islamic State's ambiguous use of prepositions, see Bunzel, "Ideology," 18.

42. In the nine-minute audio recording announcing the founding of the Islamic State, spokesman Muharib al-Juburi does not refer to al-Qaeda's role in the state, although he provides multiple justifications for the state's establishment. See Muharib al-Juburi, "al-I'lan 'an qiyam Dawlat al-'Iraq al-Islamiyya," October 15, 2006, https://archive.org/details /song-of-terror-main-8.

43. Abu Ayyub al-Masri (aka Abu Hamza al-Muhajir), "Sayuhzam al-jam' wa-yuwallun al-dubur," June 13, 2006, *al-Majmu' li-qadat Dawlat al-'Iraq al-Islamiyya* (Nukhbat al-I'lam al-Jihadi, 2010).

44. Akram Hijazi, "Ta'qiban 'ala i'lan Dawlat al-'Iraq al-Islamiyya," *Almoraqeb*, October 19, 2006, http://www.almoraqeb.net/main/articles-action-show -id-40.htm.

45. "Abu Abi" [online pseudonym], "al-Qawl al-Fasl fi mas'alat al-bay'a: Hal hiya li-Shaykh Usama am al-Mulla 'Umar am Abu 'Umar al-Baghdadi," *Shabakat Filistin li-l-Hiwar*, October 16, 2006, https://www.paldf.net/fo rum/showthread.php?t=87326.

46. Adam Gadahn, "Letter from Adam Gadahn [English translation]," personal correspondence to unknown recipient, Harmony Program, Combating Terrorism Center at West Point, January 2011, https://www.ctc .usma.edu/v2/wp-content/uploads/2013/10/Letter-from-Adam-Ga dahn-Translation.pdf. Original Arabic version available at https://www .ctc.usma.edu/v2/wp-content/uploads/2013/10/Letter-from-Adam-Ga dahn-Original.pdf.

47. See Ayman al-Zawahiri, "Shahada li-haqan dima' al-mujahidin bi-l-Sham," *Mu'assasat al-Sahab*, May 3, 2014, 5, https://pietervanostaeyen .wordpress.com/2014/05/03/dr-ayman-az-zawahiri-testimonial-to-pre serve-the-blood-of-mujahideen-in-as-sham/. A senior al-Qaeda operative, Fadil Harun, was equally critical of the timing of the Islamic State's establishment: "The decision to declare a state was improper and its timing was not appropriate. There is no doubt that al-Qaeda nowadays is not the same as it was during the era of Shaykh al-Zarqawi." Harun rightly

guessed Bin Laden had not known of the state's declaration prior to the event. "The news is relayed to him vaguely and after everything happens. Then he has no choice but to support it because we all want to have a state in Iraq, led by our brother al-Baghdadi." Rather than seeking Bin Laden's blessing, "the brothers took over some areas in some provinces and governed by the laws of God." Instead of declaring a state, Harun believes "they should have announced Islamic provinces . . . because according to my knowledge, the concept of a state is greater, requires more obligations and preserving it is more difficult." See Fadil Harun, *al-Harb 'ala al-Islam: Qissat Fadil Harun*, 2 vols., February 26, 2009, 2: 134–135; vol. 1 available at https://www.ctc.usma.edu/posts/the-war-against-islam-the -story-of-fazul-harun-part-1-original-language-2; vol. 2 available at https://www.ctc.usma.edu/posts/the-war-against-islam-the-story-of -fazul-harun-part-2-original-language-2.

48. Zawahiri, "Shahada," 1–2.
49. Abu Ayyub al-Masri, "In al-hukm illa li-Allah," November 10, 2006, *al-Majmu' li-qadat Dawlat al-'Iraq al-Islamiyya* (Nukhbat al-I'lam al-Jihadi, 2010).
50. Abu Umar al-Baghdadi, "Wa-qul ja'a al-haqq wa-zahaqa al-batil," December 22, 2006, *al-Majmu' li-qadat Dawlat al-'Iraq al-Islamiyya* (Nukhbat al-I'lam al-Jihadi, 2010).
51. Statement from the Islamic State Ministry of Media, February 13, 2007, http://forum.ma3ali.net/showthread.php?t=273221.
52. Maamoun Youssef, "Al-Qaeda Chief Appointed Minister of War," *Washington Post*, April 19, 2007, http://www.washingtonpost.com/wp-dyn /content/article/2007/04/19/AR2007041901149.html.
53. Abu al-Walid al-Ansari, "Risala nasiha li-Abi 'Umar al-Baghdadi min al-Shaykh Abi al-Walid al-Ansari," *Nukhbat al-Fikr*, October 2014, https:// ia902608.us.archive.org/11/items/Abu.al.Walid.al.Ansari.New/naseha .pdf. See Bunzel, "Ideology," 22. On Ansari, see Kévin Jackson, "Al-Qaeda's Top Scholar," *Jihadica*, September 25, 2014, http://www.jihadica .com/al-qaedas-top-scholar/#more-2457.
54. Hamid al-Ali, "al-Su'al: Hal man la yubayi'u (Dawlat al-'Iraq al-Islamiyya) 'usa?! Wa-hal huwa wajib al-'asr?!" *H-Alali.net*, April 4, 2007, http:// www.h-alali.cc/f_open.php?id=1a55240a-3422-102a-9c4c-0010dc91cf69.
55. Atiyya Abd al-Rahman, "Letter from Hafiz Sultan [English translation]," personal correspondence from Atiyya Abd al-Rahman to Mustafa Ahmad Uthman Abu al-Yazid (aka Sa'id al-Masri), SOCOM-2012-0000011, Harmony Program, Combating Terrorism Center at West Point, March 28, 2007, https://www.ctc.usma.edu/posts/letter-from-hafiz-sultan-english-translation-2. Original Arabic version available at https://www.ctc .usma.edu/posts/letter-from-hafiz-sultan-original-language-2. In his 2014 "Shahada," Zawahiri identifies the author and recipient of the letter.
56. Abd al-Rahman, "Letter from Hafiz Sultan."
57. See Gadahn, "Letter from Adam Gadahn."
58. Ayman al-Zawahiri, "al-Liqa' al-rabi' li-Mu'assasat al-Sahab ma'a Ayman al-Zawahiri," December 16, 2007, https://nokbah.com/~w3/?p=110. Accessed in December 2014 before it was taken down.
59. The video announcement of the Islamic State's founding shows its spokesman speaking in front of a generic black flag with the Muslim profession of faith inscribed on it. See "Islamic State Announcement

Subtitles Eng 15/10/2006," YouTube video, August 30, 2014, https://www
.youtube.com/watch?v=s1DsXuDHIk0. Videos and online jihadist forums from the period immediately following this announcement indi-
cate that the Islamic State was still using the flag of the Mujahidin Shura
Council that had preceded it. See "Jihadiraq001" [online pseudonym],
"al-Ihtifal bi-i'lan al-Dawla al-Islamiyya fi al-'Iraq," YouTube video, December 1, 2006, https://www.youtube.com/watch?v=Ls_vFXvXDN8;
"Mufaja'a: Suwwar wa-film li-juyush Dawlat al-'Iraq al-Islamiyya / Allahu akbar wa-li-l-Allah al-hamd," *Shabakat Filistin li-l-Hiwar*, October
27, 2006, https://www.paldf.net/forum/showthread.php?t=88987.

60. "A Religious Essay Explaining the Significance of the Banner in Islam [English translation]," Harmony Program, Combating Terrorism Center at West Point, January 2007, https://www.ctc.usma.edu
/posts/a-religious-essay-explaining-the-significance-of-the-banner-in
-islam-english-translation-2. Original Arabic version available at https://
www.ctc.usma.edu/posts/a-religious-essay-explaining-the-significance
-of-the-banner-in-islam-original-language-2. I have used my own translations. Al-Qaeda's media distributor, Fajr li-l-I'lam, released the essay
around January 23, 2007 ("al-'Alam al-jadid li-Dawlat al-'Iraq al-Islamiyya," *Shabakat Filistin li-l-Hiwar*, January 23, 2007, https://www.paldf
.net/forum/showthread.php?t=106152).

61. "Religious Essay."

62. Ibid.

63. Abdülmecit Senturk, "Nâmah Al-Saadah (Blessed Letter) Sent to the
Malik (Ruler) of Ghassan and Transfer to the Ottoman State of the Copy
of Surah Al-Qadr (chapter on Power in the Holy Qur'an) Written by
Caliph Ali," *Journal of Rotterdam Islamic and Social Sciences* 3, 1 (2012):
2–4. In a 1940 article, historian D. M. Dunlop dismissed the authenticity of the letters on the grounds that paleographic analysis conducted at
the British Museum proved the letters were written after the age of the
Prophet. See Dunlop, "Another 'Prophetic' Letter," *Journal of the Royal
Asiatic Society of Great Britain and Ireland* 1 (January 1940): 54–60.

64. Deirdre Elizabeth Jackson, *Marvellous to Behold: Miracles in Medieval
Manuscripts* (London: British Library, 2007), 66.

65. "Religious Essay."

66. Dominic Lieven, *Empire: The Russian Empire and Its Rivals* (New Haven,
CT: Yale University Press, 2001), 156.

67. Hijazi, "Ta'qiban."

68. "Religious Essay."

69. Nu'aym bin Hammad, *Kitab al-fitan* (Beirut: Dar al-Fikr li-l-Taba'a,
1992), 226, 228.

70. The Qur'an is filled with vague references to the Day of Judgment and
the end of the world but has few specifics. See Todd Lawson, "Paradise in
the Quran and the Music of Apocalypse," in *Roads to Paradise: Eschatology
and Concepts of the Hereafter in Islam*, 2 vols., eds. Sebastian Günther and
Todd Lawson (Leiden, Netherlands: Brill, 2015).

71. Ibn Khaldun, *The Muqaddimah: An Introduction to History*, transl. Franz
Rosenthal (Princeton, NJ: Princeton University Press, 1967), 196, 198.

72. Cassius Dio, *Roman History* 69.12.1–14.3. For an online edition see *Dio's
Rome [Roman History], Volume V, Books 61–76 (AD. 54–211) An Historical Narrative Originally Composed in Greek During the Reigns of Septimius*

Severus, Geta and Caracalla, Macrinus, Elagabalus and Alexander Severus: And Now Presented in English Form by Herbert Baldwin Foster, book 69, chs. 12–14, Project Gutenberg EBook #10890, http://www.gutenberg.org/files/10890/10890-h/10890-h.htm.

73. Jay Rubenstein, *Armies of Heaven: The First Crusade and the Quest for Apocalypse* (New York: Basic Books, 2011). For an overview of European apocalypticism prior to the Crusades, see James Palmer, *The Apocalypse in the Early Middle Ages* (Cambridge, UK: Cambridge University Press, 2014).

74. Bruce Hoffman, *Inside Terrorism* (New York: Columbia University Press, 2006), 98–100.

75. Jeffrey Kaplan, "The Fifth Wave: The New Tribalism," *Terrorism and Political Violence* 19, no. 4 (2007): 554; Eleanor Beevor, "Why Cults Work: The Power Games of the Islamic State and the Lord's Resistance Army," *War on the Rocks*, March 18, 2015, http://warontherocks.com/2015/03/why-cults-work-the-power-games-of-the-islamic-state-and-the-lords-resistance-army/.

76. Allen Fromherz, *The Almohads: The Rise of an Islamic Empire* (London: I.B. Tauris, 2012), 135–186.

77. Farhad Daftary, *The Ismā'īllīs: Their History and Doctrines* (Cambridge, UK: Cambridge University Press, 1990), 129.

78. Khalid bin Ibrahim al-Dubayan, "al-'Aqida al-'askariyya 'inda Ibn Tumart mu'assis Dawlat al-Muwahhidin," 20–22, https://www.google.com/url?sa=t&rct=j&q=&esrc=s&source=web&cd=5&ved=0CEUQFjAE&url=https%3A%2F%2Ffaculty.sau.edu.sa%2Ffiledownload%2Fdoc-2-doc-0cb82dbdcda47e2ad7b7aaf69573906e-original.doc&ei=6qXsVKLbC4G_ggTJ14LQDg&usg=AFQjCNFX62q9sDkibk0Owlbcx7gy0zudrA&sig2=UukgssbVL9WkzIPe1NKFZg&bvm=bv.86475890,d.eXY&cad=rja; Paul E. Walker, ed. and transl., *Orations of the Fatimid Caliphs: Festival Sermons of the Ismaili Imams* (London: I.B. Tauris, 2009), 72–76.

79. Patricia Crone, *God's Rule—Government and Islam: Six Centuries of Medieval Islamic Political Thought* (New York: Columbia University Press, 2004), 77–78.

80. Bernard Lewis, *Race and Slavery in the Middle East: An Historical Inquiry* (New York: Oxford University Press, 1990), 38.

81. Sulaym bin Qays al-Hilali, *Kitab Sulaym bin Qays al-Hilali*, ed. Muhammad Baqir al-Ansari (Qom, Iran: Nashr al-Hadi, 2000), 282. See also Crone, *God's Rule*, 85.

82. Patricia Crone, *The Nativist Prophets of Early Islamic Iran: Rural Revolt and Local Zoroastrianism* (New York: Cambridge University Press, 2012), 126.

83. Ibn Jarir al-Tabari, *Tarikh al-Tabari: Tarikh al-rusul wa-l-muluk*, vol. 7 (Cairo: Dar al-Ma'arif bi-Misr, 1960–1977), 391. See also Crone, *Nativist Prophets*, 19.

84. Hilali, *Kitab Sulaym*, 285.

85. Nu'aym bin Hammad, *Kitab al-fitan*, 118.

86. Ibid., 188.

87. Khalil Athamina, "The Black Banners and the Socio-Political Significance of Flags and Slogans in Medieval Islam," *Arabica* T. 36, Fasc. 3 (November 1989): 307–326, 313.

88. Ibn Khaldun, *Muqaddimah*, 50–51.

89. Faruq Umar, *Buhuth fi al-tarikh al-'Abbasi* (Beirut: Maktabat al-Nahda, 1977), 246.

90. Abu Hanifa Ahmad bin Dawud al-Dinawari, *al-Akhbar al-tiwal* (Leiden, Netherlands: Brill, 1888), 186.

91. Athamina, "Black Banners," 309.

92. Ibn Jarir al-Tabari, *The History of al-Tabari, Vol. XXVII: The 'Abbasid Revolution*, transl. John Alden Williams (Albany, NY: State University of New York Press, 1985), 65–66.

93. Crone, *God's Rule*, 87–88. Originally, the Arabic word *dawla* had the same ambiguous meaning as our English "revolution," meaning a turn or change.

94. Bernard Lewis, *The Language of Political Islam* (Chicago: University of Chicago Press, 1988), 35–36.

95. "The World's Muslims: Unity and Diversity," Pew Research Center, August 9, 2012, http://www.pewforum.org/2012/08/09/the-worlds-mus lims-unity-and-diversity-executive-summary/. For comparison, 41 percent of American Christians surveyed by Pew in 2010 believed Jesus would return in the next forty years. See "Public Sees a Future Full of Promise and Peril," Pew Research Center, June 22, 2010, http://www.people -press.org/2010/06/22/public-sees-a-future-full-of-promise-and-peril/.

96. Jean-Pierre Filiu, *Apocalypse in Islam*, transl. M. B. DeBevoise (Berkeley: University of California Press, 2011), 186.

97. Ibid., 121–140.

98. "Tawfiq 123" [online pseudonym], "Nahnu umma lam yukallifuna Allah bi-ma'rifat shakhs al-Mahdi qablu khurujihi," *Shabakat Ana al-Muslim li-l-Hiwar al-Islami*, April 23, 2007, http://www.muslm.org/vb/showthread. php?225702. See also Reuven Paz, "Global Jihad and the United States: Interpretation of the New World Order of Usama Bin Ladin," *Project for the Research of Islamist Movements* (PRISM), Occasional Papers 1, 1, PRISM Series of Global Jihad 1 (March 2003), http://www.google.com /url?sa=t&rct=j&q=&esrc=s&source=web&cd=1&ved=0CB4QFjAA& url=http%3A%2F%2Fwww.e-prism.org%2Fimages%2FPRISM%252 0no%25201.doc&ei=aOrPVODlG9eHsQS48YCIAQ&usg=AFQjCNH 4N9N2OqBQDD5E5M7l1Fm_726WIg&bvm=bv.85076809,d.cWc.

99. Thomas Hegghammer and Stéphane Lacroix, "Rejectionist Islamism in Saudi Arabia: The Story of Juhayman Al-'Utaybi Revisited," *International Journal of Middle East Studies* 39, no. 2 (February 2007): 103–122, 112–113. See also their book-length treatment, *The Meccan Rebellion: The Story of Juhayman al-'Utaybi Revisited* (Bristol, UK: Amal Press: 2011).

100. Ali H. Soufan and Daniel Freedman, *The Black Banners: The Inside Story of 9/11 and the War Against al-Qaeda* (New York: W. W. Norton, 2011), xvii–xix.

101. Harun, *Harb*, 2:41.

102. On the book's reception, see Brynjar Lia, *Architect of Global Jihad: The Life of Al-Qaida Strategist Abu Mus'ab al-Suri* (New York: Oxford University Press, 2009). Zawahiri mentions the book favorably in his *al-Tabri'a: Risala fi tabri'at ummat al-qalam wa-l-sayf min manqasa tuhmat al-khawar wa-l-du'f*, March 2008, http://www.ek-ls.org/forum/showthread.php?t=1 27920&highlight=%C3%ED%E3%E4. I accessed the site in December 2014 before it was taken down.

103. Filiu, *Apocalypse*, 189.

CHAPTER 2

1. "Rewards for Justice Targets al-Qaida in Iraq's New Leader," U.S. Department of State, July 3, 2006, http://iipdigital.usembassy.gov/st /english/article/2006/07/20060703141847idybeekcm0.5817835.html #axzz3Vmd3N5Cz; Mike Mount, "Reward for Wanted Terrorist Drops," *CNN*, May 13, 2008, http://edition.cnn.com/2008/WORLD /meast/05/13/pentagon.masri.value/.

2. Sadiq al-Iraqi, "Zawjat Abu [*sic*] Ayyub al-Masri: wasalna Baghdad qablu suqut nizam Saddam, wa-zawji ghamid wa-mutashaddid," *al-Riyad*, April 29, 2010, http://www.alriyadh.com/520823; "Rewards for Justice," U.S. Department of State; Dexter Filkins, "U.S. Identifies Successor to Zarqawi," *New York Times*, June 15, 2006, http://www.nytimes .com/2006/06/15/world/middleeast/15cnd-iraq.html?_r=0.

3. Abu Sulayman al-Utaybi, "Risalat al-Shaykh Abi Sulayman al-'Utaybi li-l-qiyada fi Khurasan," personal correspondence to al-Qaeda leadership, *Shabakat Ana al-Muslim li-l-Hiwar al-Islami*, April 28, 2007, http://just paste.it/do3r. The letter appeared online November 24, 2013.

4. Abu Ayyub al-Masri, "Sayuhzam al-jam' wa-yuwallun al-dubur," June 13, 2006. Abu Umar al-Baghdadi, the nominal head of the Islamic State, also anticipated going to aid the Mahdi in Mecca after consolidating gains in Iraq, then "invading the Jewish state, and retaking Jerusalem." See Abu Umar al-Baghdadi, "Hasad al-sinin bi-Dawlat al-Muwahhidin," April 17, 2007, *al-Majmu' li-qadat Dawlat al-'Iraq al-Islamiyya* (Nukhbut al-I'lam al-Jihadi, 2010).

5. Utaybi, "Risalat al-Shaykh." Abu Sulayman's allegation that Abu Umar al-Baghdadi was just Masri's puppet echoes an earlier charge made by Khalid al-Mashhadani, the head of the Islamic State's media operations, who was captured by American forces in July 2007. Mashhadani told his interrogators that Baghdadi's statements were read by an actor and that the man himself was just a myth. See Bill Roggio, "Islamic State of Iraq—an al Qaeda Front," *Long War Journal*, July 18, 2007, http:// www.longwarjournal.org/archives/2007/07/islamic_state_of_ira.php #ixzz3PrInd6mh.

6. "Abu Ahmad" [online pseudonym], "al-Haqa'iq al-mukhfa hawla Dawlat al-Baghdadi," *al-Durar al-Shamiyya*, April 5, 2014, http://eldorar.com /node/45368.

7. Abu Usama al-Iraqi, "Muhattat min jihad al-Amir al-Baghdadi," *Muntada al-Minbar al-I'lami al-Jihadi*, June 9, 2012, https://www.mnbr.info/vb /showthread.php?t=11332&langid=3&styleid=18.

8. Abu Ahmad, "Haqa'iq."

9. Utaybi, "Risalat al-Shaykh."

10. Sudarsan Raghavan, "Sunni Factions Split with al-Qaeda Group," *Washington Post*, April 14, 2007, http://www.washingtonpost.com/wp-dyn /content/article/2007/04/13/AR2007041300294.html.

11. "Islamic Army in Iraq Accuses al-Qa'ida in Iraq of 'Transgressing Islamic Law,'" Open Source Center, April 5, 2007, https://groups.yahoo.com /neo/groups/alphacity/conversations/topics/1735. For background, see "Islamic Army in Iraq," *Mapping Militant Organizations*, Stanford University, July 23, 2014, http://web.stanford.edu/group/mappingmilitants /cgi-bin/groups/view/5.

12. Brian Fishman, "Dysfunction and Decline: Lessons Learned from Inside al-Qa'ida in Iraq," Harmony Project, Combating Terrorism Center at West Point, March 16, 2009, 11–13, https://www.ctc.usma.edu/posts/dysfunction-and-decline-lessons-learned-from-inside-al-qaida-in-iraq.

13. Abu Ahmad, "al-Haqa'iq." Abu Ahmad, who claims to be a former member of the Islamic State, alleged that Syrian intelligence agents and Sunni insurgents affiliated with the Saudi government had joined.

14. "Letter from Unknown al-Qaeda Leader to Abu Ayyub al-Masri," January 25, 2008, http://iraqslogger.powweb.com/downloads/aqi_leadership_letters_sept_08.pdf. This is one of several letters in the exchange, portions of which Tony Badran translated in Bill Roggio, Daveed Gartenstein-Ross, and Tony Badran, "Intercepted Letters from al-Qaeda Leaders Shed Light on State of Network in Iraq," Foundation for the Defense of Democracy, September 12, 2008, http://www.defenddemocracy.org/media-hit/intercepted-letters-from-al-qaeda-leaders-shed-light-on-state-of-network-in/. I have used Badran's translations when I can, making a few tweaks here and there. The remaining translations are mine.

15. Utaybi, "Risalat al-Shaykh."

16. See the correspondence between Ansar al-Sunna and the Islamic State in Fishman, "Dysfunction," 8–9.

17. For Ansar al-Sunna, see Michael R. Gordon and Bernard E. Trainor, *The Endgame: The Inside Story of the Struggle for Iraq, from George W. Bush to Barack Obama* (New York: Vintage Books, 2013), 263. For the Islamic Army, see Michael Weiss and Hassan Hassan, *ISIS: Inside the Army of Terror* [Google edition] (New York: Regan Arts, 2015), 79.

18. Abu Mus'ab al-Zarqawi, "Zarqawi Letter [English translation]," personal correspondence to Osama bin Laden and Ayman al-Zawahiri, February 2004, U.S. Department of State Archive, http://2001-2009.state.gov/p/nea/rls/31694.htm.

19. Karl Vick, "Insurgent Alliance Is Fraying in Fallujah, *Washington Post*, October 13, 2004, http://www.washingtonpost.com/wp-dyn/articles/A28105-2004Oct12.html.

20. Ellen Knickmeyer and Jonathan Finer, "Insurgents Assert Control over Town near Syrian Border," *Washington Post*, September 6, 2005, http://www.washingtonpost.com/wp-dyn/content/article/2005/09/05/AR2005090500313.html.

21. "Ba'da sharit Abi Usama al-'Iraqi: Hal daqqat sa'at al-firaq bayna al-Qa'ida wa-sunnat al-'Iraq?" *Asharq al-Awsat*, October 13, 2006, http://archive.aawsat.com/details.asp?article=387171&issueno=10181#.VMUd5ivF-Ds.

22. "Islamist Sheikh Abu Osama Al-'Iraqi Denounces Al-Qaeda in Iraq for Atrocities against Sunnis," Middle East Media Research Institute (MEMRI), Jihad & Terrorism Studies Project, Special Dispatch No. 1340, October 31, 2006, http://www.memri.org/report/en/0/0/0/0/0/0/1926.htm. The video was originally released on October 12, 2006. See "Ibn Alfalojah" [online pseudonym], "Risalat al-Shaykh Abu Usama al-'Iraqi li-l-Shaykh Usama bin Ladin rahimahu Allah 'am 2006," Vimeo video, May 2014, http://vimeo.com/96742098.

23. Ibid.

24. Ibid.

25. Ibid.

26. Ibid.
27. See Cole Bunzel's translation in "From Paper State to Caliphate: The Ideology of the Islamic State," The Brookings Project on U.S. Relations with the Islamic World, Analysis Paper No. 19 (March 2015): 38, http://www.brookings.edu/~/media/research/files/papers/2015/03/ideology-of-islamic-state-bunzel/the-ideology-of-the-islamic-state.pdf.
28. Abu Umar al-Baghdadi, "Qul inni 'ala bayyina min Rabbi," March 13, 2007, al-Majmu' li-qadat Dawlat al-'Iraq al-Islamiyya (Nukhbat al-I'lam al-Jihadi, 2010). In Husaybah in 2005, residents complained that music stores and satellite dishes were banned and their women were being forced to wear full-body veils. When the Islamic Army of Iraq criticized Baghdadi for his draconian laws, the prohibition of satellite dishes and the requirement to cover women's faces were among its complaints. See Ellen Knickmeyer, "Zarqawi Followers Clash with Local Sunnis," Washington Post, May 29, 2005, http://www.washingtonpost.com/wp-dyn/content/article/2005/05/28/AR2005052800967.html; "Islamic Army in Iraq Accuses al-Qa'ida," Open Source Center.
29. Uthman bin Abd al-Rahman al-Tamimi, ed., "I'lam al-anam bi-milad Dawlat al-Islam," Minbar al-Tawhid wa-l-Jihad, January 7, 2007. For a summary of the document, see Brian Fishman, "Fourth Generation Governance: Sheikh Tamimi Defends the Islamic State of Iraq," Combating Terrorism Center at West Point, March 23, 2007, https://www.ctc.usma.edu/posts/fourth-generation-governance-sheikh-tamimi-defends-the-islamic-state-of-iraq.
30. Tamimi, "I'lam," 36.
31. Ibid., 38.
32. M. Cherif Bassiouni, The Shari'a and Islamic Criminal Justice in Time of War and Peace (New York: Cambridge University Press, 2014), 134–141.
33. Thomas Friedman, "Letter from Baghdad," New York Times, September 5, 2007, http://www.nytimes.com/2007/09/05/opinion/05Friedman.html?_r=0.
34. Mohammed M. Hafez, "Al-Qaeda Losing Ground in Iraq," CTC Sentinel 1, no. 1 (December 15, 2007): n.p., https://www.ctc.usma.edu/posts/al-qaida-losing-ground-in-iraq.
35. Wasim al-Dandashi, "Qadi Dawlat al-'Iraq al-Islamiyya Sa'udi lam yakmal dirasatihi," Elaph, April 25, 2007, http://elaph.com/ElaphWeb/Politics/2007/4/229045.htm.
36. See postscript in Utaybi, "Risalat al-Shaykh."
37. "Letter from Unknown al-Qaeda Leader to Abu Ayyub al-Masri," November 19, 2007, http://iraqslogger.powweb.com/downloads/aqi_leadership_letters_sept_08.pdf?PHPSESSID=b155c5eb6418ac653ca2ce675e6fb7f8. This is another letter in the exchange cited in note 14.
38. "Letter from Unknown al-Qaeda Leader to Abu Ayyub al-Masri," January 25, 2008. See note 14.
39. In 2013, Abu Sulayman's letter was posted online, so we know what his allegations were. See Utaybi, "Risalat al-Shaykh." Al-Qaeda also summarized his allegations in their correspondence with Masri.
40. See Utaybi, "Risalat al-Shaykh."
41. "Letter from Unknown al-Qaeda Leader to Abu Ayyub al-Masri," January 25, 2008.
42. Ibid.

43. Utaybi, "Risalat al-Shaykh."

44. "Letter from Unknown al-Qaeda Leader to Abu Ayyub al-Masri," January 25, 2008. Badran identifies the "paternal uncle" as Sayf al-Adl, but the email of the "paternal uncle" appended to the end of the message is written by Zawahiri.

45. "Letter from Unknown al-Qaeda Leader to Abu Ayyub al-Masri," January 25, 2008. Masri's predecessor, Abu Mus'ab al-Zarqawi, was equally apocalyptic in his rhetoric but avoided mentioning the Mahdi in his public statements; see David Cook, "Abu Musa'b [sic] al-Suri and Abu Musa'b [sic] al-Zarqawi: The Apocalyptic Theorist and the Apocalyptic Practitioner," unpublished, 14.

46. "Letter from Unknown al-Qaeda Leader to Abu Ayyub al-Masri," January 25, 2008.

47. Ibid.

48. "Letter from Ayman al-Zawahiri to Abu Umar al-Baghdadi," March 6, 2008. This is another letter in the batch cited in note 14.

49. "Letter from Unknown al-Qaeda Leader to Abu Ayyub al-Masri," March 10, 2008. This letter quotes Masri's earlier letter.

50. Amit Paley, "Al-Qaeda in Iraq Leader May Be in Afghanistan," *Washington Post*, July 31, 2008, http://www.washingtonpost.com/wp-dyn/content/article/2008/07/30/AR2008073003239.html.

51. William McCants, "Death of a Sulayman," *Jihadica*, May 13, 2008, http://www.jihadica.com/death-of-a-sulayman/.

52. Jessica D. Lewis, "Al-Qaeda in Iraq Resurgent: The Breaking the Walls Campaign, Part I," Institute for the Study of War, Middle East Security Report 14 (September 2013): 8, http://www.understandingwar.org/sites/default/files/AQI-Resurgent-10Sept_0.pdf.

53. See Bunzel, "Ideology," 22; Sadiq al-Iraqi, "Zawjat Abu [sic] Ayyub."

54. William McCants, "'The Painful Truth: al-Qaeda Is Losing the War in Iraq,'" *Jihadica*, October 1, 2008, http://www.jihadica.com/the-painful-truth-al-qaeda-is-losing-the-war-in-iraq/.

55. William McCants, "Lamenting Loss of Anbar, Apprehensive of Jihad's Future in Iraq," *Jihadica*, September 5, 2008, http://www.jihadica.com/lamenting-loss-of-anbar-apprehensive-of-jihads-future-in-iraq/.

56. William McCants, "Spinning the Failure of the Islamic State of Iraq," *Jihadica*, August 13, 2008, http://www.jihadica.com/spinning-the-failure-of-the-islamic-state-of-iraq/.

57. Daniel Kimmage and Kathleen Ridolfo, "Iraqi Insurgent Media—The War of Images and Ideas: How Sunni Insurgents in Iraq and Their Supporters Worldwide Are Using the Media," RadioFreeEurope/Radio-Liberty, RFE/RL Special Report, June 26, 2007, http://www.rferl.org/content/article/1077316.html.

58. Fishman, "Dysfunction," 16–20. For the original, see: https://www.ctc.usma.edu/v2/wp-content/uploads/2013/09/Analysis-of-the-State-of-ISI-Original.pdf; for the translation, see: https://www.ctc.usma.edu/v2/wp-content/uploads/2013/09/Analysis-of-the-State-of-ISI-Translation.pdf.

59. Adam Gadahn, "Letter from Adam Gadahn [English translation]," personal correspondence to unknown recipient, Harmony Program, Combating Terrorism Center at West Point, January 2011, 7–9, https://www.ctc.usma.edu/v2/wp-content/uploads/2013/10/Letter-from-Adam-Ga

dahn-Translation.pdf. Original Arabic version available at https://www
.ctc.usma.edu/v2/wp-content/uploads/2013/10/Letter-from-Adam-Ga
dahn-Original.pdf.

60. Clint Watts, Jacob Shapiro, and Vahid Brown, *Al-Qa'ida's (Mis)adven-
tures in the Horn of Africa*, Harmony Program, Combating Terrorism
Center at West Point, July 2, 2007, 89–100, https://www.ctc.usma.edu
/posts/al-qaidas-misadventures-in-the-horn-of-africa.

61. Fadil Harun, *al-Harb 'ala al-Islam: Qissat Fadil Harun*, 2 vols., February 26, 2009, 2: 68–69; vol. 1 available at https://www.ctc.usma.edu
/posts/the-war-against-islam-the-story-of-fazul-harun-part-1-original
-language-2; vol. 2 available at https://www.ctc.usma.edu/posts/the-war
-against-islam-the-story-of-fazul-harun-part-2-original-language-2.

62. Ibid., 2: 134–135.

63. Osama bin Laden, "Letter to Nasir al-Wuhayshi [English transla-
tion]," personal correspondence to Nasir al-Wuhayshi (aka Abu Basir),
SOCOM-2012-0000016, Harmony Program, Combating Terrorism
Center at West Point, 2010, 13–14, https://www.ctc.usma.edu/posts/let
ter-to-nasir-al-wuhayshi-english-translation-2. Original Arabic version
available at https://www.ctc.usma.edu/posts/letter-to-nasir-al-wuhay
shi-original-language-2. The letter was probably drafted by one of Bin
Laden's lieutenants. See Nelly Lahoud et al., "Letters from Abbottabad:
Bin Ladin Sidelined?" Harmony Program, Combating Terrorism Center at West Point, May 3, 2012, https://www.ctc.usma.edu/posts/letters
-from-abbottabad-bin-ladin-sidelined. Bin Laden also advised the Taliban and other jihadist groups in Afghanistan and Pakistan to avoid alienating the tribes, citing the Islamic State as an example of what not to
do: "As for the tribes that joined or about to join the American Awakenings project, please give them a stern warning that an excessive reac-
tion from their part towards these tribes will only increase the latter's
unity and desire to fight against them. It will be useful to clarify the
matter by citing the experience of our brothers in Iraq." See Osama bin
Laden, "Letter from Osama bin Laden to 'Atiyya Abd al-Rahman [Eng-
lish translation]," personal correspondence, 432-10-CR-019-S-4-RJD,
August 7, 2010, available at *Jihadica*, http://www.jihadica.com/wp-con
tent/uploads/2015/03/432-10-CR-019-S-4-RJD-Translation.pdf. Original Arabic version available at http://www.jihadica.com/wp-content/up
loads/2015/03/432-10-CR-019-S-4-RJD-Original.pdf.

64. Osama bin Laden, "Ila ahlina bi-l-'Iraq," audiotape message, *Mu'assasat
al-Sahab*, broadcast by *Al Jazeera* on October 22, 2007. Arabic transcript
of message available at "Sahab" [online pseudonym], "Tafrigh risalat
al-Shaykh: Usama bin Ladan—hafizahu Allah," *Shabakat Ana al-Muslim li-l-Hiwar al-Islami*, October 24, 2007, http://www.muslm.org/vb
/showthread.php?259268. English transcript by Laura Mansfield available at Andrew Cochran, "Bin Laden Sounds the Call of Defeat in Iraq
(updated 10/23 with transcript)," *Counterterrorism Blog*, October 23, 2007,
http://counterterrorismblog.org/2007/10/bin_laden_sounds_the_call
_of_d.php.

65. "DOD News Briefing with Gen. Odierno from the Pentagon," news
transcript, U.S. Department of Defense, June 4, 2010, http://www.de
fense.gov/transcripts/transcript.aspx?transcriptid=4632; Weiss and Hassan, *ISIS*, 81.

66. "Bayan min Majlis Shura Dawlat al-'Iraq al-Islamiyya," *Markaz al-Fajr li-l-I'lam*, May 15, 2010, posted by "Murasil al-Fajr" [online pseudonym] to *Muntadayat Shabakat Shumukh al-Islam* on May 16, 2010, http://www .jihadica.com/wp-content/uploads/2015/03/Bayan-min-Majlis-Shura -Dawlat-al-Iraq-al-Islamiyya.pdf.

67. Abu Bakr al-Baghdadi, "Wa-ya'ba Allah illa an yutimm nurahu," *Mu'assasat al-Furqan*, July 21, 2012, https://ia601207.us.archive.org/14/it ems/2b-bkr-bghdd/143393.pdf. See also Bunzel, "Ideology," 24.

CHAPTER 3

1. Gregory D. Johnsen, *The Last Refuge: Yemen, al-Qaeda, and America's War in Arabia* (New York: W. W. Norton, 2012), 220–221.

2. Fahd Al-Riya'i, "'Weak and Misled' Militant Not Al-Qaeda Material," *Saudi Gazette*, May 29, 2010, http://www.saudigazette.com.sa/index .cfm?method=home.regcon&contentID=2010052973772.

3. Robert Worth, "Is Yemen the Next Afghanistan?" *New York Times*, July 6, 2010, http://www.nytimes.com/2010/07/11/magazine/11Yemen-t.ht ml?pagewanted=all&_r=0.

4. Nayif Muhammad al-Qahtani, "Liqa' ma'a ahad al-matlubin (Abu Hammam al-Qahtani)," *Sada al-malahim* 1 (January 2008): 7–9, available at https://ia801403.us.archive.org/25/items/Sada-almala7em/Sada-almala 7em1.pdf.

5. *Sada al-malahim* 2 (March 2008), https://ia801403.us.archive.org/25/it ems/Sada-almala7em/Sada-almala7em2.pdf.

6. Robbie Brown and Kim Severson, "2nd American in Strike Waged Qaeda Media War," *New York Times*, September 30, 2011, http://www.nytimes .com/2011/10/01/world/middleeast/samir-khan-killed-by-drone-spun -out-of-the-american-middle-class.html?_r=0.

7. J. M. Berger, "The Myth of Anwar al-Awlaki," *Foreign Policy*, August 10, 2011, http://foreignpolicy.com/2011/08/10/the-myth-of-anwar-al-awlaki/.

8. Anwar al-Awlaki, "Shaykh Anwar's Message to the American People and Muslims in the West," *Inspire* 1 (Summer 1431/2010): 56–58, available at *Jihadology*, https://azelin.files.wordpress.com/2010/06/aqap-inspire-mag azine-volume-1-uncorrupted.pdf.

9. *Sada al-malahim* 6, 7, 8, 10, 12, 13, 14, and 15.

10. For background on the fighting, see Johnsen, *Last Refuge*, 266.

11. Xiong Tong, ed., "Al-Qaida Wing Claims to Form 12,000-Strong Army in Southern Yemen," *Xinhua*, July 30, 2010, http://news.xinhuanet.com /english2010/world/2010-07/30/c_13422488.htm.

12. Ten years ago, a team of Arabists and I used citation analysis (counting footnote references) to determine Maqdisi's rank in the jihadist scholarly hierarchy. He was at the very top. See William McCants, ed., "Militant Ideology Atlas: Executive Report," Combating Terrorism Center at West Point, November 2006, https://www.ctc.usma.edu/wp-content/up loads/2012/04/Atlas-ExecutiveReport.pdf. For Maqdisi's biography and teachings, see Joas Wagemakers, *A Quietist Jihadi: The Ideology and Influence of Abu Muhammad al-Maqdisi* (New York: Cambridge University Press, 2012).

13. Online correspondence between "Abu Abd al-Rahman al-Yamani" [online pseudonym] and Abu Muhammad al-Maqdisi, *Minbar al-Tawhid wa-*

l-Jihad, n.d., http://www.tawhed.ws/FAQ/pr?qid=3352&PHPSESSID=f
815327074d11ecd2fd01853dd03b4dc. Maqdisi is addressed respectfully
by the questioner: "The Brothers in Yemen love Shaykh Abu Muhammad al-Maqdisi and consider him their imam . . . . Perhaps the shaykh
would favor the monotheists in Yemen, who are among the youth of the
Peninsula, with his advice and guidance."

14. Ibid. AQAP published the question and Maqdisi's answer in issue 15 of its
    Sada al-malahim (October-November 2010).

15. Maqdisi, response to "Abu Abd al-Rahman al-Yamani."

16. For the full text, see Abu Mus'ab al-Suri, "Mas'uliyyat ahl al-Yaman tujah
    muqaddasat al-Muslimin wa-tharwatihim," *Minbar al-Tawhid wa-l-Jihad*,
    section 3, http://www.tawhed.ws/r?i=wksgfnyz.

17. Ibid., section 4. As for tactics, Suri suggests a range of standard terror-
    ist targets in the Arabian Peninsula: embassies, commercial interests,
    military bases, tourists, and so forth. Suri also countenanced attacks on
    targets in Yemen. See ibid., appendix.

18. Ibid., conclusion.

19. Osama bin Laden, "Letter to Nasir al-Wuhayshi [English transla-
    tion]," personal correspondence to Nasir al-Wuhayshi (aka Abu Basir),
    SOCOM-2012-0000016, Harmony Program, Combating Terrorism
    Center at West Point, 2010, 13–14, https://www.ctc.usma.edu/posts
    /letter-to-nasir-al-wuhayshi-english-translation-2. Regarding the let-
    ter's date, its author mentions AQAP attacks in Ma'rib and Ataq. The
    first attack in Ma'rib was on June 7, 2010; the first in Ataq was on July
    22, 2010. Both attacks were against military personnel. For a timeline of
    AQAP-related attacks in Yemen from 2010 to 2012, see Cody Curran et
    al., "AQAP and Suspected AQAP Attacks in Yemen Tracker 2010, 2011,
    and 2012," *AEI Critical Threats*, May 21, 2012, http://www.criticalthreats
    .org/yemen/aqap-and-suspected-aqap-attacks-yemen-tracker-2010.

20. Bin Laden, "Letter to Nasir al-Wuhayshi," 1. I have modified the
    translation.

21. Ibid., 2.

22. Osama bin Laden, "al-Sabil li-ihbat al-mu'amarat," *Mu'assasat al-Sahab*,
    December 29, 2007, www.tawhed.ws/dl?i=24041002; Cole Bunzel, "From
    Paper State to Caliphate: The Ideology of the Islamic State," The Brook-
    ings Project on U.S. Relations with the Islamic World, Analysis Paper
    No. 19 (March 2015): 28, http://www.brookings.edu/~/media/research
    /files/papers/2015/03/ideology-of-islamic-state-bunzel/the-ideology-of
    -the-islamic-state.pdf.

23. For Bin Laden's change in strategy, see Ryan Evans, "From Iraq to Ye-
    men: al-Qa'ida's Shifting Strategies," *CTC Sentinel* (October 2010), n.p.,
    https://www.ctc.usma.edu/v2/wp-content/uploads/2011/05/CTCSenti
    nel-Vol3Iss101.pdf.

24. Bin Laden, "Letter to Nasir al-Wuhayshi," 2. My translation.

25. Ibid., 3.

26. Ibid., 5.

27. Ibid., 6.

28. Ibid., 4.

29. Osama bin Laden, "Draft Letter from Osama bin Laden to Nasir al-
    Wuhayshi [English translation]," personal correspondence, SOCOM-
    2012-0000017, Harmony Program, Combating Terrorism Center at

West Point, n.d., 3, available at *Jihadica*, http://www.jihadica.com/wp
-content/uploads/2012/05/SOCOM-2012-0000017-Trans.pdf. Original
Arabic version available at http://www.jihadica.com/wp-content/uplo
ads/2012/05/SOCOM-2012-0000017-Orig.pdf. This letter seems to be
an earlier draft of SOCOM-2012-0000016; for a detailed explanation, see
Nelly Lahoud et al., "Letters from Abbottabad: Bin Ladin Sidelined?" 14,
footnote 47, Harmony Program, Combating Terrorism Center at West
Point, May 3, 2012, https://www.ctc.usma.edu/posts/letters-from-abbot
tabad-bin-ladin-sidelined. To distinguish the letter cited in this footnote
from the other letter from Bin Laden to Wuhayshi, this one will hereafter be referred to as Bin Laden, "Draft Letter."

30. Bin Laden, "Draft Letter," 3.

31. F. Gregory Gause, *Oil Monarchies: Domestic and Security Challenges in the
    Arab Gulf States* (New York: Council on Foreign Relations Press, 1994),
    24–25.

32. Bin Laden, "Letter to Nasir al-Wuhayshi," 13–14.

33. Bin Laden, "Draft Letter," 4–5.

34. Ibid., 4.

35. Ibid., 5.

36. Atiyya Abd al-Rahman, "Letter from 'Atiyya Abd al-Rahman to Osama
    bin Laden [English translation]," personal correspondence, 422-10-CR-
    109-S-4-RJD, July 17, 2010, available at *Jihadica*, http://www.jihadica.com
    /wp-content/uploads/2015/03/422-10-CR-109-S-4-RJD-Translation
    .pdf. Original Arabic version available at http://www.jihadica.com/wp
    -content/uploads/2015/03/422-10-CR-109-S-4-RJD-Original.pdf.

37. Nasir al-Wuhayshi, "Second Letter from Abu Basir to Emir of Al-Qaida
    in the Islamic Maghrib," personal correspondence to Abu Mus'ab Abd
    al-Wadud, August 6, 2012, in "Al-Qaida Papers," *Associated Press*; En-
    glish translation and original Arabic version both available at *Long War
    Journal*, http://www.longwarjournal.org/images/al-qaida-papers-how-to
    -run-a-state.pdf.

38. See Mustafa al-Sharqawi, "Tatbiq al-shari'a fi al-Yaman 'taqrir hawla An-
    sar al-Shari'a,'" YouTube video, February 24, 2013, https://www.youtube
    .com/watch?v=Yy8qv52DzVA; "Mujahidi al-Iraq" [online pseudonym],
    "al-Qa'ida tu'lin Abyan al-Yamaniyya imara Islamiyya!" *Shabakat Ana
    al-Muslim li-l-Hiwar al-Islami*, April 27, 2011, http://www.muslm.org/vb
    /archive/index.php/t-434052.html; and "Tanzim al-Qa'ida yu'lin al-
    bayan raqam 1 min idha'at Abyan imara Islamiyya'," *Barakish.net*, March
    29, 2011, http://www.barakish.net/news02.aspx?cat=0&sub=0&id=17420.

39. Letter from Abu Basir al-Tartusi, "Ila al-ikhwa Ansar al-Shari'a fi al-
    Yaman," www.abubaseer.bizland.com/hadath/Read/hadath%2092.doc.
    See also Joas Wagemakers, "Al-Qaida Advises the Arab Spring: Yemen,"
    Jihadica, June 5, 2012, http://www.jihadica.com/al-qaida-advises-the-ar
    ab-spring-yemen/.

40. Robin Simcox, "Ansar al-Sharia and Governance in Southern Ye-
    men," Hudson Institute, December 27, 2012, http://www.hudson.org
    /research/9779-ansar-al-sharia-and-governance-in-southern-yemen.

41. Agence France-Presse, "Osama Bin Laden Believed in Image, and Con-
    sidered Al Qaeda Name Change to Improve 'Brand,'" *Al Arabiya*, June 25,
    2011, http://english.alarabiya.net/articles/2011/06/25/154757.html; Peter
    Bergen, "Bin Laden: Seized Documents Show Delusional Leader and

Micromanager," *CNN*, May 3, 2012, http://www.cnn.com/2012/04/30
/opinion/bergen-bin-laden-document-trove/; Osama bin Laden, "Letter
from Osama bin Laden to Mukhtar Abu al-Zubayr [English translation],"
personal correspondence to Abu al-Zubayr (aka Ahmed Abdi Godane),
SOCOM-2012-0000005, Harmony Program, Combating Terrorism
Center at West Point, August 7, 2010, available at *Jihadica*, http://www
.jihadica.com/wp-content/uploads/2012/05/SOCOM-2012-0000005
-Trans.pdf. Original Arabic version available at http://www.jihadica
.com/wp-content/uploads/2012/05/SOCOM-2012-0000005-Orig.pdf.
See also Aaron Y. Zelin, "Know Your Ansar al-Sharia," Washington Institute for Near East Policy, September 21, 2012, http://www.washing
toninstitute.org/policy-analysis/view/know-your-ansar-al-sharia.

42. Abu Zubayr Adil al-Abab, "Online Question and Answer Session with
Abu Zubayr Adel al-Abab, Shariah Official for Member of al-Qaeda in
the Arabian Peninsula (AQAP) [English translation]," transl. Amany
Soliman, International Centre for the Study of Radicalisation and Political Violence, April 18, 2011, available at *Jihadology*, http://azelin.files
.wordpress.com/2011/04/ghorfah-minbar-al-ane1b9a3c481r-presents
-a-new-audio-message-from-al-qc481_idah-in-the-arabian-peninsulas
-shaykh-abc5ab-zc5abbayr-adc4abl-bc4abn-abdullah-al-abc481b-en.pdf.

43. Ibid., 2.

44. Ibid., 3.

45. Ibid., 7.

46. Ibid., 5.

47. Ibid., 6.

48. William McCants, "Al Qaeda Is Doing Nation-Building. Should We
Worry?" *Foreign Policy*, April 30, 2012, http://foreignpolicy.com/2012/04
/30/al-qaeda-is-doing-nation-building-should-we-worry/.

49. Simcox, "Ansar al-Sharia and Governance in Southern Yemen."

50. Sudarsan Raghavan, "In Yemen, Tribal Militias in a Fierce Battle with
al-Qaeda Wing," *Washington Post*, September 10, 2012, http://www
.washingtonpost.com/world/middle_east/in-yemen-tribal-militias-in-a
-fierce-battle-with-al-qaeda-wing/2012/09/10/0cce6f1e-f2b2-11e1-b74c
-84ed55e0300b_story.html.

51. "Conflict in Yemen: Abyan's Darkest Hour," Amnesty International, December 3, 2012, 19, http://www.amnestyusa.org/sites/default/files/mde
_31.010.2012_conflict_in_yemen_-_abyans_darkest_hour.pdf.

52. Simcox, "Ansar al-Sharia and Governance in Southern Yemen."

53. Ibid.

54. Raghavan, "Tribal Militias."

55. Casey Coombs, "Echoes of Iraq: Yemen's War Against al-Qaeda Takes a
Familiar Turn," *Time*, August 10, 2012, http://world.time.com/2012/08/10
/echoes-of-iraq-yemens-war-against-al-qaeda-takes-a-familiar-turn/.

56. Abu Zubayr Adil al-Abab, "Gains and Benefits of Ansar Al-Sharia
Control of Parts of the Wiyalah's [*sic*] of Abyan and Shabwa," Ansar al-
mujahideen English forum, July 6, 2012, 17, 21–25, 34, 41, in "Al-Qaida
Papers," *Associated Press*; English translation and original Arabic version available at *Long War Journal*, http://www.longwarjournal.org/im
ages/al-qaida-papers-how-to-run-a-state.pdf.

57. Nasir al-Wuhayshi, "First Letter from Abu Basir to Emir of Al-Qaida
in the Islamic Maghreb," personal correspondence to Abu Mus'ab Abd

al-Wadud, May 21, 2012, in "Al-Qaida Papers," *Associated Press*; English translation and original Arabic version both available at *Long War Journal*, http://www.longwarjournal.org/images/al-qaida-papers-how-to-run -a-state.pdf.

58. On the Popular Committees, see Nadwa Al-Dawsari, "The Popular Committees of Abyan, Yemen: A Necessary Evil or an Opportunity for Security Reform?" Middle East Institute, March 5, 2014, http://www .mei.edu/content/popular-committees-abyan-yemen-necessary-evil-or -opportunity-security-reform.

59. Wuhayshi, "First Letter."

60. Ibid.

61. Ibid.

62. Wuhayshi, "Second Letter."

63. Wuhayshi mentions in the second letter to Abd al-Wadud that he had learned his first letter had not reached the AQIM leader. He appended it to the second letter. See ibid.

64. Boubker Belkadi, "Ruthless Chief, Head of Al-Qaeda's NAfrica [*sic*] Branch," *Middle East Online*, December 13, 2007, http://www.middle -east-online.com/english/?id=23510.

65. Abu Mus'ab Abd al-Wadud, "Mali-Al-Qaida's Sahara Playbook," personal correspondence to the commanders of al-Qaeda in the Islamic Maghreb (AQIM), *Associated Press*, Autumn 2012, 1, http://hosted.ap.org/specials /interactives/_international/_pdfs/al-qaida-manifesto.pdf. For dating the document, see Rukmini Callimachi, "In Timbuktu, al-Qaida Left Behind a Manifesto," *Associated Press*, February 14, 2013, http://big story.ap.org/article/timbuktu-al-qaida-left-behind-strategic-plans.

66. Abd al-Wadud, "Sahara Playbook," 4.

67. Ibid., 10.

68. Ibid., 9.

69. Ibid., 4.

70. Andrew Lebovich, "The Local Face of Jihadism in Northern Mali," *CTC Sentinel* 6, no. 6 (June 2013): 4–10, 5, https://www.ctc.usma.edu/v2/wp -content/uploads/2013/06/CTCSentinel-Vol6Iss64.pdf.

71. Ibid., 6.

72. Abd al-Wadud, "Sahara Playbook," 5.

73. Ibid.

74. "Shari'ah Penalties Anger Mali Muslims," *OnIslam*, August 5, 2012, http://www.onislam.net/english/news/africa/458395-shariah-penalties -anger-mali-muslims.html.

75. "TSG IntelBrief: The Continuing Crisis in Mali," The Soufan Group, May 29, 2012, http://soufangroup.com/tsg-intelbrief-the-continuing -crisis-in-mali/.

76. Celeste Hicks, "Mali War Exposes Religious Fault Lines," *Guardian*, May 3, 2013, http://www.theguardian.com/world/2013/may/03/mali -war-religious-faultlines; see also William G. Moseley, "Assaulting Tolerance in Mali," *Al Jazeera*, July 16, 2012, http://www.aljazeera.com /indepth/opinion/2012/07/201271594012144369.html; Brian J. Peterson, "Mali 'Islamization' Tackled: The Other Ansar Dine, Popular Islam, and Religious Tolerance," *African Arguments*, April 25, 2012, http://african arguments.org/2012/04/25/confronting-talibanization-in-mali-the-oth er-ansar-dine-popular-islam-and-religious-tolerance-brian-j-peterson/.

77. "Rebels Burn Timbuktu Tomb Listed as U.N. World Heritage Site," *CNN*, May 7, 2012, http://edition.cnn.com/2012/05/05/world/africa /mali-heritage-sites/index.html.

78. Abd al-Wadud, "Sahara Playbook," 5.

79. Idrissa Fall, "A Look inside Northern Mali," *Voice of America*, July 26, 2012, http://www.voanews.com/content/a-look-inside-northern-mali/14 47183.html.

80. Adam Nossiter, "Jihadists' Fierce Justice Drives Thousands to Flee Mali," *New York Times*, July 17, 2012, http://www.nytimes.com/2012/07 /18/world/africa/jidhadists-fierce-justice-drives-thousands-to-flee-mali .html?_r=0.

81. "Malians Protest at Strict Islamic Justice," *Times of Malta*, July 14, 2012, http://www.timesofmalta.com/articles/view/20120714/world/Malians -protest-at-strict-Islamic-justice.428483.

82. Abd al-Wadud, "Sahara Playbook," 3.

83. Ibid., 9.

84. "Mali: Reform or Relapse," International Crisis Group, *Africa Report*, no. 210 (January 10, 2014): 9, http://www.crisisgroup.org/~/media/Files /africa/west-africa/mali/210-mali-reform-or-relapse-english.pdf.

85. The Shabab had made territorial gains in the south and central areas of Somalia following the Ethiopian invasion that started in 2006. Local discontent with the occupation in part enabled the group's expansion. See Jonathan Masters and Mohammed Aly Sergie, "Al-Shabab," *CFR Backgrounders*, Council on Foreign Relations, March 13, 2015, http://www .cfr.org/somalia/al-shabab/p18650.

86. Nick Grace, "Islamic Emirate of Somalia Imminent as Shabaab Races to Consolidate Power," *Long War Journal*, September 8, 2008, http://www .longwarjournal.org/archives/2008/09/islamic_emirate_of_s.php. One of the Shabab's founders, one-time al-Qaeda member Talha al-Sudani, had entertained the idea of establishing a state before the creation of the Shabab. Bin Laden's representative in Somalia, Fadil Harun, discouraged Sudani from doing so for many of the same reasons Bin Laden would later cite. See Nelly Lahoud, "Beware of Imitators: al-Qa'ida through the Lens of Its Confidential Secretary," Harmony Program, Combating Terrorism Center at West Point, June 4, 2012, https://www.ctc.usma .edu/posts/beware-of-imitators-al-qaida-through-the-lens-of-its-confid ential-secretary.

87. An example of such discussions (in Arabic) is provided as a link in William McCants, "When Will Somalia's Shabaab Movement Declare an Islamic State?" *Jihadica*, November 16, 2008, http://www.jihadica.com /when-will-somalias-shabaab-movement-declare-an-islamic-state/.

88. In a September 20, 2009, video message ("Labbayka ya Usama"), Godane addressed Bin Laden as the group's "shaykh and emir." The full video seems to have been removed from YouTube, but screenshots and detailed analysis of the video are available at Christopher Anzalone, "Leaps & Bounds: The Rapid Evolution of Harakat al-Shabab al-Mujahideen's Media," *Views from the Occident*, September 21, 2009, http://oc cident.blogspot.com/2009/09/leaps-bounds-rapid-evolution-of-harakat .html. Around the same time, soldiers affiliated with the Shabab began displaying the Islamic State flag, flying it from their trucks as they zoomed around Mogadishu and other battlefronts. See, for example,

"al-Jihad al-Sumali" [online pseudonym], "Madin ka-l-sayf ma'a junud Shabab al-Mujahidin fi al-Sumal," YouTube video, November 17, 2009, https://www.youtube.com/watch?v=EHPVsSeR77Q. The Islamic State flag was the primary flag the Shabab used thereafter.

89. According to American Shabab member Omar Hammami, AQAP reached out to the group on behalf of the leadership in Afghanistan, relaying al-Qaeda's desire that the Shabab join al-Qaeda. Prompted by the letter, the Shabab's leaders gathered to deliberate on the "option of joining al-Qaeda and the option of declaring an Islamic state." Most of the group wanted to declare a state and proclaim its merger with al-Qaeda. But the Shabab's senior leader, Godane, rejected both, arguing without explaining himself that the circumstances were not favorable for either. Hammami groused, "They continued procrastinating in announcing [their affiliation with al-Qaeda] or the [establishment of] the state." As Bin Laden's letters make clear, Godane was merely following the lead of the al-Qaeda chief. Omar Hammami's recollections are available in Aaron Y. Zelin, "New Video Message and Two Documents from Omar Hammami [Abu Mansur al-Amriki]: 'The Final Appeal from the Humble Servant???'" *Jihadology*, January 7, 2013, http://jihadology.net/2013/01/07/new-video-message -and-two-documents-from-omar-hammami-abu-man%E1%B9%A3ur -al-amriki-the-final-appeal-from-the-humble-servant/. The leader of AQAP, Nasir al-Wuhayshi, mentioned the precedent set by the Shabab's decision not to declare a state in a 2012 letter. See Wuhayshi, "Second Letter."

90. In a letter dated June 19, 2010, Atiyya Abd al-Rahman reminded Bin Laden to send a letter to the Shabab, who had been "waiting for your answers and your guidance." See Atiyya Abd al-Rahman, "Letter from Atiyya Abd al-Rahman to Osama bin Laden [English translation]," personal correspondence, 420-10-CR-019-S-4-RJD, June 19, 2010, available at *Jihadica*, http://www.jihadica.com/wp-content/uploads/2015/03/420 -10-CR-019-S-4-RJD-Translation.pdf. Original Arabic version available at http://www.jihadica.com/wp-content/uploads/2015/03/420-10-CR-01 9-S-4-RJD-Original.pdf. Atiyya nudged him again on July 17, 2010: "My dear Sheikh, the brothers in Somalia are waiting for a letter and orders from you. They are waiting for advice and a decision about the issues they brought up. It would be great if you assigned them something that we could send on, they would be happy with that." See Abd al-Rahman, "Letter from 'Atiyya Abd al-Rahman to Osama bin Laden [English translation]," 422-10-CR-109-S-4-RJD.

91. Rob Wise, "Al Shabaab," Homeland Security & Counterterrorism Program and Transnational Threats Project, Center for Strategic and International Studies, AQAM Futures Project Case Study No. 2 (July 2011): 5, http://csis.org/files/publication/110715_Wise_AlShabaab_AQAM%20 Futures%20Case%20Study_WEB.pdf.

92. "Meeting Somalia's Islamist Insurgents," *BBC News*, April 28, 2008, http://news.bbc.co.uk/2/hi/africa/7365047.stm.

93. "Somali Troops 'Capture Key Port Town' from al-Shabab," *BBC News*, October 5, 2014, http://www.bbc.com/news/world-africa-29495801; Abdulkadir Khalif, "Al-Shabaab Order Woman Stoned to Death for Sex Offence," *Africa Review*, October 26, 2012, http://www.africareview.com /News/Al-Shabaab-order-woman-stoned-to-death-for-sex-offence/-/97 9180/1598708/-/55afb2z/-/index.html.

94. Reuters, "Rape Victim Stoned to Death in Somalia was 13, U.N. Says," *New York Times*, November 4, 2008, http://www.nytimes.com/2008/11/05/world/africa/05somalia.html?_r=0.

95. Mohamed Ahmed, "Al Shabaab Amputates Hands, Feet in Jowhar," *Somalia Report*, April 12, 2011, http://www.somaliareport.com/index.php/post/512/Al_Shabaab_Amputates_Hands_Feet_In_J.

96. Mohammed Ibrahim and Jeffrey Gettleman, "Somalis Protest Against Shabab in Mogadishu," *New York Times*, March 29, 2010, http://www.nytimes.com/2010/03/30/world/africa/30shabab.html?_r=0.

97. "Somalia: Al-Shabaab—It Will Be a Long War," International Crisis Group, Africa Briefing No. 99 (June 26, 2014), http://www.crisisgroup.org/~/media/Files/africa/horn-of-africa/somalia/b099-somalia-al-shabaab-it-will-be-a-long-war.pdf.

98. "Somalia: Information on Al-Shabaab, Including Areas of Control, Recruitment, and Affiliated Groups (2012–Nov. 2013)," Immigration and Refugee Board of Canada, available at *Refworld*, United Nations High Commissioner for Refugees, November 26, 2013, http://www.refworld.org/docid/52cea4e34.html.

99. Hamza Mohamed, "Al-Shabab Bans Internet in Somalia," *Al Jazeera*, January 9, 2014, http://www.aljazeera.com/news/africa/2014/01/al-shabab-bans-internet-somalia-20141981213614575.html.

100. Ahren Schaefer and Andrew Black, "Clan and Conflict in Somalia: Al-Shabaab and the Myth of 'Transcending Clan Politics,'" *Terrorism Monitor* 9, no. 40 (November 4, 2011): 7–11, http://www.jamestown.org/single/?tx_ttnews[tt_news]=38628#.VLV0lCc7Rl8. The Shabab's relationship with Somali tribes was complex, defined by converging but temporary interests rather than shared ideology or mutual trust. Tribes often gave the Shabab nominal support in exchange for access to the group's considerable resources. See Stig Jarle Hansen, "An In-Depth Look at Al-Shabab's Internal Divisions," *CTC Sentinel* 7, no. 2 (February 2014): 9–12, 10, https://www.ctc.usma.edu/posts/an-in-depth-look-at-al-shababs-internal-divisions.

101. Bin Laden, "Letter from Osama bin Laden to Mukhtar Abu al-Zubayr."

102. Bin Laden, "Letter from Osama bin Laden to 'Atiyya Abd al-Rahman," 432-10-CR-019-S-4-RJD, 2-4. Despite Bin Laden's guidance and Godane's ultimate decision not to declare an emirate, Robow and other senior Shabab leaders again attempted to announce one. After a four-day gathering in May 2011, Robow and other senior leaders issued a statement proclaiming they would rebrand the Shabab as an Islamic state. A group of the Shabab's religious scholars also recommended that the Shabab rebrand itself as the "Islamic Emirate." Godane pointedly rejected the statement and the recommendation. See J. D. and Mohamed Odowa, "Al-Shabaab to Change Name to Imaarah Islamiyah," *Somalia Report*, May 12, 2011, http://www.somaliareport.com/index.php/post/2212/Al-Shabaab_to_Change_Name_to_Imaarah_Islamiyah; Abdul Qadir Muhammad Abdullah et al., "Final Statement of the Conference of Islamic State Scholars in Somalia," December 3, 2011, in "Al-Qaida Papers," *Associated Press*, http://hosted.ap.org/specials/interactives/_international/_pdfs/al-qaida-papers-state-scholars.pdf.

103. Geoffrey Kambere, "Financing Al Shabaab: The Vital Port of Kismayo," *CTX* 2, no. 3 (August 2012): n.p., https://globalecco.org/financing-al-shabaab-the-vital-port-of-kismayo.

104. Bin Laden, "Letter from Osama bin Laden to 'Atiyya Abd al-Rahman," 432-10-CR-019-S-4-RJD.

105. Bin Laden, "Letter from Osama bin Laden to Mukhtar Abu al-Zubayr." At least one al-Qaeda leader, possibly Ayman al-Zawahiri, disagreed with Bin Laden. He argued that al-Qaeda should publicly recognize all its affiliates. See "Letter from Unknown to Osama bin Laden [English translation]," personal correspondence from unknown author to Bin Laden, SOCOM-2012-0000006, Harmony Program, Combating Terrorism Center at West Point, December 13, 2010, available at *Jihadica*, http://www.jihadica.com/wp-content/uploads/2012/05/SOCOM-2012 -0000006-Trans.pdf. Original Arabic available at http://www.jihadica .com/wp-content/uploads/2012/05/SOCOM-2012-0000006-Orig.pdf.

106. Osama bin Laden, "Letter from Osama bin Laden to 'Atiyya Abd al-Rahman [English translation]," personal correspondence, SO-COM-2012-0000010, Harmony Program, Combating Terrorism Center at West Point, April 26, 2011, available at *Jihadica*, http://www.jihadica .com/wp-content/uploads/2012/05/SOCOM-2012-0000010-Trans.pdf. Original Arabic version available at http://www.jihadica.com/wp-con tent/uploads/2012/05/SOCOM-2012-0000010-Orig.pdf.

107. Ibid.

108. Peter Wonacott and Nicholas Bariyo, "Militants Find Symbolic Targets in Uganda," *Wall Street Journal*, July 13, 2010, http://www.wsj.com /articles/SB10001424052748704288204575362400675683926.

109. Charles Kazooba, "Somalia: AU Ministers Agree to 'Take on' Al Shabaab," *AllAfrica*, July 26, 2010, http://allafrica.com/stories/201007250021 .html.

110. Aaron Maasho, "African Union Says Military Still Weakening Somalia's al Shabaab," *Reuters*, January 7, 2015, http://www.reuters.com/art icle/2015/01/07/us-somalia-insurgency-idUSKBN0KG18C20150107.

111. Malkhadir M. Muhumed, "UN Report: Leader's Death Won't End al-Shabab," *Al Jazeera*, November 6, 2014, http://www.aljazeera.com/in depth/features/2014/11/un-report-leader-death-won-end-al-shabab -201411613375772891.html.

112. Gabriel Koehler-Derrick, ed. "A False Foundation? AQAP, Tribes and Ungoverned Spaces in Yemen," Harmony Program, Combating Terrorism Center at West Point, September 2011, 97–140, https://www.ctc .usma.edu/v2/wp-content/uploads/2012/10/CTC_False_Foundation3 .pdf.

113. Bill Roggio, "AQAP's Ansar al Sharia Executes 3 US 'Spies,'" *Long War Journal*, February 13, 2012, http://www.longwarjournal.org/archives /2012/02/aqaps_ansar_al_sharia_executes.php; Koehler-Derrick, "False Foundation?" 59.

114. Koehler-Derrick, "False Foundation?" 114.

115. Ibid., 60.

116. "Yemen al Qaeda Leader Criticises IS Beheadings as un-Islamic," *Reuters*, December 8, 2014, http://uk.reuters.com/article/2014/12/08/uk -yemen-qaeda-beheadings-idUKKBN0JM26N20141208; Alessandria Masi, "Difference Between Al-Qaeda And ISIS: Senior AQAP Leader Holds 'Press Conference,' Said Beheadings Are 'Big Mistake,'" *I. B. Times*, December 8, 2014, http://www.ibtimes.com/difference-between -al-qaeda-isis-senior-aqap-leader-holds-press-conference-said-1742818;

"TSG IntelBrief: Beyond Bombs, Bullets, and Blades: The Killer Narrative," The Soufan Group, December 11, 2014, http://soufangroup.com/tsg-intelbrief-beyond-bombs-bullets-and-blades-the-killer-narrative/.

117. When the Islamic State bombed Shi'i mosques in Sana'a, AQAP issued a statement denying its involvement. "We adhere to the directives of al-Shaykh Ayman al-Zawahiri, may God protect him, which require avoiding the targeting of mosques, markets, and places [where people] mingle in order to protect the lives of innocent Muslims and to prioritize the greater good." See "Bayan nafi al-'alaqa bi-tafjirat masajid al-Huthiyyin fi Sana'a," March 20, 2015, https://azelin.files.wordpress.com/2015/03/al-qc481_idah-in-the-arabian-peninsula-22 denying-a-relationship-with-the-bombings-of-the-e1b8a5c5abthc4ab -mosques-in-e1b9a3anac48122.pdf; Daniel Byman and Jennifer R. Williams, "Will al Qaeda Be the Great Winner of Yemen's Collapse?" *Foreign Policy*, April 9, 2015, http://foreignpolicy.com/2015/04/09/will -al-qaeda-be-the-great-winner-of-yemens-collapse/.

118. Jean-Luc Marret was probably the first person to apply the term to an al-Qaeda affiliate. He used it to describe the ideology and behavior of al-Qaeda's North African affiliate, which called for attacks on the West but focused its own attacks locally. See his "Al-Qaeda in the Islamic Maghreb: A 'Glocal' Organization," *Studies in Conflict & Terrorism* 31 (2008): 541–552.

119. "al-Islah" [online pseudonym], "al-'Alim kullahu yansur rayat Dawlat al-'Iraq al-Islamiyya (al-Yaman—al-Sumal—Indunisiyya. Idkhal wa-shuf)," *Arrawan*, June 27, 2010, http://z3tr.arrawan.com/showthread.php?45965.

120. Reuters, "Factbox-Ansar Dine—Black Flag over Northern Mali," *Faith World*, July 3, 2012, http://blogs.reuters.com/faithworld/2012/07/03/fact box-ansar-dine-black-flag-over-northern-mali/.

121. Thomas Joscelyn, "From al Qaeda in Italy to Ansar al Sharia Tunisia," *Long War Journal*, November 21, 2012, http://www.longwarjournal.org /archives/2012/11/from_al_qaeda_in_ita.php.

122. "al-Barlaman al-Libi yurahhib bi-qarar tasnif 'Ansar al-Shari'a' ka-jama'a irhabiyya," *Ennahar El Djadid*, November 22, 2014, http://www.ennahar online.com/ar/arabic_news/227646.html.

123. William McCants, "Black Flag," slideshow, *Foreign Policy*, November 7, 2011, http://foreignpolicy.com/slideshow/black-flag/.

124. Tara Todras-Whitehill, "In Cairo, Protesters Didn't Pledge Allegiance to a Flag," *Al-Monitor*, September 12, 2012, http://www.al-monitor.com /pulse/originals/2012/al-monitor-scenes-from-cairos-embassy-prote .html.

125. William McCants, "The Sources of Salafi Conduct," *Foreign Affairs*, September 19, 2012, http://www.foreignaffairs.com/articles/138129/wil liam-mccants/the-sources-of-salafi-conduct?page=show.

CHAPTER 4

1. Charles Lister, "Profiling the Islamic State," Brookings Doha Center, Analysis Paper No. 13 (November 2014): 10–11, http://www.brookings .edu/~/media/Research/Files/Reports/2014/11/profiling%20islamic %20state%20lister/en_web_lister.pdf.

2. A large number of Baghdadi's personal documents were collected by German news agencies. See Volkmar Kabisch et al., "Auf der Spur des

IS-Anführers," *ARD*, February 18, 2015, http://www.tagesschau.de/aus
land/baghdadi-101.html. In an email, Volkmar Kabisch related to me
that Ibrahim was born in Samarra, spent his very early childhood in the
town of al-Jelam (fifteen miles northeast of Samarra), and then moved
with his family to the Jibriyya district of Samarra where he grew up.
See also Hisham al-Hashimi, "Ashya' min hayat al-Baghdadi," *Almada
Newspaper*, September 6, 2014, http://almadapaper.net/ar/printnews.aspx
?NewsID=471187; Janine di Giovanni, "Who Is ISIS Leader Abu Bakr
al-Baghdadi?" *Newsweek*, December 8, 2014, http://www.newsweek.com
/2014/12/19/who-isis-leader-abu-bakr-al-baghdadi-290081.html; and;
"al-Kashf 'an watha'iq hawla haqiqat Abu [*sic*] Bakr al-Baghdadi," *All-
4Syria*, February 27, 2015, http://all4syria.info/Archive/196498.

3. Giovanni, "Who Is ISIS Leader Abu Bakr al-Baghdadi?"

4. The brother, Shamsi, is in prison. See "al-Kashf 'an watha'iq hawla
haqiqat Abu Bakr al-Baghdadi," *All4Syria*, February 27, 2015, http://all
4syria.info/Archive/196498.

5. Kabisch et al., "Auf der Spur des IS-Anführers"; Bashir al-Wandi,
"al-Baghdadi . . . irhab bi-nakhat al-Ba'th," *al-Hiwar al-Mutamaddin*,
March 11, 2015, http://www.ahewar.org/debat/print.art.asp?t=0&aid=45
8880&ac=1.

6. Kabisch et al., "Auf der Spur des IS-Anführers."

7. See Turki bin Mubarak al-Bin'ali (aka Abu Hummam Bakr bin Abd al-
'Aziz al-Athari), "Madd al-ayadi li-bay'at al-Baghdadi," https://archive
.org/details/baghdadi-001, and chapter 6 on Baghdadi's caliphate in this
volume.

8. Abu Yusuf al-Tunisi, "Li-awwal marra . . . al-Sira al-dhatiyya li-l-Shaykh
Abu Bakr al-Baghdadi," July 15, 2013, available at Pieter Van Ostaeyen,
"Abu Bakr al-Baghdadi—a Short Biography of the ISIS Sheikh," *pietervanostaeyen*, July 15, 2013, https://pietervanostaeyen.wordpress.com
/2013/07/15/abu-bakr-al-baghdadi-a-short-biography-of-the-isis-
sheikh/. For an English translation, see "A Biography of Abu Bakr al-
Baghdadi," *INSITE Blog on Terrorism and Extremism*, SITE Intelligence
Group, August 12, 2014, http://news.siteintelgroup.com/blog/index.php
/entry/226-the-story-behind-abu-bakr-al-baghdadi.

9. Hashimi, "Ashya' min hayat al-Baghdadi."

10. Martin Chulov, "ISIS: The Inside Story," *Guardian*, December 11, 2014,
http://www.theguardian.com/world/2014/dec/11/-sp-isis-the-inside
-story; Giovanni, "Who Is ISIS Leader Abu Bakr al-Baghdadi?";
Hashimi, "Ashya' min hayat al-Baghdadi."

11. Hashimi, "Ashya' min hayat al-Baghdadi."

12. "al-Kashf 'an watha'iq," *All4Syria*.

13. Loveday Morris, "Is This the High School Report Card of the Head
of the Islamic State?" *Washington Post*, February 19, 2015, http://www
.washingtonpost.com/blogs/worldviews/wp/2015/02/19/is-this-the
-high-school-report-card-of-the-head-of-the-islamic-state/.

14. "Neue Erkenntnisse über IS-chef Baghdadi: Der kurzsichtige Kalif,"
Spiegel Online, February 19, 2015, http://www.spiegel.de/politik/ausland
/abu-bakr-al-baghdadi-das-leben-des-is-anfuehrers-a-1019227.html;
"al-Kashf 'an watha'iq," *All4Syria*. Other accounts say Baghdadi got his
bachelor's degree at Saddam University for Islamic Studies; for example,
Hashimi, "Ashya' min hayat al-Baghdadi."

15. The date on his physical when he matriculated at Saddam University for Islamic Studies is 1996. See Kabisch et al., "Auf der Spur des IS-Anführers."

16. Amatzia Baram, "From Militant Secularism to Islamism: The Iraqi Ba'th Regime 1968–2003," Woodrow Wilson International Center for Scholars, October 2011, 16–17, http://www.wilsoncenter.org/sites/default/files /From%20Militant%20Secularism%20to%20Islamism.pdf.

17. The book Baghdadi edited, *Ruh al-murid fi sharh al-'iqd al-farid fi nuzum al-tajwid* by Muhammad al-Samarqandi (who died in Baghdad around AD 1378), is obscure, which is why Baghdadi chose it. It wouldn't make sense for an aspiring editor of manuscripts to choose a published work. See the online record here: http://quran-c.com/display/DispBib .aspx?BID=4167. For background on Samarqandi, see Umar Rida Kahhala, *Mu'jam al-mu'allifin: Tarajim musannafi al-kutub al-'Arabiya*, vol. 12 (Beirut: Dar Ihya' al-Turath al-'Arabi, n.d.), 4–5.

18. "al-Kashf 'an watha'iq," *All4Syria*.

19. For a detailed discussion of Baghdadi's intellectual journey, see my biography of him in "The Believer," *The Brookings Essay*, Brookings Institution (August 2015).

20. Wael Essam, "'al-Baghdadi' kharaja min sijn Bukka akthar tatarrufan wa-kafara bi-l-'Ikwhan' . . . wa-darrasahu 'alim sufi," *al-Quds al-Arabi*, October 19, 2014, http://www.alquds.co.uk/?p=237500.

21. "Video: Weltspiegel Extra: Das Phantom des IS Terrors," *Das Erste*, February 18, 2015, http://www.daserste.de/information/talk/anne-will /videosextern/weltspiegel-extra-das-phantom-des-is-terrors-100.html. Ibrahim would finish his doctorate in 2007, after he was already a senior leader in the Islamic State.

22. Chulov, "Isis: The Inside Story."

23. Michael Weiss and Hassan Hassan, *ISIS: Inside the Army of Terror* [Google Edition] (New York: Regan Arts, 2015), 116.

24. Hunter Walker, "Here Is the Army's Declassified Iraq Prison File on the Leader of ISIS," *Business Insider*, February 18, 2015, http://www.business insider.com/abu-bakr-al-baghdadi-declassified-iraq-prison-file-2015-2.

25. Some accounts say Baghdadi had already helped found an insurgent group, the Jaysh Ahl al-Sunna wa-l-Jama'a (Chulov, "Isis: The Inside Story"; Weiss and Hassan, *ISIS*, 116). Others say he hadn't yet taken up arms. See Ruth Sherlock, "How a Talented Footballer Became World's Most Wanted Man, Abu Bakr al-Baghdadi," *Telegraph*, November 11, 2014, http://www.telegraph.co.uk/news/worldnews/middleeast /iraq/10948846/How-a-talented-footballer-became-worlds-most-wanted-man-Abu-Bakr-al-Baghdadi.html.

26. "al-Kashf 'an watha'iq," *All4Syria*.

27. Chulov, "Isis: The Inside Story."

28. Ibid.

29. Tim Arango and Eric Schmitt, "U.S. Actions in Iraq Fueled Rise of a Rebel," *New York Times*, August 10, 2014, http://www.nytimes.com /2014/08/11/world/middleeast/us-actions-in-iraq-fueled-rise-of-a-rebel.html?_r=0; Hashimi, "Ashya' min hayat al-Baghdadi"; Giovanni, "Who Is ISIS Leader Abu Bakr al-Baghdadi"; Weiss and Hassan, *ISIS*, 121–122.

30. Aaron Y. Zelin, "Abu Bakr al-Baghdadi: Islamic State's Driving Force," *BBC News*, July 31, 2014, http://www.bbc.com/news/world-middle-east-28560449.

31. "al-Kashf 'an watha'iq," *All4Syria*.

32. The medieval book was *al-La'ali' al-farida fi sharh al-qasida*, Abu Abd Allah Muhammad bin Hasan al-Fasi's thirteenth-century commentary on al-Shatibi's twelfth-century *Hirz al-amani wa-wajhuhu al-tahani fi al-qira'at al-sab'*. Baghdadi edited the portion from the introduction to the chapter on two *hamza*s ("Protokoll der Disputationskommission," a German translation of the Arabic minutes from Baghdadi's dissertation defense kindly provided to me by Volkmar Kabisch.)

33. A screenshot of the Arabic comments is found in "Video: Weltspiegel Extra."

34. "al-Kashf 'an watha'iq," *All4Syria*. All the copies of Baghdadi's dissertation reportedly have been stolen.

35. Hashimi, "Ashya' min hayat al-Baghdadi."

36. Weiss and Hassan, *ISIS*, 85–86.

37. McCants, "Believer."

38. Chulov, "Isis: The Inside Story."

39. Abu Ahmad, "al-Haqa'iq al-mukhfa hawla dawlat al-Baghdadi," al-Durar al-Shamiyya, April 5, 2014, http://eldorar.com/node/45368.

40. Tunisi, "al-Sira al-dhatiyya."

41. Chulov, "Isis: The Inside Story"; Weiss and Hassan, *ISIS*, 113.

42. Abu Ahmad, "al-Haqa'iq."

43. Sherlock, "Footballer."

44. Letter from Atiyya Abd al-Rahman to the Islamic State, April 21, 2010, quoted in Zawahiri, "Shahada li-haqan dima' al-mujahidin bi-l-Sham," *Mu'assasat al-Sahab*, May 3, 2014, 2, https://pietervanostaeyen.wordpress.com/2014/05/03/dr-ayman-az-zawahiri-testimonial-to-preserve-the-blood-of-mujahideen-in-as-sham/. In "Shahada," Zawahiri seems to be mistaken when he says Atiyya's letter was sent after Baghdadi's appointment, unless he means Baghdadi had already been selected before the letter arrived. In the same letter of condolence, Atiyya suggested the Islamic State should unite with other jihadist factions and contemplate a "new structure."

45. Abu Ahmad, "al-Haqa'iq."

46. "@wikibaghdady" [online pseudonym], "Asrar dawlat al-Baghdadi," Twitter post, circa December 14, 2013, https://docs.google.com/document/d/1wEQ0FKosa1LcUB3tofeub1UxaT5A-suROyDExgV9nUY/edit; Abu Ahmad, "al-Haqa'iq." According to @wikibaghdady, Hajji Bakr's knowledge of Iraq's army and his loyalty to Abu Umar al-Baghdadi and Abu Ayyub al-Masri endeared him to them

47. Abu Ahmad, "al-Haqa'iq."

48. Tunisi, "al-Sira al-dhatiyya"; Chulov, "Isis: The Inside Story."

49. Hashimi, "Ashya' min hayat al-Baghdadi."

50. Tunisi, "al-Sira al-dhatiyya."

51. On June 19, 2010, Atiyya forwarded a letter from the Islamic State to Bin Laden about the "new command taking charge." See Abd al-Rahman, "Letter from 'Atiyya Abd al-Rahman to Osama bin Laden [English translation]," 420-10-CR-019-S-4-RJD.

52. Osama bin Laden, "Letter from Osama bin Laden to 'Atiyya Abd al-Rahman [English translation]," SOCOM-2012-0000019, Harmony Program, Combating Terrorism Center at West Point, July 6, 2010, http://www.docexdocs.com/ctc/SOCOM-2012-0000019Trans.pdf. Original Arabic available at http://www.docexdocs.com/ctc/SOCOM -2012-0000019Orig.pdf. In his "Shahada," Zawahiri dates the letter July 6, 2010. Bin Laden wanted to know about Abu Bakr al-Baghdadi, his "first deputy," and his minister of war, Abu Sulayman al-Nasir li-Din Allah.

53. On July 17, 2010, Atiyya informed Bin Laden that he would ask for "information about Abu Bakr al-Baghdadi and his deputy," as well as information about Abu Sulayman al-Nasir li-Din Allah, the minister of war. See Abd al-Rahman, "Letter from 'Atiyya Abd al-Rahman to Osama bin Laden," 422-10-CR-109-S-4-RJD. (For a biography of Abu Sulayman, see Thomas Joscelyn, "The Islamic State of Iraq and the Sham's Quiet War Minister," *Long War Journal*, June 16, 2014, http://www.longwar journal.org/archives/2014/06/the_islamic_states_q.php). Atiyya also wanted to ask members of other jihadist groups, including "al-Ansar," about the Islamic State's new leaders. The Ansar probably refers to Ansar al-Islam, an Iraqi insurgent group with which the Islamic State had butted heads. Bin Laden alludes to the conflict in an August 7, 2010, letter: "As for what the brothers in Iraq mentioned about the contention they have with Ansar Al Islam group, continue your correspondence with them. Advise them to do their best to avoid disagreement and conflict if possible. Advise them to seek the help of the tribal leaders, ulema and the former members of Ansar Al-Sunnah to resolve the issue." (See Bin Laden, "Letter from Osama bin Laden to Atiyya Abd al-Rahman," 432-10-CR-019-S-4-RJD.) Ansar al-Islam would later merge with the Islamic State when it declared its caliphate in 2014.

54. Letter from Atiyya Abd al-Rahman to the Islamic State's Ministry of Media, September 29, 2010, quoted in Zawahiri, "Shahada," 3.

55. Letter from a representative of the Islamic State's Majlis al-Shura to Atiyya Abd al-Rahman, October 9, 2010, quoted in Zawahiri, "Shahada," 3.

56. "Tanzim al-Qa'ida bi-l-'Iraq yata'ahhad bi-ta'yid al-Zawahiri wa-shann hajamat," *Reuters*, May 9, 2011, http://ara.reuters.com/article/topNews /idARACAE7480SO20110509; Zawahiri, "Shahada," 3.

57. Letter from a Representative for Communications with the Islamic State to Atiyya Abd al-Rahman, May 23, 2011, quoted in Zawahiri, "Shahada," 4.

58. Giovanni, "ISIS Leader"; "@wikibaghdady" [online pseudonym], "Asrar dawlat al-Baghdadi," December 15, 2013, https://docs.google.com/doc ument/d/1wEQ0FKosa1LcUB3tofeub1UxaT5A-suROyDExgV9nUY /edit. For background on Hajji Bakr and his contribution to the organization of the Islamic State, see Christoph Reuter, "The Terror Strategist: Secret Files Reveal the Structure of the Islamic State," *Spiegel Online*, April 18, 2015, http://www.spiegel.de/international/world/islamic-state -files-show-structure-of-islamist-terror-group-a-1029274.html.

59. The insider who went by the Twitter handle @wikibaghdady tweeted a lot of the Islamic State's dirty laundry in the winter of 2013 (see "@ wikibaghdady" [online pseudonym], "Asrar dawlat al-Baghdadi"). A few months later, an "Abu Ahmad" spoke to a news outlet and related similar information (see Abu Ahmad, "al-Haqa'iq"). See also Hashimi, "Ashya'

min hayat al-Baghdadi"; Mitchell Prothero, "How 2 Shadowy ISIS Commanders Designed Their Iraq Campaign," *McClatchy DC*, June 30, 2014, http://www.mcclatchydc.com/2014/06/30/231952/how-2-shadowy-isis-commanders.html. Baghdadi has preferred to put Iraqis in charge of the war machine (this includes many former officers in the Iraqi army) and to install foreigners in the functional offices, such as the offices of recruitment and media. See Hisham al-Hashimi, "Haykaliyyat tanzim Da'ish," *Kitabat fi al-Mizan*, February 24, 2014, http://www.kitabat.info/subject .php?id=43152.

60. "Khitta istratijiyya li-ta'ziz al-mawqif al-siyasi li-Dawlat al-'Iraq al-Islamiyya," *Mufakkirat al-Fallujah*, December 2009 or January 2010, https://ia802604.us.archive.org/16/items/Dirasa_dawla_03/khouta.pdf. The document is dated Muharram 1431 (December 18, 2009–January 10, 2010).

61. Ibid., 3.

62. Ibid., 8.

63. Ibid., 4.

64. Ibid., 6.

65. Ibid., 25.

66. Ibid., 34.

67. Ibid., 36–37.

68. Ibid., 36.

69. See *Majallat al-Ansar*, vols. 1–28 (January 15, 2002–April 3, 2003), https://www.tawhed.ws/c?i=325.

70. "Khitta istratijiyya," 38–39.

71. Ibid., 39–40.

72. Ibid., 43–45.

73. Ibid., 50.

74. Ibid., 51.

75. Ibid., 51–52.

76. For my translation of the book, see Abu Bakr Naji, *The Management of Savagery: The Most Critical Stage through Which the Umma Will Pass*, transl. William McCants, John M. Olin Institute for Strategic Studies at Harvard University, May 23, 2006, https://azelin.files.wordpress .com/2010/08/abu-bakr-naji-the-management-of-savagery-the-most -critical-stage-through-which-the-umma-will-pass.pdf.

77. A major jihadist insider, Husayn bin Mahmud, alluded to Naji's death in an article online with the phrase "may God bless him," which is used only for those who have died ("Sahil al-jiyad fi jam' masadir al-jihad," *al-Jabha al-I'lamiyya al-Islamiyya al-'Alamiyya*, June 25, 2007).

78. Imam al-Sharif, the former head of Egyptian Islamic Jihad, claims the author is Muhammad al-Hukayma, an Egyptian member of the Islamic Group. In a 2014 interview, Sharif stated that Hukayma had a professional background in media and was working in the al-Qaeda media wing in Iran when he wrote *The Management of Savagery*. A 2008 *Asharq Al-Awsat* article reported that Hukayma moved from Iran to Pakistan in 2005. Hukayma announced the merger of the Islamic Group with al-Qaeda in a 2006 video in which he appeared next to Zawahiri (most of the Islamic Group rejected the merger). With a $1 million U.S. bounty on his head, Hukayma was killed in a U.S. air strike in Pakistan in 2008. See "Sabil al-Rishad" [online pseudonym], "Ba'da haqa'iq al-'alaqa bayna

al-Qa'ida wa Iran," YouTube video, February 19, 2014, https://www
.youtube.com/watch?v=RHQLpR2dLts&sns=tw; "Maqtal Abu Jihad
al-Masri mas'ul al-i'lam bi-tanzim al-Qa'ida," *Asharq Al-Awsat*, November 2, 2014, http://classic.aawsat.com/details.asp?issueno=10626&article
=493173#.VJBI0Sc7Rl8. For discussion of Hukayma as the author of *The
Management of Savagery* in the Arabic press, see Mustafa Zahran, "Ansar
Bayt al-Maqdis. wa 'Da'ishna' al-mashhad al-Masri," *Al Jazeera*, November 26, 2014, http://www.aljazeera.net/home/Getpage/6c87b8ad-70ec
-47d5-b7c4-3aa56fb899e2/e5785718-db70-4f05-bb3e-7fda7f466b0f;
Tariq al-Shaykh, "al-Hajma al-fikriyya al-qadima," *Al Ahram*, November
24, 2014, http://www.ahram.org.eg/NewsQ/341613.aspx.

79. Naji, *Management of Savagery*, 19.
80. Ibid., 11.
81. Ibid., 111–112.
82. Ibid., 34.
83. Ibid., 31.
84. Ibid., 98.
85. "The Messenger of God forbade the killing of women and children" (tradition from *Sunan Abi Dawud*).
86. For the ways the Islamic State circumvents the medieval Islamic scholarly tradition on war, see Sohaira Siddiqui, "Beyond Authenticity: ISIS and the Islamic Legal Tradition," *Jadaliyya*, February 24, 2015, http://www.jadaliyya.com/pages/index/20944/beyond-authenticity_isis-and-the-islamic-legal-tra.
87. Naji, *Management of Savagery*, 7. This seems to be a paraphrase of the following: "if a state overextends itself strategically—by, say, the conquest of extensive territories or the waging of costly wars—it runs the risk that the potential benefits from external expansion may be outweighed by the great expense of it all" (Paul Kennedy, *The Rise and Fall of the Great Powers* [New York: Random House, 1987], xvi).
88. Naji, *Management of Savagery*, 98.
89. William McCants, "Managing Savagery in Saudi Arabia," *Jihadica*, June 26, 2008, http://www.jihadica.com/managing-savagery-in-saudi-arabia/.
90. William McCants, "Al Qaeda Is Doing Nation-Building. Should We Worry?" *Foreign Policy*, April 30, 2012, http://foreignpolicy.com/2012/04/30/al-qaeda-is-doing-nation-building-should-we-worry/.
91. Hassan Hassan, "The Secret World of Isis Training Camps—Ruled by Sacred Texts and the Sword," *Guardian*, January 24, 2015, http://www.theguardian.com/world/2015/jan/25/inside-isis-training-camps. See also Jack Jenkins, "The Book That Really Explains ISIS (Hint: It's Not the Qur'an)," *Think Progress*, September 10, 2014, http://thinkprogress.org/world/2014/09/10/3565635/the-book-that-really-explains-isis-hint-its-not-the-quran/; David Ignatius, "The Manual That Chillingly Foreshadows the Islamic State," *Washington Post*, September 25, 2014, http://www.washingtonpost.com/opinions/david-ignatius-the-mein-kampf-of-jihad/2014/09/25/4adbfc1a-44e8-11e4-9a15-137aa0153527_story.html.
92. "Alaslami" [online pseudonym] (@M_Alaslami1), Twitter post *(account since deleted)*, November 2014, https://twitter.com/M_Alaslami1/status/536781484250497024.

93. "al-Muhami Adil al-Turki" [online pseudonym] (@laweradelturki), Twitter post, September 13, 2012, https://twitter.com/laweradelturki/status/246294423527383040.

94. "al-Dar'awi" [online pseudonym] (@der3am), Twitter post, February 9, 2014, https://twitter.com/der3am/status/432414102598606848.

95. Lister, "Profiling the Islamic State," 12.

96. Brian Fishman and Joseph Felter, "Al-Qa'ida's Foreign Fighters in Iraq: A First Look at the Sinjar Records," Harmony Project, Combating Terrorism Center at West Point, January 2, 2007, https://www.ctc.usma.edu/posts/al-qaidas-foreign-fighters-in-iraq-a-first-look-at-the-sinjar-records.

97. Weiss and Hassan, *ISIS*, 99–111.

98. Ibid., 139.

99. Phil Sands, Justin Vela, and Suha Maayeh, "Assad Regime Set Free Extremists from Prison to Fire Up Trouble during Peaceful Uprising," *The National*, January 22, 2014, http://www.thenational.ae/world/syria/assad-regime-set-free-extremists-from-prison-to-fire-up-trouble-during-peaceful-uprising.

100. Abu Ahmad, "al-Haqa'iq."

101. Lister, "Profiling the Islamic State," 12.

102. Weiss and Hassan, *ISIS*, 168.

103. Lister, "Profiling the Islamic State," 13.

104. Thomas Joscelyn, "Syrian Rebel Leader Was Bin Laden's Courier, Now Zawahiri's Representative," *Long War Journal*, December 17, 2013, http://www.longwarjournal.org/archives/2013/12/aq_courier_rebel_leader_zawahiri.php.

105. Thomas Joscelyn, "Zawahiri Eulogizes al Qaeda's Slain Syrian Representative," *Long War Journal*, April 4, 2014, http://www.longwarjournal.org/archives/2014/04/zawahiri_eulogizes_a.php. For the date of Abu Khalid's capture, see Abd al-Rahman al-Hajj, "'Abu Khalid al-Suri' min 'al-Tali'a al-Muqatila' ila 'Ahrar al-Sham' maruran bi 'al-Qa'ida," *Al Hayat*, February 28, 2014, http://alhayat.com/Articles/794946.

106. Joscelyn, "Zawahiri Eulogizes al Qaeda's Slain Syrian Representative."

107. See Brynjar Lia, *Architect of the Global Jihad: The Life of Al-Qaida Strategist Abu Mus'ab al-Suri* (New York: Oxford University Press, 2009).

108. Alan Cullison, "Inside Al-Qaeda's Hard Drive," *Atlantic*, September 1, 2004, http://www.theatlantic.com/magazine/archive/2004/09/inside-al-qaeda-s-hard-drive/303428/.

109. Abu Mus'ab al-Suri, *Da'wat al-muqawama al-Islamiyya al-'alamiyya [The Call of the Global Islamic Resistance]*, published on jihadist websites in December 2004, 750.

110. Ibid., 1518.

111. A September 2014 *Al Jazeera* article describes Uraydi as Nusra's "Sharia official." Nusra also issued a video recording of a dialogue with Uraydi in 2013 titled "Our Method and Creed," addressing Uraydi as "our shaykh." See "Wusul al-junud al-fijiyyin al-mufraj 'anhum ila al-Qunaytra," *Al Jazeera*, September 11, 2014, http://www.aljazeera.net/home/Getpage/f6451603-4dff-4ca1-9c10-122741d17432/b539af9c-294b-494e-b503-2a8cd5cda739; Ansar Jabhat al-Nusra, "Jabhat al-Nusra muqabila ma'a al-Duktur Sami al-Uraydi (hafazuhu Allah) bi-'unwan (manhajuna wa-'aqidatuna)," YouTube video, al-Manara al-Bayda', October 21, 2013, https://www.youtube.com/watch?v=pYb8Rh_Kwpo.

112. D. Sami Oride (@sami_oride), Twitter post, August 13, 2014, https://twitter.com/sami_oride/status/499554084543029248.

113. D. Sami Oride (@sami_oride), Twitter post, March 18, 2014, https://twitter.com/sami_oride/status/445987493125427200/photo/1.

114. D. Sami Oride (@sami_oride), Twitter post, February 12, 2014, https://twitter.com/sami_oride/status/433474436339990528/photo/1.

115. Suri, *The Call of the Global Islamic Resistance*, 909.

116. Nusra's popular support inside Syria derives in part from public perceptions of its heavily Syrian composition, although exact numbers are not known. There are reports that Nusra recruits Syrian adolescents as soldiers through its free "educational" programs in local schools and by offering protection or salaries. See "Maybe We Live and Maybe We Die: Recruitment and Use of Children by Armed Groups in Syria," Human Rights Watch, June 2014, 25–26, http://www.hrw.org/sites/default/files/reports/syria0614_crd_ForUpload.pdf; "The Islamic Front and Jabhat an-Nusra: Assessing the Sustainability and Future Trajectory of the Syrian Opposition's Most Important Alliance through Analysis of Rhetoric and Local Governance Activity," Courage Services, Inc., April 2014, 3, http://www.courageservices.com/documents/Islamic%20Front%20and%20Jabhat%20an-Nusra_Courage%20Services_Apr2014.pdf.

117. Charles C. Caris and Samuel Reynolds, "ISIS Governance in Syria," Institute for the Study of War, *Middle East Security Report* 22 (July 2014), http://www.understandingwar.org/sites/default/files/ISIS_Governance.pdf.

118. "The Islamic Front and Jabhat an-Nusra," 8.

119. In cities where the Islamic State lacks manpower, it relies more on locals to manage day-to-day affairs. See Weiss and Hassan, *ISIS*, 212–213.

120. Maqdisi quotes the line in his statement "Bayan hawla 'al-Dawla al-Islamiyya fi al-'Iraq wa-l-Sham' wa-l-mawqif al-wajib tujahaha," *Minbar al-Tawhid wa-l-Jihad*, May 26, 2014, 11-12, https://tawhed.ws/r?i=26051401. See the partial translation by Cole Bunzel, "From Paper State to Caliphate: The Ideology of the Islamic State," The Brookings Project on U.S. Relations with the Islamic World, Analysis Paper No. 19 (March 2015): 29, http://www.brookings.edu/~/media/research/files/papers/2015/03/ideology-of-islamic-state-bunzel/the-ideology-of-the-islamic-state.pdf.

121. During the period, I kept a record of every report I could find in English and Arabic of the Islamic State and Nusra governing, abusing civilians, and fighting with other rebel groups.

122. Weiss and Hassan, *ISIS*, 203.

123. Ibid., 208–211.

124. Plato, *Republic* 8:565d. See *Plato in Twelve Volumes*, Vols. 5 & 6 translated by Paul Shorey (Cambridge: Harvard University Press, 1969), http://www.perseus.tufts.edu/hopper/text?doc=Perseus%3Atext%3A1999.01.0168%3Abook%3D8%3Apage%3D565.

125. The strategic differences between the two groups blurred somewhat in late 2014 when Nusra began to seize territory from other Sunni rebel groups in northern Syria. Reflecting this change, Nusra leaders began to publicly praise Naji's work for its advice on governance. "It should be the reference for the leaders of the mujahids administering the regions" tweeted one official. "Despite all our differences with the State group, it is the organization that has most applied what is in the book, after

Jabhat al-Nusra." See "Abu al-Jamajem" [online pseudonym] (@AbuJ-amajem), Twitter post, March 6, 2015, https://twitter.com/AbuJamajem/status/573714693828800512/photo/1. My thanks to Sam Heller for the reference.

126. Theo Padnos, "My Captivity," *New York Times Magazine*, October 29, 2014, http://www.nytimes.com/2014/10/28/magazine/theo-padnos-american-journalist-on-being-kidnapped-tortured-and-released-in-syria.html?_r=1.

127. Weiss and Hassan, *ISIS*, 190.

128. "@wikibaghdady" [online pseudonym], "Asrar dawlat al-Baghdadi," Twitter posts, December 17 and December 18, 2013, https://docs.google.com/document/d/1wEQ0FKosa1LcUB3tofeub1UxaT5A-suROyDExgV9nUY/edit.

129. See Zawahiri, "Shahada," 6.

130. Abu Ahmad, "al-Haqa'iq"; @wikibaghdady, "Asrar dawlat al-Baghdadi," December 17 and December 18. Abu Ahmad asserts that @wikibaghdady's account of Baghdadi's meetings with Nusra leaders is generally correct but that he was wrong when he said Jawlani never met with Baghdadi.

131. Abu Bakr al-Baghdadi, "Wa-bashshir al-mu'minin," April 9, 2013, posted online by "tawtheek00jihad00dawlah" [online pseudonym], February 20, 2014, http://tawtheek00jihad00dawlah.wordpress.com/2014/02/20/وبشر-المؤمنين-أبو-بكر-البغدادي/. Baghdadi sent several other Islamic State leaders with Jawlani, including the Islamic State's spokesman Abu Muhammad al-Adnani. See Hashimi, "Ashya' min hayat al-Baghdadi."

132. "Jabhat al-Nusra," *Mapping Militant Organizations*, Stanford University, November 12, 2014, http://web.stanford.edu/group/mappingmilitants/cgi-bin/groups/view/493#note24.

133. Abu Muhammad al-Jawlani, "About the Fields of al-Sham," audio message, *al-Manara al-Bayda'*, April 10, 2013, original Arabic audio message and English translation available at Aaron Y. Zelin, "al-Manarah al-Baydah' Foundation for Media Production presents a new audio message from Jabhat al-Nusrah's Abu Muhammad al-Jawlani (al-Golani): 'About the Fields of al-Sham,'" April 19, 2013, *Jihadology*, http://jihadology.net/2013/04/10/al-manarah-al-bay%E1%B8%8Da-foundation-for-media-production-presents-a-new-audio-message-from-jabhat-al-nu%E1%B9%A3rahs-abu-mu%E1%B8%A5ammad-al-jawlani-al-golani-about-the-fields-of-al-sham/.

134. Letter from Abu Bakr al-Baghdadi to Ayman al-Zawahiri, April 10, 2013, quoted in Zawahiri, "Shahada."

135. Ayman al-Zawahiri, "Letter from Ayman al-Zawahiri to Abu Bakr al-Baghdadi and Abu Muhammad al-Jawlani [English translation]," personal correspondence, May 22, 2013, http://s3.documentcloud.org/documents/710588/translation-of-ayman-al-zawahiris-letter.pdf.

136. Letter from Abu Bakr al-Baghdadi to one of the "officials of the group," July 29, 2013, quoted in Zawahiri, "Shahada," 4–5. It's unclear if the "group" refers to al-Qaeda or the Islamic State.

137. Tradition from *Sahih Bukhari*. Adam Gadahn quotes the tradition in a letter to an unknown recipient in late January 2011. See Adam Gadahn, "Letter from Adam Gadahn [English translation]," SOCOM-2012-0000004, Harmony Program, Combating Terrorism Center at West Point, January

2011, https://www.ctc.usma.edu/posts/letter-from-adam-gadahn-en glish-translation-2. Original Arabic version available at https://www.ctc .usma.edu/posts/letter-from-adam-gadahn-original-language-2.

138. Abu Muhammad al-Adnani, "Fa-dharhum wa-ma yaftarun," audio message, *Mu'assasat al-Furqan*, June 19, 2013, audio message and Arabic transcript both available at Pieter Van Ostaeyen, "An internal Jihadi strife—Jabhat an-Nusra and the Islamic State in Iraq and as-Sham," *pietervanostaeyen*, June 22, 2013, https://pietervanostaeyen.wordpress .com/2013/06/22/an-internal-jihadi-strife-jabhat-an-nusra-and-the-is lamic-state-in-iraq-and-as-sham/. See also Bunzel, "Ideology," 26.

139. "Bayan bi-sha'ni 'alaqat jama'at Qa'idat al-Jihad bi-jama'at al-Dawla al-Islamiyya fi al-'Iraq wa-l-Sham," *Tanzim Qai'dat al-Jihad—al-Qiyada al-'Amma*, January 22, 2014, http://justpaste.it/ea9k. Al-Qaeda has always had a complicated relationship with its affiliate in Iraq. In his 2011 private letter, Adam Gadahn claims the Islamic State technically answered to al-Qaeda but "operational relations between the leadership of al-Qaeda and the State have been cut off for quite some time." Gadahn was probably referring to operations inside Iraq because the Islamic State continued to take direction from al-Qaeda for external operations, at least in the early years. In a private letter written on November 19, 2007, Bin Laden asks al-Masri for an update on a plot against Halliburton, and repeated this question on January 25, 2008. Six weeks later, a March 6, 2008, letter asks al-Masri to carry out attacks on the Danes for printing cartoons lampooning the Prophet. See "Letter from unknown al-Qaeda leader to Abu Ayyub al-Masri," November 19, 2007, and January 28, 2008. The letters are part of the batch of letters discussed in chapter 2, note 14.

140. Abu Muhammad al-Adnani, "Ma kana hadha manhajuna wa-lan yakun," April 17, 2014, http://justpaste.it/makan.

141. "al-Garshi Gwantanimu" [online pseudonym] (@MKST1111), Twitter post *(account since deleted)*, February 3, 2014, https://twitter.com/MKS T1111/status/430293977561329665.

142. "Muhib al-Dawla Baqiya" [online pseudonym] (@klklklkl1234), Twitter post *(account since deleted)*, February 9, 2014, https://twitter.com/kl klklkl1234/status/432604752359481344.

143. See, for example, "Abu Abd al-Muhsin" [online pseudonym] (@ma-jed9432), Twitter post, February 16, 2014, https://twitter.com/majed9432 /status/435196345948078080; "Munasir al-Islam" [online pseudonym] (@ gzrawi9), Twitter post *(account since deleted)*, February 3, 2014, https:// twitter.com/gzrawi9/status/430244970210275328.

144. Zawahiri, "Shahada."

145. "The brethren in the Shura required an oath from the martyred (as we consider him) Shaykh Abu Umar al-Baghdadi that his emir is Shaykh Usama bin Laden (may God bless him) and that the State follows the Qa'idat al-Jihad group." See Zawahiri, "Shahada," 1–2.

146. Abu Muhammad al-Adnani, "'Udhran amir al-Qa'ida," *Wakalat al-Anba' al-Islamiyya*, May 11, 2014, http://www.dawaalhaq.com/?p=12828.

147. The spokesman, Abu Muhammad al-Adnani, was in prison during the first incarnation of the Islamic State so he might be unfamiliar with the correspondence between its leaders and al-Qaeda. Although Adnani is right that the group ignored al-Qaeda's instructions regarding what the State was to target inside Iraq, internal al-Qaeda memos disprove his

claim that al-Qaeda never asked about the disposition of its forces inside the country. "Very quickly write us a report on your conditions and your assessment of the situation in the current stage" an al-Qaeda leader wrote al-Masri on January 25, 2008. "How are things and conditions on the ground especially in Diyala, Mosul, and Baghdad?" the leader asked in the same letter. "We would also like to reiterate our request that you write us complete and detailed reports about your current conditions" instructed a member of al-Qaeda's leadership to the Islamic State's leader on March 10, 2008. Al-Qaeda's leaders framed their instructions as "advice" rather than orders, but that doesn't mean they expected the Islamic State to ignore them. In a letter dated March 6, 2008, Zawahiri "advises" the Islamic State to set up a human resources department "to look for hidden capabilities among the brothers who have joined the State and activate them." Zawahiri further advises the State to establish an independent legal council and Shari'a court to resolve disputes for all Muslims whether they belonged to the State or not. See chapter 2, note 14.

148. Walid Ghanim, "Man huwa 'Abu Khalid al-Suri' wa-kayfa qutila??!" *All 4Syria*, February 24, 2014, http://www.all4syria.info/Archive/132991.

149. "Snafi al-Nasr" [online pseudonym] (@Snafialnasr), Twitter post, February 23, 2014, https://twitter.com/Snafialnasr/status/437590454604136448. See also Ghanim, "Man huwa 'Abu Khalid al-Suri' wa-kayfa qutila??!"; Hajj, "'Abu Khalid al-Suri.'"

150. See Cole Bunzel, "The Islamic State of Disobedience: al-Baghdadi Triumphant," *Jihadica*, October 5, 2013, http://www.jihadica.com/the -islamic-state-of-disobedience-al-baghdadis-defiance/.

151. Abu Qatada, "Risala min al-Shaykh Abi Qatada ila ikhwanihi al-mujahi-din," January 20, 2014, http://twitmail.com/email/620473351/30/.

152. Abu Muhammad al-Maqdisi, "Allahumma inni abra' ilayka mimma san'a' ha'ula'," *Minbar al-Tawhid wa-l-Jihad*, January 25, 2014, http:// www.tawhed.ws/r?i=25011401. See Cole Bunzel, "The Islamic State of Disunity: Jihadism Divided," *Jihadica*, January 30, 2014, http://www .jihadica.com/the-islamic-state-of-disunity-jihadism-divided/.

153. Bunzel, "Jihadism Divided."

154. Ibid. See also Bunzel, "Ideology," 34.

155. "Shami Witness" [online pseudonym] (@ShamiWitness), Twitter post, May 17, 2014, https://twitter.com/ShamiWitness/status/467790551777 959936.

156. "Shami Witness" [online pseudonym] (@ShamiWitness), Twitter post, July 12, 2014, https://twitter.com/ShamiWitness/status/487865881276 739584.

157. Bunzel, "Ideology," 28.

158. Statement by Abu Khalid al-Suri, January 17, 2014, http://www.hanein .info/vb/image/imgcache/2014/01/1941.jpg.

159. The following account is based on Lulu's videotaped confes-sion: "al-Ard al-Mubarika" [online pseudonym], "I'tirafat munas-siq 'amaliyyat ightiyyal al-Shaykh Abi Khalid al-Suri yatluha kalimat li-l-Shaykh Abi 'Abd Allah," YouTube video, April 24, 2014, https:// www.youtube.com/watch?v=Fvh79FdaBbg. For a summary, see Ah-mad al-Uqda, "Ahrar al-Sham takshif 'an huwiyyat qatil Abu Khalid al-Suri," *Siraj Press*, April 25, 2014, http://www.sirajpress.com/1517

مقال/(أحرار-الشام)-تكشف-عن-هوية-قاتل-أبو-خالد-السوري/; see also "'Zaman al-Wasl' tanshur nass i'tirafat 'munassiq ightiyyal Abi Khalid al-Suri'," *Zaman al-Wasl*, n.d., https://www.zamanalwsl.net/mobile/readNews.php ?id=49018.

160. "Syria Rebel Leader Abu Khaled al-Suri Killed in Aleppo," *BBC News*, February 24, 2014, http://www.bbc.com/news/world-middle-east-26318 646.

161. "Syria: Countrywide Conflict Report #4," Syria Conflict Mapping Project, Carter Center, September 11, 2014, 25, https://www.cartercenter .org/resources/pdfs/peace/conflict_resolution/syria-conflict/Nationwi deUpdate-Sept-18-2014.pdf; Weiss and Hassan, *ISIS*, 184.

162. See Weiss and Hassan for an overview of the different motives that drew recruits to the Islamic State (*ISIS*, 146–159).

CHAPTER 5

1. Yasmine Fathi, "Mubarak's Fall Spawns End of Times Prophecies," *Ahram Online*, September 25, 2011, http://english.ahram.org.eg/NewsContent Print/1/0/22476/Egypt/0/Mubaraks-fall-spawns-End-of-Times-proph ecies.aspx; Charles Cameron, "Arab Spring and Apocalyptic Dawn," *Zenpundit*, October 2, 2011, http://zenpundit.com/?p=4358.

2. "The World's Muslims: Unity and Diversity," Pew Research Center, August 9, 2012, http://www.pewforum.org/2012/08/09/the-worlds-muslims -unity-and-diversity-executive-summary/.

3. Musa Cerantonio, "Syria Lecture—Melbourne—Talk 1—Musa Cerantonio," YouTube video, December 24, 2012, https://www.youtube.com /watch?v=yrt4AMMA2vg&feature=youtube_gdata_player.

4. Muhammad Nasir al-Din al-Albani, *Takhrij ahadith fada'il al-Sham wa-Dimashq* (Riyadh: Maktabat al-Ma'arif, 2000), 10.

5. Ibid., 14.

6. Ibid., 38.

7. Ibid., 64.

8. Abu Bakr al-Baghdadi, "Baqiya fi al-'Iraq wa-l-Sham," audio recording, June 2014, https://archive.org/details/seham_201307.

9. Nour Malas, "Ancient Prophecies Motivate Islamic State Militants," *Wall Street Journal*, November 18, 2014, http://www.wsj.com/articles /ancient-prophecies-motivate-islamic-state-militants-1416357441.

10. Louise Cheer, "Facebook Page Calls for Release of Australian Hate Preacher Who Claimed to Be Waging Jihad in the Middle East," *Daily Mail*, July 12, 2012, http://www.dailymail.co.uk/news/article-2689850 /Facebook-page-calls-release-Australian-hate-preacher.html. For Cerantonio's apocalyptic worldview, see Graeme Wood, "What ISIS Really Wants," *The Atlantic*, March 2015, http://www.theatlantic.com/features /archive/2015/02/what-isis-really-wants/384980/.

11. *Sunan Ibn Majah* (http://sunnah.com/ibnmajah/36/63).

12. On Zarqawi's nickname, see Loretta Napoleoni, *Insurgent Iraq: Al Zarqawi and the New Generation* (New York: Seven Stories Press, 2005), 42.

13. See the "Kitab al-fitan" chapter of Ibn Majah's *Sunan*, http://sunnah .com/ibnmajah/36. Abu Mus'ab al-Suri devoted a few pages to the topic of the strangers in his discussion of the End-Time prophecies. See David Cook, "Abu Musa'b [*sic*] al-Suri and Abu Musa'b [*sic*] al-Zarqawi: The

Apocalyptic Theorist and the Apocalyptic Practitioner," unpublished, 14.

14. Mariam Karouny, "Apocalyptic Prophecies Drive Both Sides to Syrian Battle for End of Time," *Reuters*, April 1, 2014, http://www.reuters.com/article/2014/04/01/us-syria-crisis-prophecy-insight-idUSBREA3013420140401.

15. Robert Mackey, "The Case for ISIS, Made in a British Accent," *New York Times*, June 20, 2014, http://www.nytimes.com/2014/06/21/world/middleeast/the-case-for-isis-made-in-a-british-accent.html?_&_r=0.

16. For information on the Strangers' media operation, see Cole Bunzel, "A Jihadi Civil War of Words: The Ghuraba' Media Foundation and Minbar al-Tawhid wa'l-Jihad," *Jihadica*, October 21, 2014, http://www.jihadica.com/a-jihadi-civil-war/.

17. Abu Umar al-Hurani, "Ghuraba'—al-Dawla al-Islamiyya fi al-'Iraq wa-l-Sham—Suwwar min ard al-malahim," YouTube video *(video has since been deleted)*, October 29, 2013, https://www.youtube.com/watch?v=i9JPc4R_oDM.

18. *Ghuraba' bilad al-Sham*, personal blog, http://williamhamdan.blogspot.com/.

19. "'Da'ish' yudashshan futuhat jadida fi 'Marj Dabiq'," *Al Hayat*, August 15, 2014, http://alhayat.com/Articles/4133949/.

20. Abu Mus'ab al-Zarqawi, "Ayna ahl al-muru'at?" *Kalimat mudi'a: al-Kitab al-jami' li-khutab wa-kalimat al-shaykh al-mu'taz bi-dinihi*, September 11, 2004, 159, http://e-prism.org/images/AMZ-Ver1.doc.

21. Tradition from *Sahih Muslim*, http://sunnah.com/muslim/54/44.

22. Ibid. Zarqawi's public statements were suffused with apocalyptic rhetoric. See Cook, "Abu Musa'b al-Suri and Abu Musa'b al-Zarqawi."

23. Abu Umar al-Baghdadi, "Innama al-mu'minun ikhwatun," January 1, 2009, *al-Majmu' li-qadat Dawlat al-'Iraq al-Islamiyya* (Nukhbat al-I'lam al-Jihadi, 2010).

24. E. W. Brooks, "The Campaign of 716–718, from Arabic Sources," *Journal of Hellenic Studies* 19 (1899): 19–31, 20.

25. Ibn Jarir al-Tabari, *The History of al-Tabari, Vol. 24: The Empire in Transition*, transl. David Powers (New York: State University of New York Press, 1989), 41.

26. Abu Muhammad al-Adnani, "Wa-la yumakkinanna lahum dinahum al-ladhi irtada lahum" (April 2014).

27. *Dabiq* 1 (Ramadan 1435): 3–5.

28. "'Da'ish' yudashshan," *Al Hayat*.

29. "8 qutila li-tanzim 'al-Dawla' fi ishtibakat ma'a al-Jaysh al-Hurr 'inda qaryat Dabiq bi-Halab," *Smart News*, September 24, 2014, http://smartnews-agency.com/news/8-في-اشتباكات-مع-الجيش-الحر-عند-قرية-دابق-بحلب-قتلى-لتنظيم-الدولة-.

30. Malas, "Ancient Prophecies."

31. "There will be a truce between you and [the Romans]. They will betray you and march against you under eighty banners, under each banner 12,000 troops." In another version, "They will gather for the battle. At that time, they will come under eighty banners, under each banner 12,000 troops." See "Kitab al-fitan" in the *Sunan* of Ibn Majah.

32. "Casey" [online pseudonym], "Video: Message from Dabiq, Wait. We Are Also Waiting," *WorldAnalysis.net*, October 15, 2014, http://worldanalysis.net/14/2014/10/video-message-dabiq-wait-also-waiting/.

33. "@Otaibiah_n511" [online pseudonym], Twitter post *(account since deleted)*, https://twitter.com/Otaibiah_n511/status/510669519354748928.

34. "@88adee" [online pseudonym], Twitter post *(account since deleted)*, https://twitter.com/88adee/status/517764254762414080.

35. "@999Rhs" [online pseudonym], Twitter post *(account since deleted)*, https://twitter.com/999Rhs/status/517764791398440960.

36. *Dabiq 5* (Muharram 1436): 33.

37. "al-'Abd al-abiq . . . ila Marj Dabiq," *Platform Media*, September 11, 2014, https://www.alplatformmedia.com/vb/showthread.php?p=457470. My thanks to Cole Bunzel for this source; "Why Islamic State Chose Town of Dabiq for Propaganda," *BBC News*, November 17, 2014, http://www.bbc.com/news/world-middle-east-30083303.

38. Michael D. Danti, "Planning for Safeguarding Heritage Sites in Syria," ASOR Syrian Heritage Initiative, Weekly Report 1 (August 11, 2014), http://www.asor-syrianheritage.org/wp-content/uploads/2015/03/ASOR_CHI_Weekly_Report_01r.pdf. Over a thousand years earlier, apocalyptic partisans of the Abbasids had desecrated Sulayman's remains. See Eric Schroeder, *Muhammad's People: An Anthology of Muslim Civilization* (Mineola, NY: Dover Publications, Inc., 2002), 262.

39. "ISIS and Obama's Summit," *The Wall Street Journal*, February 16, 2015, http://www.wsj.com/articles/isis-and-obamas-summit-1424132931.

40. Abu Umar al-Baghdadi, "Risala ila hukkam al-bayt al-abyad . . . wa-sa'ir ahlafihim min ru'asa' al-duwal al-nasraniyya," November 7, 2008, *al-Majmu' li-qadat Dawlat al-'Iraq al-Islamiyya* (Nukhbat al-I'lam al-Jihadi, 2010).

41. The "White Minaret" is the name of Nusra's media outlet, founded before the group split from the Islamic State.

42. Abu Muhammad al-Adnani, "Lan yadurrukum illa adhan," audio recording, February 2013, https://archive.org/details/forKan.001.

43. Abu Bakr al-Baghdadi, "Baqiya fi al-'Iraq wa-l-Sham" (June 2014), https://archive.org/details/seham_201307.

44. David Cook, *Studies in Muslim Apocalyptic (Studies in Late Antiquity and Early Islam, No. 21)* (Princeton, NJ: Darwin Press, 2002), 96–97.

45. "@dAwLa_KiLaFa1" [online pseudonym], Twitter post *(account since deleted)*, https://twitter.com/dAwLa__KiLaFa1/status/551438259356983296.

46. Guy Taylor, "Apocalypse Prophecies Drive Islamic State Strategy, Recruiting Efforts," *Washington Times*, January 5, 2015, http://www.washingtontimes.com/news/2015/jan/5/apocalypse-prophecies-drive-islamic-state-strategy/?page=all.

47. "Batirashvili Badria" [online pseudonym] (@BadriaArvi), Twitter post *(account since deleted)*, October 23, 2014, https://twitter.com/BadriaArvi/status/525210983489236992. Islamic State supporters are not the only group to invoke the Antichrist in the Syrian context: Anti-Assad factions have regularly tweeted about Hizballah commander Hassan Nasrallah under the Arabic hashtag #The_Antichrist_of_the_Resistance," referring to his support for the Assad regime.

48. "Abd al-Malak al-Matiri" [online pseudonym] (@superbinilly), Twitter post, January 11, 2015, https://twitter.com/katfqanoni203/status/554282910891515904.

49. Tradition from *Sahih Muslim*. Abu Qatada al-Filistini, a jihadist critic of the Islamic State, quotes the prophecy favorably in his "Qira'at fi

al-Nubu'at: al-Masih al-Dajjal." See Abu Qatada al-Filistini, "Qira'at fi al-Nubu'at: al-Masih al-Dajjal," *Minbar al-Tawhid wa-l-Jihad,* n.d., 16, https://www.tawhed.ws/r?i=p4qqi3j8.

50. "Twelver" Shi'a believe there were twelve legitimate leaders or imams after Muhammad died, beginning with the Prophet's son-in-law Ali and running through his descendants. Twelvers believe the last of these imams went into hiding and will reappear as the Mahdi. See Najam Haider, *Shi'i Islam: An Introduction* (New York: Cambridge University Press, 2014), 145–166.

51. Karouny, "Apocalyptic Prophecies."

52. Nu'aym bin Hammad, *Kitab al-fitan* (Beirut: Dar al-Fikr li-l-Taba'a, 1992), 190.

53. "kemowen5" [online pseudonym], "Amin 'amm Hizb Allah al-'Iraqi al-Jaysh al-Hurr huwa jaysh al-Sufyani alladhi yuqatil al-Imam al-Mahdi," YouTube video, May 4, 2013, https://www.youtube.com/watch?v=sZjIF91kog4.

54. Cook, *Studies in Muslim Apocalyptic,* 133.

55. Ibid.

56. Tabari, *The History of al-Tabari, Vol. 27: The 'Abbasid Revolution,* 177–178. See Asad Ahmed, *The Religious Elite of the Early Islamic Hijaz: Five Prosopographical Case Studies* (Oxford: Prosopographica et Genealogica, 2011), 119.

57. Barbara Roggema, *The Legend of Sergius Bahira: Easter Christian Apologetics and Apocalyptic in Response to Islam* (Boston: Brill, 2008), 76.

58. Wilferd Madelung, "Abu 'l-'Amaytar the Sufyani," *Jerusalem Studies in Arabic and Islam* 24 (2000): 327–343, 329.

59. Moshe Gil, *A History of Palestine, 634–1099* (New York: Cambridge University Press, 1992), 293–294.

60. "Fidiyu: al-'Ar'ur yad'u wa-yatamanna bi-anna yakun tahtu rayat jaysh al-Sufyani alladhi sayazhur fi akhir al-zaman wa-yuharib jaysh al-Imam al-Mahdi 'alayhi al-salam," *Makadait,* January 2, 2014, http://www.makadait.com/?p=15659.

61. Jean-Pierre Filiu, *Apocalypse in Islam,* transl. M.B. DeBevoise (Berkeley: University of California Press, 2011), 199.

62. Nu'aym b. Hammad, *Kitab al-Fitan* (1993), 162.

63. Ruhollah Hosseinian, "Istishmam bu-yi havadith akhir al-zamani," *Fars News Agency,* 6 Tir 1362 (June 27, 2013), http://farsnews.com/newstext.php?nn=13920403000166.

64. "Subhan Allah" [online pseudonym] (@ahmd878), Twitter post, May 31, 2013, https://twitter.com/ahmd878/status/340489376469504003.

65. Wilferd Madelung, "The Sufyani between Tradition and History," *Studia Islamica* 63 (1986): 4–48, 13.

66. Ibid., 22.

67. Ibid., 20.

68. Robert Windrem, "ISIS by the Numbers: Foreign Fighter Total Keeps Growing," *NBC News,* March 1, 2015, http://www.nbcnews.com/storyline/isis-terror/isis-numbers-foreign-fighter-total-keeps-growing-n314731.

69. Barbara Slavin, "Shiite Militias Mixed Blessing in Iraq, Syria," *Al-Monitor,* February 9, 2015, http://www.al-monitor.com/pulse/originals/2015/02/shiite-militias-mixed-blessing-iraq-syria.html.

70. Zack Beauchamp, "Iraq's Yazidis: Who They Are and Why the US Is Bombing ISIS to Save Them," *Vox,* August 8, 2014, http://www.vox.com

/2014/8/8/5982421/yazidis-yezidis-iraq-crisis-bombing; Gerard Russell, "The Peacock Angel and the Pythagorean Theorem," *Foreign Policy*, August 8, 2014, http://foreignpolicy.com/2014/08/08/the-peacock-angel-and-the-pythagorean-theorem/.

71. *Dabiq* 4 (Dhul-Hijjah 1435): 15.

72. John D. Sutter, "Slavery's Last Stronghold," *CNN*, http://www.cnn.com/interactive/2012/03/world/mauritania.slaverys.last.stronghold/.

73. Ruth Sherlock, "Islamic State Commanders 'Using Yazidi Virgins for Sex,'" *Telegraph*, October 18, 2014, http://www.telegraph.co.uk/news/worldnews/islamic-state/11171874/Islamic-State-commanders-using-Yazidi-virgins-for-sex.html.

74. Tradition from *Sahih Muslim*.

75. *Dabiq* 4: 14–17.

76. *Dabiq* 4: 17.

77. "ISIS militants speak about taking Yazidi girls," *The Telegraph*, November 11, 2014, https://www.youtube.com/watch?v=LJHW-xQ4XgE. See Y. Yehoshua, R. Green, and A. Agron, "Sex Slavery In The Islamic State—Practices, Social Media Discourse, And Justifications"; "Jabhat Al-Nusra: ISIS Is Taking Our Women As Sex Slaves Too," MEMRI, August 17, 2015, http://www.memrijttm.org/sex-slavery-in-the-islamic-state-practices-social-media-discourse-and-justifications-jabhat-al-nusra-isis-is-taking-our-women-as-sex-slaves-too.html.

78. Hadir Mahmud, "Bi-l-fidiyu . . . jara'im Da'ish fi al-'Iraq wa-Suriya. al-nisa' mathalan," *El Badil*, November 4, 2014, http://elbadil.com/2014/11/04/بالفيديو-جرائم-داعش-في-العراق-وسوريا/.

79. "Manshur jadid li 'Da'ish' . . . as'ila wa-ajwiba hawla sabi wa muwaqa'at 'al-nisa' al-kafirat' jinsiyyan," *CNN Arabic*, December 13, 2014, http://arabic.cnn.com/middleeast/2014/12/13/isis-justification-female-slaves.

80. Russell Myers, "British Female Jihadis Running ISIS 'Brothels' Allowing Killers to Rape Kidnapped Yazidi Women," *Mirror*, September 10, 2014, http://www.mirror.co.uk/news/uk-news/british-female-jihadis-running-isis-4198165; Ruth Sherlock, "Islamic State Commanders 'Using Yazidi Virgins for Sex.'"

81. Anna Steele, "Woman Uses Hidden Camera to Expose Life under Islamic State (+video)," *Christian Science Monitor*, September 25, 2014, http://www.csmonitor.com/World/Middle-East/2014/0925/Woman-uses-hidden-camera-to-expose-life-under-Islamic-State-video.

82. Damien Gayle, "All-Female Islamic State Police Squad Tortured New Mother with Spiked Clamp Device Called a 'Biter' after She Was Caught Breastfeeding in Public," *Daily Mail*, December 31, 2014, http://www.dailymail.co.uk/news/article-2890911/All-female-Islamic-State-police-squad-tortured-woman-device-called-biter-caught-breastfeeding-public.html.

83. al-Hasan al-Yusi, *Zahr al-akam fi al-amthal wa-l-hikam* (Dar al-Thaqafa, 1981), 833 (the passage is available online here: http://www.madinahnet.com/books40/833-صفحة-الحكم-والأمثال-في-الأكم-زهر/).

84. Khaled Abd al-Muhsin, "'Nisa' fi firash Da'ish' riwayat haqiqiyya li-ahdath damiya. Katib yakshif asrar 'jawari al-khalifa al-Baghdadi'," *Al Ahram*, December 14, 2014, http://gate.ahram.org.eg/News/572214.aspx.

85. Shadiya Sarhan, "Akhtar nisa' Da'ish tanshur 'dalil aramil al-jihadiyyin' 'ala Twitir,": 24, January 26, 2015, http://24.ae/article/133546/.aspx.

86. Ali Rajab, "Bi-l-suwwar . . . abraz 'danjawanat Da'ish'," *Veto*, December 10, 2014, http://www.vetogate.com/1370965.

87. Hani al-Zahiri, "'Niswan Da'ish' al-shaqrawat," *Al Hayat*, December 23, 2014.

88. Carolyn Hoyle, Alexandra Bradford, and Ross Frenett, "Becoming Mulan? Female Western Migrants to ISIS," Institute for Strategic Dialogue, January 2015, 10–15, http://www.strategicdialogue.org/ISDJ2969_Becoming_Mulan_01.15_WEB.PDF. The tweeter, Umm Ubaydah, was living in the Islamic State when she made her comments online. See Joshi Herrmann, "Internet Brides of Jihad: How Islamic State Is Using Social Media to Lure Young British Women to Syria," *London Evening Standard*, December 2, 2014, http://www.standard.co.uk/lifestyle/london-life/internet-brides-of-jihad-how-islamic-state-is-using-social-media-to-lure-young-british-women-to-syria-9846143.html.

89. Herrmann, "Internet Brides."

90. "UN Terror Expert: One Austrian 'Jihad Poster Girl' Is Dead after Moving to Syria to Join ISIS," *NY Daily News*, December 18, 2014, http://www.nydailynews.com/news/world/expert-austrian-teen-girl-dead-joining-isis-article-1.2049826.

91. Abu Muhammad al-Adnani, "Ma kana hadha manhajuna wa-lan yakun," audio message, *Mu'assasat al-Furqan*, April 17, 2014, audio message and English translation available at Pieter Van Ostaeyen, "Message by ISIS Shaykh Abu Muhammad al-'Adnani as-Shami," *pietervanostaeyen*, April 18, 2014, https://pietervanostaeyen.wordpress.com/2014/04/18/message-by-isis-shaykh-abu-muhammad-al-adnani-as-shami/.

92. The Arabic word *khalifa*, Anglicized as "caliph," means successor.

93. See, for example, Muhammad Nasir al-Din al-Albani, *Silsilat al-ahadith al-sahiha*, vol. 1 (Riyadh: Maktabat al-Ma'arif li-l-Nashar wa-l-Tawzi'), 34–36; Abd Allah bin Wakil, "*al-Malik al-'Adud wa-l-Malik al-Jabari*," *Ahl al-Hadith*, June 14, 2003, http://www.ahlalhdeeth.com/vb/showthread.php?t=155508.

94. Ayman al-Zawahiri, "Tawjihat 'amma li-l-'aml al-jihadi," *Minbar al-Tawhid wa-l-Jihad*, September 16, 2013, https://www.tawhed.ws/r?i=16091301. Bin Laden's secretary in Africa, Fadil Harun, alludes to the prophecy several times in his autobiography, connecting the event with the End Times and the appearance of the Muslim savior, the Mahdi: "The caliph, who is not yet present, will definitely appear when the prerequisite conditions are fulfilled. He will pave the way for the appearance of the Mahdi (peace be upon him) and the descent of Jesus (peace be upon him). We will unite under him for the benefit of the entire world because Islam is ordained for the whole of mankind and not for Muslims alone" (Harun, *al-Harb 'ala al-Islam: Qissat Fadil Harun*, 2 vols., February 26, 2009, 2:723).

95. "al-Bin'ali . . . Mufti Da'ish 'al-Damawi'," *Bawabat al-Harakat al-Islamiyya*, January 27, 2015, http://www.islamist-movements.com/25818.

96. Turki ibn Mubarak al-Bin'ali, "al-Qiyafa fi 'adm ishtirat al-tamkin al-kamil li-l-khilafa," April 30, 2014, 1, available at *Jihadica*, http://www.jihadica.com/wp-content/uploads/2014/07/اشتراط-التمكين-الكامل-للخلافة-في-عدم-القيافة.doc. See Cole Bunzel, "The Caliphate's Scholar-in-Arms," *Jihadica*, July 9, 2014, http://www.jihadica.com/the-caliphate%E2%80%99s-scholar-in-arms/.

97. Bin'ali, "al-Qiyafa," 2.
98. Ibid., 3.
99. Ibid., 3.
100. Ibid., 4.
101. Ibid., 6.
102. Ibid., 7–8.
103. Ibid., 10.
104. Ibid., 14–15.
105. Ibid., 12–14.
106. Bin'ali, "Madd al-ayadi li-bay'at al-Baghdadi," July 21, 2013, https://ar chive.org/details/baghdadi-001. See Joas Wagemakers, "Al-Qaida Advises the Arab Spring: The Case for al-Baghdadi," *Jihadica*, September 21, 2013, http://www.jihadica.com/al-qaida-advises-the-arab-spring-the -case-for-al-baghdadi/.
107. Bin'ali, "Madd al-ayadi," 3. Juhayman al-Utaybi, the man who stormed the Meccan mosque after declaring his companion the Mahdi, believed the Mahdi would be a descendent of Muhammad's grandsons. In his treatise on the End of Days, Utaybi quotes a prophecy by Muhammad: "The Mahdi is from my descendants from the son of Fatima." See Juhayman al-Utaybi, "al-Fitan wa-akhbar al-Mahdi wa-nuzul Isa ('alayhi al-salam) wa-ashrat al-sa'a," *Minbar al-Tawhid wa-l-Jihad*, 18.
108. Twelver Shi'a call Ja'far "the Liar" because he denied his brother had a son, which would have made Ja'far the twelfth imam instead of the son. See Moojan Momen, *An Introduction to Shi'i Islam: The History and Doctrines of Twelver Shi'ism* (New Haven, CT: Yale University Press, 1987), 59–60, 161.
109. Bin'ali, "Madd al-ayadi," 4–5.
110. Ibid., 6–7.
111. Ibid., 11–12.
112. Ibid., 12–13.
113. Ibid., 13–15.
114. Ibid., 15–16.
115. Ibid., 6.
116. Abu Muhammad al-Maqdisi, "Hadha ba'da ma 'indi wa-laysa kulluhu," *Minbar al-Tawhid wa-l-Jihad* (June–July 2014), http://tawhed.ws /r?i=01071401.

CHAPTER 6

1. "The Capture of Mosul: Terror's New Headquarters," *Economist*, June 14, 2014, http://www.economist.com/news/leaders/21604160-iraqs-sec ond-city-has-fallen-group-wants-create-state-which-wage-jihad.
2. Zana Khasraw Gul, "Who Is in Control of Mosul?" *openDemocracy*, July 7, 2014, https://www.opendemocracy.net/zana-khasraw-gul/who-is -in-control-of-mosul.
3. Associated Press, "Fear, Sectarianism behind Iraq Army Collapse," *Haaretz*, June 13, 2014, http://www.haaretz.com/news/middle-east/1.5 98575; Nico Prucha, "Is This the Most Successful Release of a Jihadist Video Ever?" *Jihadica*, May 19, 2014, http://www.jihadica.com /is-this-the-most-successful-release-of-a-jihadist-video-ever/.
4. Alexander Mikaberidze, *Conflict and Conquest in the Islamic World: A Historical Encyclopedia*, vol. 1 (Santa Barbara, CA: ABC-CLIO, 2011), 663–663.

5. Aaron Y. Zelin, "ISIS is Dead, Long Live the Islamic State," *Foreign Policy*, June 30, 2014, http://foreignpolicy.com/2014/06/30/isis-is-dead-long-live-the-islamic-state/.

6. Abu Muhammad al-Adnani, "Hadha wa'd Allah," Al-Battar Media Foundation, June 29, 2014, available at *Jihadica*, http://www.jihadica.com/wp-content/uploads/2014/07/هذا-وعد-الله.pdf. Full video of the speech is available at "Ajil wa-hamm" [online pseudonym], "Kalimat li-l-shaykh al-mujahid Abi Muhammad al-'Adnani—hadha wa'd Allah," Youtube video, June 29, 2014, https://www.youtube.com/watch?v=d4OZcLlMAOs.

7. Fadil Harun, *al-Harb 'ala al-Islam: Qissat Fadil Harun*, 2 vols., February 26, 2009, 1:686; available at https://www.ctc.usma.edu/posts/the-war-against-islam-the-story-of-fazul-harun-part-1-original-language-2. See Kévin Jackson, "The Forgotten Caliphate," *Jihadica*, December 31, 2014, http://www.jihadica.com/the-forgotten-caliphate/.

8. Anwar al-Awlaki, "Allah Is Preparing Us for Victory," transcr. Amatullah, ed. Mujahid fe Sabeelillah, 25–26, https://ia600609.us.archive.org/31/items/AllahIsPreparingUsForVictory-AnwarAlAwlaki/AllahIsPreparingUsForVictory.pdf.

9. Ayman al-Zawahiri, "Tawjihat 'amma li-l-'aml al-jihadi," *Minbar al-Tawhid wa-l-Jihad*, September 16, 2013, https://www.tawhed.ws/r?i=16091301.

10. Stern and Berger argue that the shift in discourse from weakness to strength was a major change in jihadist rhetoric; see Jessica Stern and J. M. Berger, *ISIS: The State of Terror* (New York: HarperCollins, 2015), 108–109, 117.

11. "Li-madha zahara 'al-khalifa' al-Da'ishi bi-l-'imama al-suda'?" *Al Arabiya*, July 6, 2014, http://www.alarabiya.net/ar/arab-and-world/iraq/2014/07/06/محمد-داعش-البغدادي-ليس-عمامة-سوداء-اقتفاءً-بالنبي--.html.

12. "Faris al-Dawla" [online pseudonym] (@M_N_B_A), Twitter post (*account since deleted*), July 5, 2014, https://twitter.com/M_N_B_A/status/485437010169982976; "Li-madha zahara 'al-khalifa' al-Da'ishi bi-l-'imama al-suda'?"

13. Abu Bakr al-Baghdadi, Mosul sermon, July 1, 2014, Arabic transcript available at http://justpaste.it/gtdd.

14. Ibid.

15. "Was It a Rolex? Caliph's Watch Sparks Guesses," *Al Arabiya*, July 6, 2014, http://english.alarabiya.net/en/variety/2014/07/06/Was-it-a-Rolex-Caliph-s-watch-sparks-guesses.html.

16. "Li-madha zahara 'al-khalifa' al-Da'ishi bi-l-'imama al-suda'?"

17. "al-Nafir ila ard al-Sham" [online pseudonym] (@daaghu345h), Twitter post, July 3, 2014, https://twitter.com/daaghu345h/status/484719022441648129.

18. "Muzmajir al-Sham" [online pseudonym] (@saleelalmajd1), Twitter post, July 3, 2014, https://twitter.com/saleelalmajd1/status/484745347697479680.

19. "Abu Hadhifa al-Maqdisi" [online pseudonym] (@glaopalo2), Twitter post (*account since deleted*), July 3, 2014, https://twitter.com/glaopalo2/status/484746768199192577.

20. "@salman15n" [online pseudonym], Twitter post (*account since deleted*), https://twitter.com/salman15n/status/529306591896809472.

21. "@khansaa000" [online pseudonym], Twitter post (*account since deleted*), https://twitter.com/khansaa000/status/526113636637757440; "Abu Yusuf

al-Zahiby" [online pseudonym] (@prince_zahab), Twitter post, February 8, 2015, https://twitter.com/prince_zahab/status/564576740836933632.

22. "Harad al-Mu'minin" [online pseudonym] (@RBG011), Twitter post (*account since deleted*), November 13, 2014, https://twitter.com/RBG011 /status/533238697848610816.

23. "Suwwar al-Dawla al-Islamiyya" [online pseudonym] (@isis_pic), Twitter post (*account since deleted*), January 17, 2015, https://twitter.com/isis_pic /status/556557099094663169/photo/1.

24. "Zakariyya al-Salami #Khilafa" [online pseudonym] (@zakjdidi), Twitter post (*account since deleted*), November 26, 2014, https://twitter.com /zakjdidi/status/537517046675034112.

25. *Dabiq* 6: 59.

26. *Dabiq* 5: 18.

27. Robert Hoyland, "Writing the Biography of the Prophet Muhammad," *History Compass* 5 (2007): 581–602.

28. "S'adat al-Wazira" [online pseudonym] (@s3adt_alwazera), Twitter post, March 11, 2015, https://twitter.com/s3adt_alwazera/status/575637105520 480256; "Belal" [online pseudonym] (@Faglal), Twitter post, March 7, 2015, https://twitter.com/Faglal/status/574248240834543616.

29. "#Asifa_al-Hazm" [online pseudonym] (@alhawazni), Twitter post, March 27, 2015, https://twitter.com/alhawazni/status/581779621370195968.

30. "Tania" [online pseudonym] (@TANIA_IRAQ), Twitter post, March 21, 2015, https://twitter.com/TANIA_IRAQ/status/579326527294160896.

31. Nearly a decade ago, I directed a team of Arabists who counted the citations in jihadist scholarly texts. Maqdisi was cited most, followed by Abu Qatada. See William McCants, "Militant Ideology Atlas: Executive Report," Combating Terrorism Center at West Point, November 1, 2006, https://www.ctc.usma.edu/posts/militant-ideology-atlas. In a strange twist, Maqdisi once cited the study and my blog as proof he was the jihadist big dog (see Robert Worth, "Credentials Challenged, Radical Quotes West Point," *New York Times*, April 29, 2009, http://www .nytimes.com/2009/04/30/world/middleeast/30jihad.html?_r=0).

32. Muhammad al-Da'ma, "Abu Qatada: Jama'at al-Baghdadi laysu ikhwanuna," *Asharq Al-Awsat*, December 7, 2014, http://aawsat.com/home /article/238521/أبو-قتادة-جماعة-البغدادي-ليسوا-إخواننا.

33. Abu Muhammad al-Maqdisi, "Wa-la takunu ka-allati naqadat ghazlaha min ba'da quwwatin ankanthan," *Minbar al-Tawhid wa-l-Jihad*, July 12, 2014, https://www.tawhed.ws/r?i=12071401, English translation available at "Sheikh Abu Muhammad al-Maqdisi on Proclamation of Caliphate," Kavkaz Center, July 20, 2014, http://www.kavkazcenter.com/eng/con tent/2014/07/20/19483.shtml.

34. "Ittisa' mubaya'at Da'ish fi al-mashraq wa-l-maghrab yuthir al-jadal wa-yada' nihayat li 'al-Qa'ida'," *Alkarama Press*, October 8, 2014, http://www .karamapress.com/arabic/?Action=ShowNews&ID=94643.

35. Muhammad bin Salih al-Muhajir, "al-Khulasa fi munaqashat i'lan al-khilafa," *Minbar al-Tawhid wa-l-Jihad*, August 2014, http://www .jihadica.com/wp-content/uploads/2014/10/al-Khulasa-fi-munaqashat -ilan-al-khilafa.doc. See Cole Bunzel, "A Jihadi Civil War of Words: The Ghuraba' Media Foundation and Minbar al-Tawhid wa'l-Jihad," *Jihadica*, October 21, 2014, http://www.jihadica.com/a-jihadi-civil-war/.

36. Muhajir, "Khulasa," 6–9.

37. Abu Dujana al-Basha, "Hadhihi risalatuna," audio message, *Mu'assasat al-Sahab*, posted by "Murasil" [online pseudonym] to Shabakat al-Jihad, September 26, 2014, http://www.shabakataljahad.com/vb/showthread .php?t=40231. See Kévin Jackson, "Al-Qaeda Revives Its Beef with the Islamic State," *Jihadica*, October 15, 2014, http://www.jihadica.com/al -qaeda-revives-its-beef-with-the-islamic-state/.

38. Cole Bunzel, "Al-Qaeda's Quasi-Caliph: The Recasting of Mullah 'Umar," *Jihadica*, July 23, 2014, http://www.jihadica.com/al-qaeda%E2%80%99s -quasi-caliph-the-recasting-of-mullah-%E2%80%98umar/. See also Cole Bunzel, "From Paper State to Caliphate: The Ideology of the Islamic State," The Brookings Project on U.S. Relations with the Islamic World, Analysis Paper No. 19 (March 2015): 33–34, http://www.brook ings.edu/~/media/research/files/papers/2015/03/ideology-of-islamic -state-bunzel/the-ideology-of-the-islamic-state.pdf. Similarly, Al-Qaeda's representative in Somalia, Fadil Harun, believed he had pledged allegiance to Mullah Omar as the commander of the faithful but his authority was confined to Afghanistan. See Harun, *Harb*, 2:90.

39. See Abu Khalid's and Abu Mus'ab al-Suri's letter scolding Bin Laden for defying Mullah Omar's command in Alan Cullison, "Inside Al-Qaeda's Hard Drive," *Atlantic*, September 1, 2004, http://www.theatlantic.com /magazine/archive/2004/09/inside-al-qaeda-s-hard-drive/303428/.

40. Bunzel, "Al-Qaeda's Quasi-Caliph."

41. William McCants, "Zawahiri's Counter-Caliphate," *War on the Rocks*, September 5, 2014, http://warontherocks.com/2014/09/zawahiris-count er-caliphate/.

42. "Tunisi min tanzim Da'ish watawa"ad al-Tunisiyyin bi-fath Tunis dhabh Rashid al-Ghannushi," YouTube video, September 24, 2014, https:// www.youtube.com/watch?v=dLgW_CdX2b0. YouTube terminated the account for violating its terms of service.

43. Conflict Studies, "ISIS Propaganda Video—Destroying Passports," YouTube video, September 14, 2014, https://www.youtube.com/watch ?v=8hKo9Y2XHkM. The video has now been made private.

44. "al-Tayf Niyuz" [online pseudonym], "Yamani: tafaja'a bi-ibnihi al-mukhtafi fi sharit li-'Da'ish'," YouTube video, June 21, 2014, https://www .youtube.com/watch?v=OlFy4USKL1Y.

45. https://www.youtube.com/watch?v=dxQ7xElti0k. YouTube terminated the account for violating its terms of service.

46. Richard Barrett, "Foreign Fighters in Syria," The Soufan Group, June 2014, http://soufangroup.com/wp-content/uploads/2014/06/TSG-Fore ign-Fighters-in-Syria.pdf.

47. Jamie Dettmer, "ISIS and Al Qaeda Ready to Gang Up on Obama's Rebels," *Daily Beast*, November 11, 2014, http://www.thedailybeast.com/ar ticles/2014/11/11/al-qaeda-s-killer-new-alliance-with-isis.html.

48. Barrett, "Foreign Fighters," 24. Barrett quotes an Ahrar al-Sham interviewee claiming that "60% to 70%" of Nusra's foreign fighters and "30% to 40%" of Ahrar's foreign fighters joined ISIS in 2013. There were also practical reasons why Nusra foreign fighters joined the Islamic State. Nusra and other al-Qaeda recruitment materials are often in Arabic, in contrast to the State's multilingual media machine. Nusra is more selective in who it allows in the group, preferring foreigners who bring military skills and experience to the table, while the Islamic State usually accepts anyone who will hop aboard. See Jaysh Jabhat Jabhat [*sic*] al-Nusra

al-ilaktruni, "al-Liqa' al-sawti al-awwal ma'a al-shaykh al-fatih Abi Muhammad #al-Jawlani," YouTube video, November 4, 2014, https://www.youtube.com/watch?v=hFpIMi_hmRE.

49. Edward N. Luttwak, "Caliphate Redivivus? Why a Careful Look at the 7th Century Can Predict How the New Caliphate Will End," *Strategika*, August 1, 2014, http://www.hoover.org/research/caliphate-redivivus-why-careful-look-7th-century-can-predict-how-new-caliphate-will-end.

50. The phrase "al-Rashid" is not a common epithet for Baghdad in medieval books of Islamic history. When the phrase is used, it usually refers to events in the city of al-Rashid's own day. See, for example, al-Yafi'i's *Mirat al-jinan wa-'ibrat al-yaqzan*, vol. 2 (Beirut: Dar al-Kutub al-'Ilmiyya, 1997), 92. In modern discourse, the phrase "the Baghdad of al-Rashid" is sometimes contrasted with "the Damascus of al-Walid," one of the great Umayyad caliphs who ruled from the city. The Islamist Hakim al-Mutayri, for example, tweeted: "The battle today into which the Baghdad of al-Rashid and the Damascus of al-Walid have plunged represents the entire Muslim community." Hakim al-Mutayri (@DrHAKEM), Twitter post, June 16, 2014, https://twitter.com/DrHAKEM/status/478457595229769728. See also William McCants, "Why ISIS Really Wants to Conquer Baghdad," *Markaz*, Brookings Institution, November 12, 2014, http://www.brookings.edu/blogs/markaz/posts/2014/11/12-baghdad-of-al-rashid-mccants.

51. Muharib al-Jaburi, "al-I'lan 'an qiyam Dawlat al-'Iraq al-Islamiyya," January 15, 2007, *al-Majmu' li-qadat Dawlat al-'Iraq al-Islamiyya* (Nukhbat al-I'lam al-Jihadi, 2010).

52. Abu Umar al-Baghdadi, "Wa-yamkurun wa-yamkur Allah," September 15, 2007, *al-Majmu' li-qadat Dawlat al-'Iraq al-Islamiyya* (Nukhbat al-I'lam al-Jihadi, 2010).

53. Abu Muhammad al-Adnani, "al-Iqtihamat afja'," November 2012; al-Adnani, "Lan yadurrukum illa adha," February 2013; al-Adnani, "al-Ra'id la yakdhib ahlaha," January 2014; al-Adnani, "Ma asabaka min husna famin Allah," June 11, 2014.

54. Hugh Kennedy, *When Baghdad Ruled the Muslim World: The Rise and Fall of Islam's Greatest Dynasty* (Boston: Da Capo Press, 2004), 123, quoting Julia Bray's translation in Julia Ashtiany, *Abbasid Belles Lettres: Cambridge History of Arabic Literature*, vol. 2 (Cambridge, UK: Cambridge University Press, 1990), 294–5.

55. Ibid., 72.

56. Ibid., 126–127.

57. Hugh Kennedy, *When Baghdad Ruled the Muslim World: The Rise and Fall of Islam's Greatest Dynasty* (Boston: Da Capo Press, 2004), 74.

58. On the translation of Greek texts into Arabic during Harun's reign, see L. E. Goodman, "The Translation of Greek Materials into Arabic," in M. J. L. Young et al., *Religion, Learning and Science in the 'Abbasid Period* (Cambridge, UK: Cambridge University Press, 1990), 482–484. For the translation movement in general, see Dimitri Gutas, *Greek Thought, Arabic Culture* (New York: Routledge, 1998).

59. Edward Granville Browne, *A Literary History of Persia*, vol. 1 (New York: Charles Scribner's Sons, 1902), 307.

60. Gene Heck, *Charlemagne, Muhammad, and the Arab Roots of Capitalism* (Berlin: Walter de Gruyter, 2006), 269–271.

61. Joseph F. O'Callaghan, *A History of Medieval Spain* (Ithaca, NY: Cornell University Press, 1975), 106; Heck, *Charlemagne*, 172.

62. Colin Freeman, "Iraq crisis: Baghdad's Shia militia in Defiant 50,000-Strong Rally as Isis Make [*sic*] Further Gains," *Telegraph*, June 21, 2014, http://www.telegraph.co.uk/news/worldnews/middleeast/iraq /10916926/Iraq-crisis-Baghdads-Shia-militia-in-defiant-50000-strong -rally-as-Isis-make-further-gains.html.

63. Janine di Giovanni, "The Militias of Baghdad," *Newsweek*, November 26, 2014, http://www.newsweek.com/2014/12/05/militias-baghdad-287142 .html.

64. Phillip Smyth, "The Shiite Jihad in Syria and Its Regional Effects," Washington Institute for Near East Policy, *Policy Focus* 138 (2015): 43, http://www.washingtoninstitute.org/uploads/Documents/pubs/Policy Focus138_Smyth-2.pdf.

65. Abu Ayyub al-Masri, "al-Dawla al-Nabawiyya," September 19, 2008, *al-Majmu' li-qadat Dawlat al-'Iraq al-Islamiyya* (Nukhbat al-I'lam al-Jihadi, 2010).

66. Ibid., 165.

67. Ibid., 166.

68. Ibid., 168.

69. Ibid., 171.

70. Ibid., 175.

71. Ibid., 180.

72. Ibid., 165.

73. Michael Weiss and Hassan Hassan, *ISIS: Inside the Army of Terror* [Google edition] (New York: Regan Arts, 2015), 215–216; Sarah Birke, "How ISIS Rules," *New York Review of Books*, February 5, 2015, http:// www.nybooks.com/articles/archives/2015/feb/05/how-isis-rules/. For a good summary of the Islamic State's ordinances, see Andrew F. Marsh and Mara Revkin, "Caliphate of Law," *Foreign Affairs*, April 15, 2015, https://www.foreignaffairs.com/articles/syria/2015-04-15/caliphate -law.

74. Maggie Fick, "Special Report: For Islamic State, Wheat Season Sows Seeds of Discontent," *Reuters*, January 20, 2015, http://www.reuters .com/article/2015/01/20/us-mideast-crisis-planting-specialreport-id USKBN0KT0W420150120.

75. For the Islamic State's tribal politics in Syria, see Charles Lister, "Profiling the Islamic State," Brookings Doha Center, Analysis Paper No. 13 (November 2014): 10–11, http://www.brookings.edu/~/media/Research /Files/Reports/2014/11/profiling%20islamic%20state%20lister/en _web_lister.pdf. 24.

76. Hassan Hassan, "Isis Exploits Tribal Fault Lines to Control Its Territory," *Guardian*, October 25, 2014, http://www.theguardian.com /world/2014/oct/26/isis-exploits-tribal-fault-lines-to-control-its-terri tory-jihadi; Weiss and Hassan, *ISIS*, 195.

77. "Islamic State Abducts Sons of Tribal Leader in Eastern Syria," *ARA News*, January 2, 2015, http://aranews.net/2015/01/islamic-state-abducts -sons-tribal-leader-eastern-syria/.

78. Reuters, "Syria: Mass Grave May Hold Bodies of 230 Members of Anti-ISIS Tribe," *New York Times*, December 17, 2014, http://www.nytimes

.com/2014/12/18/world/middleeast/syria-mass-grave-may-hold-bodies -of-230-members-of-anti-isis-tribe.html?_r=0; "Iraqi Tribal Leader Calls for Help After ISIS Massacre," *Al Arabiya*, October 30, 2014, http:// english.alarabiya.net/en/News/middle-east/2014/10/30/ISIS-kills-220 -from-opposing-Iraqi-tribe.html.

79. Martin Chulov, "Lack of Political Process in Iraq 'Risks Further Gains for ISIS,'" *Guardian*, January 18, 2015, http://www.the guardian.com/world/2015/jan/18/lack-politial-process-iraq-renders-us -coalition-bombs-grave-mistake.

80. The Gulf Institute (@GulfInstitute), Twitter post, October 8, 2013, https:// twitter.com/GulfInstitute/status/387596457596837890; David D. Kirkpatrick, "ISIS' Harsh Brand of Islam Is Rooted in Austere Saudi Creed," *New York Times*, September 24, 2014, http://www.nytimes.com/2014/09/25 /world/middleeast/isis-abu-bakr-baghdadi-caliph-wahhabi.html?_r=1.

81. "'Shari' al-Baghdadi' . . . Qat' ru'us wa-ayadi wa-rajm wa-sulb (suwwar wa-fidiu)," *al-Masry al-Youm*, December 21, 2014, http://www.almasry alyoum.com/news/details/607192; Mary Atkinson and Rori Donaghy, "Crime and Punishment: Islamic State vs Saudi Arabia," *Middle East Eye*, February 13, 2015, http://www.middleeasteye.net/news/crime-and -punishment-islamic-state-vs-saudi-arabia-1588245666.

82. *Rule of Terror: Living under ISIS in Syria*, Report of the Independent International Commission of Inquiry on the Syrian Arab Republic, United Nations Office of the High Commissioner for Human Rights, November 14, 2014, 6, http://www.ohchr.org/Documents/HRBodies/HRCouncil /CoISyria/HRC_CRP_ISIS_14Nov2014.pdf; "'Shari' al-Baghdadi.'"

83. For the Islamic State's use of ultraviolence to attract recruits, see Stern and Berger, *ISIS: The State of Terror*, 72–73.

84. See, for example, the *Jami'* of Tirmidhi: "Do not punish with God's punishment," http://sunnah.com/tirmidhi/17/42.

85. "Ma hukm tahriq al-kafir bi-l-nar hatta yamut?" Fatwa 60, January 20, 2015, available at *Jihadica*, http://www.jihadica.com/wp-content/uploads/20 15/02/IS-fatwas-35-38-40-53-55-57-59-62-65-71.pdf. English translation available at Cole Bunzel, "32 Islamic State Fatwas," *Jihadica*, March 2, 2015, http://www.jihadica.com/32-islamic-state-fatwas/.

86. James Grehan, "Smoking and 'Early Modern' Sociability: The Great Tobacco Debate in the Ottoman Middle East (Seventeenth to Eighteenth Centuries)," *American Historical Review* 111, no. 5 (December 2006): 1352, 1356–1358.

87. Ibid., 1360, 1373–1374.

88. Ibid., 1361–1362.

89. Ibid., 1363–1364.

90. Ibid., 1367.

91. "Somalia's Al-Shabaab Bans Smoking Cigarettes, Chewing Khat," Bloomberg, May 9, 2011, http://www.bloomberg.com/news/articles/2011 -05-09/somalia-s-al-shabaab-bans-smoking-cigarettes-chewing-khat.

92. Loveday Morris, "In Syrian Civil War, Emergence of Islamic State of Iraq and Syria Boosts Rival Jabhat al-Nusra," *Washington Post*, October 28, 2013, http://www.washingtonpost.com/world/middle_east/in-syrian-civil -war-emergence-of-islamic-state-of-iraq-and-syria-boosts-rival-jabhat -al-nusra/2013/10/25/12250760-3b4b-11e3-b0e7-716179a2c2c7_story

.html; Balint Szlanko, "Jabhat Al Nusra's New Syria," *The National*, December 15, 2012, http://www.thenational.ae/news/world/middle-east/jabhat-al-nusras-new-syria.

93. Morgan Winsor, "ISIS Beheads Cigarette Smokers: Islamic State Deems Smoking 'Slow Suicide' Under Sharia Law," *IB Times*, February 12, 2015, http://www.ibtimes.com/isis-beheads-cigarette-smokers-islamic-state-deems-smoking-slow-suicide-under-sharia-1815192; "'Da'ish' tastathmir fi al-tadkhin bi-tahrimihi," *Al-Alam*, March 29, 2015, http://www.alalam.ir/news/1689723; "Shabaka Kurdiyya: Tatbiq 'Da'ish' li-'uqubat al-tadkhin tawaqqa'a 12 qatilan min 'anasir al-tanzim," *Youm7*, February 20, 2015, http://www.youm7.com/story/2015/2/20/-من-قتيلا-12-توقع-التدخين 2075304/عناصر-تطبيق-داعش-لعقوبة-شبكة-كردية#.VSUtDPnF9KI.

94. "ISIS Reverts Smoking Ban in Kirkuk 'to Gain Popularity,'" *Al Arabiya*, September 22, 2014, http://english.alarabiya.net/en/variety/2014/09/22/ISIS-reverts-smoking-ban-in-Kirkuk.html.

95. Abu Umar al-Baghdadi, "Hasad al-sinin bi-Dawlat al-Muwahhidin," April 17, 2007, *al-Majmu' li-qadat Dawlat al-'Iraq al-Islamiyya* (Nukhbat al-I'lam al-Jihadi, 2010).

96. *Dabiq* 5: 3, 12–13, 24.

97. Abu Bakr al-Baghdadi, "Even If the Disbelievers Despise Such," English translation available at http://ia902205.us.archive.org/17/items/bghd_20141113/english.pdf; original Arabic version available at http://ia902205.us.archive.org/17/items/bghd_20141113/arabic.pdf.

98. *Dabiq* 5: 25–30.

99. Katie Zavadski, "ISIS Now Has a Network of Military Affiliates in 11 Countries Around the World," *New York Magazine*, November 23, 2014, http://nymag.com/daily/intelligencer/2014/11/isis-now-has-military-allies-in-11-countries.html. AQIM had rejected the Islamic State's caliphate soon after it was announced. See Thomas Joscelyn, "AQIM Rejects Islamic State's Caliphate, Reaffirms Allegiance to Zawahiri," *Long War Journal*, July 14, 2014, http://www.longwarjournal.org/archives/2014/07/aqim_rejects_islamic.php.

100. Paul Cruickshank et al., "ISIS Comes to Libya," *CNN*, November 18, 2014, http://www.cnn.com/2014/11/18/world/isis-libya/; Thomas Joscelyn, "Islamic State 'Province' in Libya Claims Capture of Town," *Long War Journal*, February 15, 2015, http://www.longwarjournal.org/archives/2015/02/islamic_state_provin_1.php; Frederick Wehrey and Ala' Alrababa'h, "Rising Out of Chaos: The Islamic State in Libya," Carnegie Endowment for International Peace, March 5, 2015, http://carnegieendowment.org/syriaincrisis/?fa=59268.

101. Bunzel, "Ideology," 32.

102. "Al-Qaeda in Yemen Denounces 'Expansionist' ISIS," *Al Arabiya*, November 22, 2014, http://english.alarabiya.net/en/News/middle-east/2014/11/22/Al-Qaeda-in-Yemen-denounces-ISIS-.html.

103. David D. Kirkpatrick, "Militant Group in Egypt Vows Loyalty to ISIS," *New York Times*, November 10, 2014, http://www.nytimes.com/2014/11/11/world/middleeast/egyptian-militant-group-pledges-loyalty-to-isis.html?_r=3.

104. Jack Moore, "Spiritual Leader of Libya's Biggest Jihadi Group Pledges Allegiance to ISIS," *Newsweek*, April 8, 2015, http://www.newsweek.com/top-judge-libyas-biggest-jihadi-group-pledges-allegiance-isis-320408.

105. "ISIS Claims Increasing Stake in Yemen Carnage," *CBS News/Associated Press*, March 23, 2015, http://www.cbsnews.com/news/isis-yemen-carnage-houthi-rebels-advance-in-aqap-territory-toward-hadi/.

106. David Blair, "Boko Haram Is Now a Mini-Islamic State, with Its Own Territory," *Telegraph*, January 10, 2015, http://www.telegraph.co.uk/news/worldnews/africaandindianocean/nigeria/11337722/Boko-Haram-is-now-a-mini-Islamic-State-with-its-own-territory.html.

107. Harun Maruf, "Experts Say al-Shabab-Islamic State Linkup 'Unlikely,'" *Voice of America*, March 18, 2015, http://www.voanews.com/content/experts-say-al-shabab-islamic-state-linkup-unlikely/2684247.html.

108. David D. Kirkpatrick, "ISIS Finds New Frontier in Chaotic Libya," *New York Times*, March 10, 2015, http://www.nytimes.com/2015/03/11/world/africa/isis-seizes-opportunity-in-libyas-turmoil.html.

109. For a terrific discussion of this principal-agent problem, see Jacob Shapiro, *The Terrorist's Dilemma: Managing Violent Covert Organizations* (Princeton, NJ: Princeton University Press, 2013).

110. Kamil al-Tawil, "al-Zawahiri yattajih ila hall 'al-Qa'ida,'" *Al Hayat*, April 3, 2015, http://www.alhayat.com/Articles/8371259/.

111. *Dabiq* 5: 3.

112. Rachael Levy, "Could Saudi Arabia Be the Next ISIS Conquest?" *Vocativ*, June 23, 2014, http://www.vocativ.com/world/iraq-world/saudi-arabia-next-isis-conquest/.

113. Abu Ayyub al-Masri, "Sayuhzam al-jam' wa-yuwallun al-dubur," June 13, 2006.

114. Abu Muhammad al-Adnani, "Lan yadurrukum illa adhan," audio recording, February 2013, https://archive.org/details/forKan.001.

115. Baghdadi, "Hasad al-sinin."

116. See Nu'aym b. Hammad, *Kitab al-fitan* (1993), 211; David Cook, *Studies in Muslim Apocalyptic* (Studies in Late Antiquity and Early Islam, No. 21) (Princeton, NJ: Darwin Press, 2002), 156.

117. On the apocalyptic moment, see Richard Landes, *Heaven on Earth: The Varieties of Millennial Experience* (New York: Oxford University Press, 2011), 16.

118. *Dabiq* 5: 40.

CONCLUSION

1. Jean-Pierre Filiu, *Apocalypse in Islam*, transl. M. B. DeBevoise (Berkeley: University of California Press, 2011), 121, 140.

2. Ibid., 80–103; David Cook, *Contemporary Muslim Apocalyptic Literature* (Syracuse, NY: Syracuse University Press, 2005), 59–83.

3. Filiu, *Apocalypse*, 121–140.

4. Ibid., 131.

5. Ayman al-Zawahiri, "Zawahiri's Letter to Zarqawi [English translation]," personal correspondence to Abu Mus'ab al-Zarqawi, Harmony Program, Combating Terrorism Center at West Point, July 9, 2005, https://www.ctc.usma.edu/posts/zawahiris-letter-to-zarqawi-english-translation-2. Original Arabic version available at https://www.ctc.usma.edu/v2/wp-content/uploads/2013/10/Zawahiris-Letter-to-Zarqawi-Original.pdf. I have modified the translation.

6. Paul D. Buell, "Massacre," *Historical Dictionary of the Mongol World Empire* (Lanham, MD: Scarecrow Press, 2003), 190.

7. For example, see the account of Joshua's conquest of Jericho (Joshua 6:17–22). For an overview of the doctrine of slaughtering one's enemies, see Susan Niditch, *War in the Hebrew Bible: A Study in the Ethics of Violence* (New York: Oxford University Press, 1993).

8. Ali Bey al-Abbasi, *Travels of Ali Bey in Morocco, Tripoli, Cyprus, Egypt, Arabia, Syria, and Turkey: Between the Years 1803 and 1807*, 2 vols. (Longmans, 1816), vol. 2, 152.

9. Alastair Crooke, "You Can't Understand ISIS If You Don't Know the History of Wahhabism in Saudi Arabia," *Huffington Post*, August 27, 2014, http://www.huffingtonpost.com/alastair-crooke/isis-wahhabism-saudi-arabia_b_5717157.html.

10. For a list of the massacres and the related literature, see Khaled Abou El Fadl, *Reasoning with God: Reclaiming Shari'ah in the Modern Age* (Lanham, MD: Rowman and Littlefield, 2014), 456, footnote 82.

11. Frank Clements, *Conflict in Afghanistan: A Historical Encyclopedia* (Santa Barbara, CA: ABC-CLIO, 2003), 112.

12. See, for example, Madawi al-Rasheed's explanation of why tribes joined the Wahhabi movement in *A History of Saudi Arabia* (New York: Cambridge University Press, 2005), 13–23.

13. Max Boot, *Invisible Armies: An Epic History of Guerilla Warfare from Ancient Times to the Present* (New York: Liveright Publishing, 2013), 64–79.

14. Mehdi Hasan, "This Is What Wannabe Jihadists Order on Amazon Before Leaving for Syria," *New Republic*, August 22, 2014, http://www.newrepublic.com/article/119182/jihadists-buy-islam-dummies-amazon.

15. Aaron Zelin, "The Islamic State of Iraq and Syria Has a Consumer Protection Office," *Atlantic*, June 13, 2014, http://www.theatlantic.com/international/archive/2014/06/the-isis-guide-to-building-an-islamic-state/372769/.

16. Letter from Abd al-Hamid Abu Yusuf, a commander in "Northern Baghdad Province," to Abu Bakr al-Baghdadi, n.d. The Arabic handwritten letter was given to me by the German journalist Volkmar Kabisch. The word for "bribing" here is *irsha'*.

17. Jamie Crawford and Laura Koran, "U.S. Officials: Foreigners Flock to Fight for ISIS," *CNN*, February 11, 2015, http://www.cnn.com/2015/02/10/politics/isis-foreign-fighters-combat/.

18. Yasir al-Shadhili, "Dirasa Amirkiyya: 5 fi al-mi'a faqat min al-Sa'udiyyin man yata'atif ma'a 'Da'ish'," *Al Hayat*, October 17, 2014, http://alhayat.com/Articles/5095664/داعش-مع-يتعاطف-من-السعوديين-من-فقط-المئة-في -دراسة-أميركية--5-.

APPENDICES

1. I've consulted the translations and texts on *Sunnah.com* where possible.

APPENDIX 1

1. Arthur John Arberry, *The Koran Interpreted: A Translation* (New York: Touchstone, 1955).

2. Ibid., 29 (tradition from *Mustadrak al-Hakim*).

3. The last sentence alludes to Qur'an 6:158.

APPENDIX 3

1. Jawad Bahr al-Natsha, *al-Mahdi Masbuq bi-Dawla Islamiyya* (Al-Khalil/ Hebron: Markaz Dirasat al-Mustaqbal, 2009), 59–60, 66, 74, 99.
2. That is, between the corner (*rukn*) of the Ka'ba and the "place" (*maqam*) where Abraham stood.

APPENDIX 4

1. Turki ibn Mubarak al-Bin'ali, "Al-Qiyafa fi 'adm ishtirat al-tamkin al-kamil li-l-khilafa."
2. "The religion will abide until the Hour comes or there are twelve caliphs over you, each of them from the Quraysh tribe" (tradition from *Sahih Muslim*).
3. "The caliphate in my community will be thirty years, then there will be monarchy after that" (tradition from *Jami' al-Tirmidhi*).

INDEX

al-Abab, Adil, 57–9
Abbasids, 15, 26–9, 32, 110–11, 116,
     118, 123, 131–3, 147, 180, 219n38
Abd al-Rahman, Atiyya, 13–14,
     18–19, 55, 77–8, 208n44, 208n51
Abd al-Wadud, Abu Mus'ab, 60–4
Abdullah, Abu, 104
Abdulmutallab, Umar Farouk, 50
Abu Bakr, 116, 123–4
Abu Muslim, 26–7
Abu Nuwas, 132
Abu Sufyan, 108. *See also* Sufyani
al-Adl, Sayf, 7–10, 184nn5–6,
     186n38, 194n44
al-Adnani, Abu Muhammad, 93–4,
     97, 215–16n147
Afghanistan, 25, 28, 31, 39, 87, 91,
     101, 155
   Herat training camp, 8
   and Taliban, 7, 9–10, 18, 44, 80,
     129–30, 149
Africa
   Central African Republic, 24
   Ethiopia, 65, 201n85
   Kenya, 44, 67
   Nigeria, 141
   Somalia, 29, 53, 64–8, 69–70, 84,
     153
   See also North Africa
African Union, 67
ahadith, 23, 150
Ahmed, Abu, 75–6
Ahrar al-Sham, 96–8

al-Qaeda
   al-Fajr (media distribution), 20
   and apocalypticism, 27–9
   full name (Qa'idat al-Jihad), 56
   and Islamic State, 6–7, 76, 78–9,
     90–5, 124–5, 129–30, 141–2, 148,
     151–2
   Vanguards of Khorasan (magazine),
     28
   See also Bin Laden, Osama; al-
     Zawahiri, Ayman
al-Qaeda affiliates
   al-Qaeda in Iraq, 12, 15–17, 19,
     31–3, 36–7, 40, 43
   al-Qaeda in Yemen, 47–9, 52, 158
   al-Qaeda in the Arabian Peninsula
     (AQAP), 48–68, 197n19, 202n89,
     205n117
   al-Qaeda in the Indian
     Subcontinent, 129–30
   al-Qaeda in the Islamic Maghreb
     (AQIM), 60–5, 68–9, 158,
     230n99
   and "glocalization," 69
   and Islamic State flag, 69–71
   Nusra Front (Jabhat al-Nusra,
     Syria), 85–93, 95–6, 98, 107, 125,
     131, 139, 213n116, 213–14n125,
     226–7n48
   al-Shabab (Somalia), 44, 64–8,
     84, 141, 158, 184n13, 201n85,
     201n86, 201–2nn88–9, 203n100,
     203n102

al-Qaeda in the Arabian Peninsula
(AQAP)
Ansar al-Shari'a (Supporters of the
Shari'a), 56–9, 70, 141
attacks in Ma'rib and Ataq, 197n19
The Echo of Battles (online
magazine), 47–50
Inspire (online magazine), 49–50
merger with al-Qaeda in Yemen,
48, 202n89
Aleppo, Syria, 1, 96–8, 101–2, 109,
121
Algeria, 13–14, 61, 64, 86–7, 140
Ali (Muhammad's son-in-law), 25,
74, 108, 110, 116–17, 127, 180,
220n50
al-Ali, Hamid, 18
Almohads, 24, 147
al-Amaytar, Abu, 109
American Revolution, 149
Ansar al-Din, 70
Ansar al-Shari'a, 56–9, 70, 141
Ansar al-Sunna, 35
Ansar Bayt al-Maqdis, 140
al-Ansari, Abu al-Walid, 18
Antichrist, 10, 99, 106–7, 145–7,
166–8, 219n47
apocalyptic prophecies
and Antichrist, 106–7, 145–7,
166–8, 219n47
appearance of Gog and Magog,
169–70
conquest of Constantinople, 166,
173–4
conquest of Rome, 166, 173
and Dabiq, 102–5, 112, 147, 165, 173
and Damascus, 100, 106, 109–10,
136, 166, 168
death of the believers, 170–1
destruction of Mecca and Medina,
170–1
End of Days, 12, 22–4, 142, 145,
223n107
End-Time, 23, 28, 51, 99, 101, 109,
111, 119, 140, 145, 163–71, 173–5,
217n13
establishing the caliphate in
accordance with the prophetic
method, 12, 114–17, 122, 126–9,
131, 163–4, 174, 178–9
fighting Rome, 165–6

fighting the Jews, 168–9, 174
Final Hour, 23, 29, 146–7, 164
and flags/banners, 22, 25–9,
109–11
great universal signs, 171
and Hashimites, 25
invasion of India, 174
and Jesus, 105–6, 142, 168–70,
174–5, 190n95, 222n94
and Muhammad, 23, 25–6, 99–101,
106, 112, 114, 116, 144, 150,
163–71, 173–5
sectarian dimension of, 107–11
and al-Sham, 99–102, 105, 107–8,
110, 118, 164, 166–7, 171, 177,
180–1
and Shi'i Islam, 24, 107–8, 111, 147
spread of Islam, 174–5
and strangers/foreigners, 100–2
and the Sufyani, 108–9
and Sunni Islam, 24, 28, 100,
108–9, 115, 122, 145–7, 161,
163–71, 173–5
twelve caliphs, 114–18, 179–81
"twelve thousand," 50–2, 60
and Yazidis, 111–14
See also Mahdi (Muslim savior, "the
Rightly-Guided One")
apocalypticism
and Abbasids, 27, 147
and Abu Mus'ab al-Suri, 29, 86
and al-Qaeda, 27–9
and AQAP, 50–1
apocalyptic propaganda and
rhetoric, 24, 27–8, 147, 154,
194n45, 218n22
and generational change, 28, 147
and Iraq War, 146
and Islamic State, xiii, 1–2, 6, 15,
100–19, 126, 139–40, 142–3,
146–7, 153–5, 177–8
and Masri, 31–2, 40–1
and violence, 107–12, 147, 158–9
and Zarqawi, 102–3, 146, 194n45,
218n22
Arab Spring, 45, 55, 69–71, 99, 152
Ark of the Covenant, 24
Army of the Caliphate, 140
al-Ar'ur, Adnan, 109
al-Assad, Bashar, 85–6, 90, 97–8,
100–1, 108, 125, 134, 153, 157

al-Assad, Hafez, 86
Atatürk, Mustafa Kemal, 115
al-Awlaki, Anwar, 49–50

al-Badri, Ibrahim Awwad Ibrahim.
    See al-Baghdadi, Abu Bakr (nom
    de guerre)
Baghdad, Iraq, 10, 31–2, 75–7, 103,
    131–4, 136, 227n50
al-Baghdadi, Abu Bakr (renamed
    Caliph Ibrahim al-Baghdadi,
    nom de guerre), 1, 77, 85, 97
    and al-Qaeda, 76, 90–6, 129, 140–2
    apocalypticism of, 100, 103
    appointment as commander of the
        faithful, 45, 73, 77–8
    and Bin Laden, 78
    black clothing as caliph, 123–4
    as caliph of Islamic State, 116–18,
        122–4, 132, 146
    in Camp Bucca (American
        detention center), 75–6
    education, 74–6
    family and early years, 73–4
    and Nusra Front, 90–5
    and Zawahiri, 78–9, 90–6
al-Baghdadi, Abu Umar (nom de
    guerre), 43, 82, 94, 103, 131, 142,
    191n4–5
    allegiance pledged to Bin Laden,
        17, 94
    appointment as commander of the
        faithful, 15–18
    and black flag, 20
    death of, 45, 77, 146
    and Masri, 32–5, 40–1
    and nineteen tenants of Islamic
        State, 37–8
    as nominal head of Islamic State,
        18–9, 37, 40–1, 76
    and proclamation of Islamic State,
        15–16
    status of, 76–7, 82, 146
al-Bahlul, Ali, 29
banners. See flags and banners
Bar Kokhba, Simon, 24
Barmakids, 132
beheading, 13, 38, 58, 68, 105–6, 114,
    137, 143, 148
Benghazi, Libya, 141
Berbers, 110–11

Bin Laden, Osama
    and Abu Usama al-Iraqi video,
        36–7
    and al-Qaeda affiliates, 53–6, 60,
        64–9, 135, 152
    allegiance pledged to Mullah
        Omar, 16, 33, 87, 129
    and apocalypticism, 28, 146–7
    family, 8, 28
    and Islamic State, 3, 16–18, 33–4,
        36–7, 44–5, 48–9, 77–8, 93–4,
        125, 136, 152
    strategy of, xiii, 7–8, 11–12, 14–15,
        53–6, 141, 151–2
al-Bin'ali, Turki ibn Mubarak, 89,
    115–18, 179–81
Boko Haram, 141
Book of Tribulations, 29, 143

Cairo, Egypt, 70–1
caliphate, 6, 9–10, 22–7, 50–1, 56,
    103–9
    Abbasid, 15, 26–9, 32, 110–11, 116,
        118, 123, 131–3, 147, 180, 219n38
    Almohad, 24, 147
    countercaliph, 129–30, 141
    and debate over popular support, 7,
        11–12, 53, 68, 122–5, 151–3
    Fatimid, 24, 147
    Islamic State as, xii, 1, 15–17, 20,
        121–44, 151–3, 159
    Mamluk, 104
    and Management of Savagery, 82–3
    Ottoman, 21, 104, 115, 122, 153
    prophecy of establishing "in
        accordance with the prophetic
        method," 12, 114–18, 122, 126–7,
        129, 131, 163–4, 174, 178–9
    Rashidun, 131–4, 227n50
    Umayyad, 22, 24–7, 103, 108–11,
        116, 127, 133, 180, 227n50
caliphs, 22, 25–6, 103–9, 113–17,
    127–33, 146
    Abu Bakr, 116, 123–4
    Abu Bakr al-Baghdadi as, 1, 15, 96,
        116–18, 122–4, 132, 146
    and Abu Umar al-Baghdadi as, 15,
        33
    Ali, 25, 74, 108, 110, 116–17, 127,
        180, 220n50
    Hasan, 116, 180

caliphs (continued)
  Mehmed II, 104
  Mu'awiya, 22, 108, 180
  and Mullah Omar, 129–30
  and prophecy, 146, 164, 177–8,
    179–81
  Rashid, 131–4, 227n50
  Saffah, 27, 133
  Selim I, 105–6
  Sulayman, 103, 105
  twelve caliphs prophecy, 114–18,
    179–81
  Umar, 113
  See also Mahdi (Muslim savior, "the
    Rightly-Guided One")
Call of the Global Islamic Resistance, 87
Camp Bucca (American detention
  center), 75–6
Cerantonio, Musa, 99–100
Charlie Hebdo attacks, 106–7
chemical weapons, xii
Christ. See Jesus
Christianity, 23, 37, 44, 105–6, 109,
  112, 133, 138, 145–6, 190n95
Clausewitz, Carl von, 13, 81
Constantinople, 103, 105, 166, 173–4
countercaliph, 129–30, 141
Crusades, 8–9, 24, 121

Dabiq, Syria, 102–5, 112, 147, 165, 173
Damascus, Syria, 22, 25, 32, 85, 100,
  106, 109–10, 136, 166, 168
dawla, 9, 15, 27
dawla mubaraka, 27
Day of Judgment, 12, 23, 32, 40,
  100–2, 109, 112, 173, 188n70
Deceiver, see Antichrist
al-Din, Ansar, 70
Dunaway, Mark, 5–6

Egypt, 7–9, 24, 44, 70–1, 99, 104,
  140, 147
bring down of Russian airliner in,
  xi–xii
emirate, use of the term, 9
End of Days, 12, 22–4, 142, 145,
  223n107
End-Time prophecies, 23, 28, 51,
  99, 101, 109, 111, 119, 140, 145,
  217–18n13
Ethiopia, 65, 201n85

Fallujah, Iraq, 36, 75
Fatimids, 24, 147
fatwas, 2, 96, 115
Fertile Crescent, 7, 29
al-Filistini, Abu Qatada, 96, 128,
  219-20n49
Filiu, Jean-Pierre, 145
Final Hour, 23, 29, 146–7, 164
flags and banners
  black flag, 1, 5, 19–22, 25–8, 48, 70,
    109–10, 126
  of Islamic State, 5–6, 19–22, 45,
    48–9, 64, 69–71, 104, 110–11,
    121, 124–6
  in legend and history, 22, 25–8,
    32, 124
  and prophecy, 22, 25–9, 109–11
  yellow flag, 20–1, 110–11
French Revolution, 149

Gadahn, Adam, 16, 43–4, 215n139
gharib/ghuraba (stranger, foreigner), 101
Godane, Ahmed Abdi, 64, 201-
  2nn88–9, 203n102
Gush Emunim, 24

Hadrian, 24
Hajji Bakr (nom de guerre), 79, 90
Hammad, Nu'aym bin, 29, 143
Harun, Fadil, 29, 44, 186-7n47,
  201n86, 222n94, 226n38
Harun al-Rashid, 131–4, 227n50
al-Hasan, 116, 180
Hasan, Nidal, 50
Hashim (Muhammad's
  greatgrandfather), 25
Hashimites, 25–6
hearts-and-minds strategy, 56–8, 60,
  68–9, 86–7, 139, 148–51
Hijazi, Akram, 16
Hizb al-Islam, 66
Hizballah, 110
Hosseinian, Ruhollah, 110
hudud (fixed punishments in Islamic
  scripture), 38–9, 57–8, 67–8, 82,
  128, 136, 152
Hurayra, Abu, 97
Husayn (Muhammad's grandson),
  15, 116
Hussein, Saddam, 10, 34, 52, 73–6,
  78–9, 121, 126–7, 153–4

Ibn Khaldun, 23–4, 26, 179
imara (emirate), 9
Imru al-Qays, 26
Iran, 6–9, 25–6, 94, 108, 110, 133–4,
    158, 210-11n78
Iran-Iraq War, 73
Iraq, xii
    al-Qaeda in Iraq, 12, 15–17, 19,
        31–3, 36–7, 40, 43
    Anbar Province, 35, 45, Ba'ath
        party, 127, 153–4
    Baghdad, 10, 31–2, 75–7, 103,
        131–4, 136, 227n50
    Fallujah, 36, 75
    Hawija, 127, 139
    Islamic State's expansion, xiii
    Kurds in, 156–7
    Mosul, 1, 9, 113, 121–4, 131–4, 157
    Shi'a in, 10–11, 32, 108, 110, 125,
        133, 136, 156–7
    Sunni in, 12, 14, 35–9, 60, 121, 134,
        157–8
    and US invasion, 1, 9–10, 33, 49,
        117, 145–6
    and US withdrawal, 80, 125
    and Yazidis, 111–13
al-Iraqi, Abu Maryam, 98
al-Iraqi, Abu Usama (nom de guerre),
    36–7
Iraqi Hizballah, 108
ISIS (Islamic State of Iraq and al-
    Sham/the Levant). *See* Islamic
    State
Islam
    fear and hostility to Muslims, xii
    hudud (fixed punishments), 38–9,
        57–8, 67–8, 82, 128, 136, 152
    Ka'ba (shrine), 22, 28, 142–3, 167,
        171, 233n2
    origins of, 56–7, 101
    Qur'an, 23, 58, 74–6, 79, 106,
        112, 117, 150, 161, 169–71, 181,
        188n70
    refugees, xii
    Salafism, 53, 63, 74–5, 96, 109
    Shari'a law, 37, 56, 61–2, 67, 83–4,
        181
    Wahhabism, 138, 148–51
    See also apocalyptic prophesies;
        caliphate; caliphs; mosques;
        Muhammad; Shari'a law; Shi'I

Islam; Sunni Islam
Islamic Army, 34–5, 193n28
Islamic Jihad, 31
Islamic State
    and Ahrar al-Sham, 96–8
    and al-Qaeda, 6–7, 76, 78–9, 90–5,
        124–5, 129–30, 141–2, 148, 151–2
    and apocalypticism, xiii, 1–2, 6,
        15, 100–19, 126, 139–40, 142–3,
        146–7, 153–5, 177–8
    and Bin Laden, 3, 16–18, 33–4,
        36–7, 44–5, 48–9, 77–8, 93–4,
        125, 136, 152
    branding of, 126–8
    as caliphate, xii, 1, 15–17, 20,
        121–44, 151–3, 159
    coins of, 127
    contradictions of, 154–5
    Dabiq (magazine), 142–3
    Da'wa Gathering, 126–7
    declaration as caliphate, 123, 126,
        128–30
    and debate over popular support, 7,
        11–12, 53, 68, 122–5, 151–3
    and "Enduring and Expanding"
        slogan, 139–42
    establishment of Islamic State of
        Iraq and al-Sham (the Levant)
        (2013), 91–2
    expansion of, xii, xiii–xiv
    flag of, 5–6, 19–22, 45, 48–9, 64,
        69–71, 104, 110–11, 121, 124–6
    and jihadism, xiv, 3, 19, 21, 33, 36,
        42, 79–81, 95–7, 115, 123–6, 128,
        130, 151–2
    and Mahdi, 22, 142–4, 146–7
    and *Management of Savagery*, 82–4,
        87, 210-11n78, 211n87
    proclamation of Islamic State of
        Iraq (2006), 6, 14–17, 19, 32
    and Shi'a, 94, 117, 125, 127, 132–3,
        158
    Shura Council, 77–8
    and slavery, 111–14
    and "Strategic Plan for Reinforcing
        the Political Position of the
        Islamic State of Iraq," 79–82
    strategy of, xiii, 148–51
    and Sunni Islam, 33–9, 42, 44,
        79–82, 98, 103–4, 111, 122–5,
        136, 151–2, 156–7

Islamic State *(continued)*
    tense used to describe capabilities and intentions of, xi, xiii–xiv
    terror war chest of, xii–xiii
    use of the term, 15–16
    and Yazidis, 111–13
    and young women recruits, 113–14
    See also al-Masri, Abu Ayyub; al-Baghdadi, Abu Bakr; al-Baghdadi, Abu Umar
Istanbul, Turkey, 105. *See also* Constantinople

Ja'far the Barmakid, 132, 223n108
Jandal, Abu, 29
al-Jawlani, Abu Muhammad, 85, 90–2, 214nn130–1
Jerusalem, 24, 29, 32, 100, 103, 140, 169, 191n4
Jesus, 105–6, 142, 168–70, 174–5, 190n95, 222n94
Jews, 24, 37, 82, 106, 133, 140, 145–6, 167–9, 174
jihad, 3, 5–6, 10–12, 51, 55–6, 62, 83, 86–7, 121, 123, 135
jihadism and jihadists
    and 9/11, 87
    Algerian, 86
    and apocalyptic prophecies, 100–3, 115, 122–3, 143, 146
    global movement, 6, 45, 64, 69–70, 95, 130, 140–1, 146, 158
    global recruitment, 130–1
    hearts-and-minds strategy, 56–8, 60, 68–9, 86–7, 139, 148–51
    historical, 133
    and Hizballah, 110
    and Islamic State, xiv, 3, 19, 21, 33, 36, 42, 79–81, 95–7, 115, 123–6, 128, 130, 151–2
    and Islamic State flag, 5–6, 69–70
    and *Management of Savagery*, 82–4, 87, 210-11n78, 211n87
    as mujahidin, 11
    online forums and social media, 48, 64, 104, 187-8n59
    and razing of shrines, 63
    and smoking tobacco, 138–9
    and "Strategic Plan for Reinforcing the Political Position of the Islamic State of Iraq," 79–82
    See also al-Qaeda; al-Qaeda affiliates; Bin Laden, Osama
Jordan, 7–8, 10, 32, 128, 137–8
Judaism, 57, 88. *See also* Jews

Ka'ba (Islamic shrine), 22, 28, 142–3, 167, 171, 233n2
Kampala, Uganda, July 2010 attacks, 67
al-Kasasbeh, Moath, 137
Kassig, Peter, 114
Kennedy, Paul, 84
Kenya, 67
Khan, Samir, 49, 60
Khansa Brigade, 113
Khorasan, 25–6, 28–9, 42, 91, 167
Kony, Joseph, 24
Kurds, 156–8

Last Days, 106, 108, 114
Lebanon, 8, 110
Leibowitz, Marc, 5
Libya, xiv, 60, 64, 70, 86, 94, 105, 140–1, 155
Lind, William, 81
Lord's Resistance Army, 24
Lulu, Ahmad, 97–8, 216-17n159

Machiavelli, Niccolò, 3
Maghrib. *See* North Africa
Mahdi (Muslim savior, "the Rightly-Guided One"), 22–9, 111, 194n45
    and al-Qaeda, 28–9
    Bin Laden on, 222n94
    Bin'ali on, 116, 180–1
    claimants to title of, 24–5, 27
    historic origins of, 22–9
    and Islamic State, 22, 142–4, 146–7
    Masri on, 32, 40, 142, 146
    Muhammad on, 164–5, 223n107
    Natsha on (in *The Mahdi Is Preceded by an Islamic State*), 178
    and popular belief, 23–4, 99, 107–8
    and Saffah, 27
    and Shi'a, 28, 107–8, 110, 116–17
    and Sunni Islam, 24, 28, 108–9
    al-Utaybi on, 223n107

Mahdi Army, 133
Mahmood, Aqsa, 113
Majlis Shura al-Mujahidin, 76
Mali, 60–4, 67, 69–70, 158
al-Maliki, Nuri, 36, 136
Mamluk Sultanate, 104
Management of Savagery, 82–4, 87, 210-11n78, 211n87
Mao Zedong, 81
al-Maqdisi, Abu Muhammad, 50–1, 96, 118, 128, 184n8, 196-97nn12–13, 213n120, 225n31
al-Masri, Abu Ayyub, (aka Abu Hamza al-Muhajir), 76–7, 94
  apocalypticism of, 31–2, 40–1, 142
  and bounty on, 31
  death of, 45, 77, 146
  and founding of Islamic State, 16–17, 31–5, 146
  as leader of Islamic State, 16–17, 31–5, 38–42, 44, 134–5, 146
  as leader of al-Qaeda in Iraq, 16–17, 31–2
  and Islamic State of Iraq, 33
  and Twelver Shi'i Islam, 220n50
  and Utaybi, 39–42
  and Zarqawi, 31–2
Mehmed II, 105
al-Mejjati, Adam Karim, 105
messiahs, 24, 106. *See also* Mahdi (Muslim savior, "the Rightly-Guided One")
monotheism, 51, 61, 121–2, 131, 135, 196-7n13
Monotheism and Jihad, 10, 12, 56
mosques, 63, 70, 113
  Aqsa Mosque (Jerusalem), 32
  attacks on, 10, 34, 37, 44, 79, 205n117, 223n107
  Grand Mosque (Mecca), 28
  Imam Ali Mosque (Najaf), 10
  Nuri Mosque (Mosul), 123
  Prophet's Mosque (Medina), 32
  Umayyad Mosque (Damascus), 32, 106
Mosul, Iraq, 1, 9, 113, 121–4, 131–4, 157
Mu'awiya, 22, 108, 180
Mubarak, Hosni, 99

Muhammad, 20, 22, 51, 53, 56–7, 78, 107, 126–7
  ahadith, 23, 150
  and battle of Uhud, 26, 134
  prophecies attributed to, 23, 25–6, 99–101, 106, 112, 114, 116, 144, 150, 163–71, 173–5
  and punishment for apostasy, 137–8
  and Shi'i doctrine of leadership, 7, 15
  mujahidin, use of the term, 11, 45, 53, 93. *See also* jihadists
al-Mukhtar, 24
Muslim Brotherhood, 75
Muslim Brotherhood of Syria, 86
Muthanna, Abu, 101–2

9/11 attacks, xii, xiii, 8, 49, 69, 87
Naji, Abu Bakr (nom de guerre), 82–4, 87, 210n77, 213-14n125
Nigeria, 141
North Africa, xii, xiii, 15, 24, 27, 82, 133
  and al-Qaeda in the Islamic Maghreb (AQIM), 60–5, 68–9, 158, 229n99
  Algeria, 13–14, 61, 64, 86–7, 140
  and Almohads, 24, 147
  Egypt, xi–xii, 7–9, 24, 44, 70–1, 99, 104, 140, 147
  Libya, xiv, 60, 64, 70, 86, 94, 105, 140–1, 155
  Mali, 60–4, 67, 69–70, 158
  Tunisia, 70, 94, 99, 102, 110, 130
Nur al-Din Zengi, 8–9, 121, 123

Obama, Barack, 71, 105
oil, 83, 90, 98
Omar, Mullah Muhammad, 16, 18, 33, 87, 129–30, 226n38
Ottoman Empire, 21, 104, 115, 122, 153

Padnos, Theo, 90
Pakistan, 18, 39, 42–4, 49, 86, 91, 153, 195n63, 210n78
Palestine, 8, 24, 128
Paris attack, xi–xiii
Pasha, Ahmad Cevdet, 21
prophecies. *See* apocalyptic prophecies
Prophet. *See* Muhammad

al-Qahtani, Nayif, 47–9, 60
Qur'an, 23, 58, 74–6, 150, 161,
    169–71, 181
  and end of days, 169–70, 181,
    188n70
  portrayal of Jesus in, 106
  recitation of, 74–5, 79, 117
  and slavery, 112
Qur'anic studies, 74, 117
al-Qurashi, Abu Ubayd, 81
Quraysh tribe, 116, 165, 177, 179–80,
    233n2

Ramadan, 27
al-Rashid, Harun, 131–4, 227n50
Robow, Mukhtar (aka Abu Mansur),
    64, 203n102
Russian airliner bombing, xi–xiii

al-Saffah, 27, 133. See also Abbasids
Saladin, 9
Salafism, 53, 63, 74–5, 96, 109
Sana'a, Yemen, 52, 205n117
Saydnaya military prison, 86
Saudi Arabia, 12, 47–9, 74, 94, 105–6,
    136–40, 142, 148, 151
  Mecca, 22, 28, 32, 53, 56, 103, 108,
    123, 133, 142, 177
  Medina, 53, 82, 102–3, 142, 165,
    168, 171, 173, 177
Selim I, 104–5
September 11, 2011, attacks of, 8, 49,
    69, 87
al-Shabab (al-Qaeda affiliate in
    Somalia), 44, 64–8, 84, 141, 158,
    184n13, 201n85, 201n86, 201-
    2nn88–9, 203n100, 203n102
al-Sham, 91, 99–102, 105, 107–8, 110,
    118, 164, 166–7, 171, 177, 180–1
Shami Witness (online pseudonym),
    96
Shari'a committees, 115–16, 179
Shari'a law, 37, 56, 61–2, 67, 83–4, 181
Shi'a Islam
  and apocalyptic prophecies, 24,
    107–8, 111, 147
  and Baghdadi, 74, 117
  doctrine of leadership, 7
  and flags, 110
  in Iraq, 10–11, 32, 108, 110, 125,
    133, 136, 156–7

and Islamic State, 94, 117, 125, 127,
    132–3, 158
  in Syria, 108, 136, 156
  and Taliban, 149
  Twelver Shi'a Islam, 220n50,
    223n108
  and the U.S., 37
  and Zarqawi, 7–8, 10–11, 13, 36, 146
Sistani, Grand Ayatollah, 133
slavery, 1, 111–14, 149
smoking tobacco, 63, 65, 89, 138–9
social media, 95
  blogs, 102
  Twitter, 1, 6, 43, 48, 84, 93–4, 96,
    104, 114, 126–7, 140, 209n59
  YouTube, 94, 102
Soleimani, Qasem, 134
Somalia, 29, 53, 64–8, 69–70, 84,
    153. See also al-Shabab (al-Qaeda
    affiliate in Somalia)
Soufan, Ali, 29
Spain, 24, 16, 133, 147
strangers, 101–2
Strangers Media Foundation, 102
"Strategic Plan for Reinforcing the
    Political Position of the Islamic
    State of Iraq," 79–82
Sufism, 74, 63
Sufyani, 108–9
Sulayman, 103, 105
Sun Tzu, 81
Sunni Islam
  1920 Revolution Brigade, 37
  and al-Qaeda, 35–9
  and apocalyptic prophecies, 24, 28,
    100, 108–9, 115, 122, 145–7, 161,
    163–71, 173–5
  and Baghdadi, 74–5
  and flags, 110
  in Iraq, 12, 14, 35–9, 60, 121, 134,
    157–8
  and Islamic State, 33–9, 42, 44,
    79–82, 98, 103–4, 111, 122–5,
    136, 151–2, 156–7
  in Syria, 85–6, 88–9, 96, 98, 103–4,
    153
  and Zarqawi, 7–8, 10–14, 36
  See also Taliban
al-Suri, Abu Khalid, 86–8
al-Suri, Abu Mus'ab, 29, 51–2, 86–7,
    97, 197n17, 217-18n13

Syria
  al-Bab, 89
  Aleppo, 1, 96–8, 101–2, 109, 121
  Dabiq, 102–5, 112, 147, 165, 173
  Damascus, 22, 25, 32, 85, 100, 106, 109–10, 136, 166, 168
  Free Syrian Army, 104, 108, 131
  Ghouta, 100, 103
  Islamic State's expansion, xiii
  Kurds in, 156–7
  Nusra Front (Jabhat al-Nusra), 85–93, 95–6, 98, 107, 125, 131, 139, 213n116, 213-14n125, 226-7n48
  Raqqa, 113, 126, 131, 136
  Russian bombing in, xi–xii
  al-Sham, 91, 99–102, 105, 107–8, 110, 118, 164, 166–7, 171, 177, 180–1
  Shi'a in, 108, 136, 156
  Sunni in, 85–6, 88–9, 96, 98, 103–4, 153
  See also al-Assad, Bashar
Syria Khayr, 97

al-Tabari, 109
Taber, Robert, 81
Taha, Adnan, 163
Taliban, 16, 44, 52, 87, 195n63
  and Afghanistan, 7, 9–10, 18, 44, 80, 129–30, 149
  See also Omar, Mullah Muhammad
Timbuktu, Mali, 62–3
Tunisia, 70, 99, 102, 110, 130
Turkey, 8, 20, 97, 102, 104, 122, 131
"twelve thousand" prophecy, 50–2, 60

Uganda, Kampala, 67
Uhud, battle of, 26, 134
Umayyads, 22, 24–7, 103, 108–11, 116, 127, 133, 180, 227n50
United Nations, bombing of Baghdad U.S. headquarters, 10, 32
United States
  9/11 attacks, xii, xiii, 8, 49, 69, 87
  and al-Qaeda, 8, 11–12, 14–15, 37–9, 41–2, 52–3, 56, 59–61
  American Revolution, 149

attack on Benghazi consulate, 141
  and Bin Laden, 11, 44–5, 52–3, 55
  Camp Bucca (detention center), 75–6
  and deaths of Masri and Abu Umar al-Baghdadi, 45, 73, 77, 146
  and death of Utaybi, 42
  and death of Zarqawi, 15, 32
  drone strikes, 67
  embassies, 44, 70–4
  fear and hostility to Muslims, xii
  Fort Hood shooting, 50
  and invasion of Iraq, 1, 9–10, 33, 49, 117, 145–6
  and Islamic State, xii–xiv, 14–15, 35, 79–81, 84, 88, 104–5, 139, 155–7
  and Israel, 88
  and Nusra Front, 85–8
  San Bernardino shooting, xii
al-Uraydi, Sami, 87–8, 93, 212n111
al-Utaybi, Abu Sulayman, 39–42, 191n5, 193n39, 223n107

Wadoud, Abdul, 104
Wahhabism, 138, 148–51
World War I, 115, 122
al-Wuhayshi, Nasir, 47–8, 52, 55, 59–61, 200n63, 202n89

Yazidis, 111–13
Yemen, 47–55, 59, 61, 69, 74, 140–1, 153, 155, 167, 171, 196-7n13
  al-Qaeda in Yemen, 47–9, 52, 158

al-Zarqawi, Abu Mus'ab, 7–15, 35–6, 61
  and Abd al-Rahman, 19–20, 55
  admiration for Nur al-Din Zengi, 8–9, 121, 123
  and al-Qaeda, 7–15, 148
  apocalypticism of, 102–3, 146, 194n45, 218n22
  death of, 15, 32
  as al-Gharib ("the Stranger"), 101
  and Maqdisi, 50
  and Masri, 31–2
  and Monotheism and Jihad, 10, 12, 56
  and Shi'a Islam, 7–8, 10–11, 13, 36, 146
  and Sunni Islam, 7–8, 10–14, 36

al-Zawahiri, Ayman, 7, 11–17, 19, 31, 36, 142
   and Abu Khalid al-Suri, 86
   and apocalypticism, 28, 115, 146, 218n22
   assumes leadership of al-Qaeda, 78
   hearts-and-minds approach of, 8, 11–13, 41, 68, 141, 148
   and Islamic State, 41, 78–9, 85, 90–7, 129–30
   and Zarqawi, 11–14, 148
al-Zawi, Hamid, 33